"Reality, a friend of mine once said, is what you run into when you're wrong. *Reframing the Soul* is a wonderful guide to navigating reality with grace and truth. It is honest, hopeful, literate, and faith-filled. His framework for daily life is brilliant!"

— John Ortberg, senior pastor of Menlo Church and author of *I'd Like You More If You Were More Like Me*

"With remarkable clarity, thoughtfulness, wisdom, and humor, Gregory Spencer has taken this difficult to understand subject and shown how deeply and broadly it reaches into every aspect of our lives. Masterfully weaving together real-life stories of tragedy and hope, a lifetime of learning about communication, and the role that faith plays in helping us see beyond our limited perspectives, *Reframing the Soul* is the best introduction I've read to both why and how we should reframe as an essential daily practice."

— Don Waisanen, PhD, associate professor of communication, Baruch College

"We live and die in stories. They tell us who we are, what to believe, and what to do. Gregory Spencer's *Reframing the Soul* helps us see that even though some of our stories are toxic, they can be recast in ways that are healthier and still true. He uses stories from his own life, along with many stories from others, to help us become better tellers of our own stories."

— Daniel Taylor, author of *Death Comes for the Deconstructionist* and *Do We Not Bleed?*

"Years ago, Dr. Spencer gave me the greatest gift: he taught me that words can shape our world. Today, he's giving that gift to you in this profoundly meaningful book. *Reframing the Soul* is equal parts caring and challenging, inspiring and insightful—and its message has never been more relevant. Diving into these pages will give you a renewed faith and an invigorated hope for humanity."

— Allison Trowbridge, author of *Twenty-Two: Letters to a Young Woman Searching for Meaning*

"For more than a decade, I've known Gregory Spencer as one of the most transformative teachers I've ever encountered. In this book, he gifts us with a liberating framework for making new meaning out of old, often haunting, memories that replay through our minds and shows us how to use the tools we already have to restore and reconstruct our lives so that we can engage others in love."

— Josh Daneshforooz, author of *Loving Our Religious Neighbors*

"Read *Reframing the Soul* to discover the transformative power of reframing. You will unearth more truth-filled words to frame your past, present, and future—and experience greater freedom. When I was in college, Gregory Spencer taught me truths that changed my life. With this book, he has done it again."

—Justin Buzzard, founding pastor of Garden City Church, cofounder of
Three Sons Club, and author of *Date Your Wife*.

"This book is for anyone who wants to live well. If you have endured loss, heart-break, disappointment, or any of life's other inevitable bumps, Spencer's words will help you organize your experience in a fresh way that gives life. Give yourself the gift of feasting on these beautiful, wise words."

—Margot Starbuck, author of *Small Things with Great Love*

"What story are you living? Where are you going? Where have you been? In this powerful and poetic book, Dr. Spencer invites you to answer these questions with intentionality and honesty, to understand fully the story you tell yourself, so that you can choose the future story you want to live."

—Paul Angone, author of *101 Secrets for Your Twenties* and creator of allgroanup.com

"Words frame the way we see the world, so if we want to see differently, we must learn to speak differently. *Reframing the Soul* has the power to impact your speech, transform your sight, and renew your spirit. Eminently readable and frequently brilliant, I wish I'd had this book years ago."

—Jonathan Merritt, contributing writer for *The Atlantic* and author of *Jesus Is Better Than You Imagined*

Reframing the
SOUL

Reframing the
SOUL

How Words
Transform
Our Faith

GREGORY SPENCER

LEAFWOOD
PUBLISHERS
an imprint of Abilene Christian University Press

REFRAMING THE SOUL
How Words Transform Our Faith

an imprint of Abilene Christian University Press

Copyright © 2018 by Gregory Spencer

ISBN 978-0-89112-477-1 | LCCN 2017051336

Printed in the United States of America

Reprint permissions for previously published materials continue on page 253.

LIBRARY OF CONGRESS CATALOGING-IN-PUBLICATION DATA
Names: Spencer, Gregory H. (Gregory Horton), 1953- author.
Title: Reframing the soul : how words transform our faith / Gregory Spencer.
Description: Abilene : Leafwood Publishers, 2018. | Includes bibliographical
    references.
Identifiers: LCCN 2017051336 | ISBN 9780891124771 (pbk.)
Subjects: LCSH: Language and languages—Religious aspects—Christianity. |
    Vocabulary. | Rhetoric—Religious aspects—Christianity. | Thought and
    thinking—Religious aspects—Christianity. | Change
    (Psychology)—Religious aspects—Christianity.
Classification: LCC BR115 .L25 S63 2018 | DDC 248.4—dc23
LC record available at https://lccn.loc.gov/ 2017051336

Cover design by Bruce Gore | Gore Studios, Inc.
Interior text design by Sandy Armstrong, Strong Design

Leafwood Publishers is an imprint of Abilene Christian University Press
ACU Box 29138
Abilene, Texas 79699

1-877-816-4455
www.leafwoodpublishers.com

18 19 20 21 22 23 / 7 6 5 4 3 2 1

Contents

Acknowledgments

I've read that novelist Isaac Asimov typed his manuscripts in a single draft and sent each one to his editor after typing the last page. I am no Isaac Asimov. This book needed a lot of assistance from many faithful sources.

My wife, Janet, is First Reader and First Editor Supreme. Not only is she beautiful inside and out, she's an insightful and encouraging reviewer, asking important, even difficult questions—and making indispensable contributions to the book. Other discerning readers include Gary Moon, Rick Pointer, Jim Taylor, June Michealsen, Lesa Stern, Elizabeth Gardner, Mary Given, Ken Kornelis, Jane Wilson, Laura Wilson, and Cheryl Smith. My extended family has offered wise and compelling advice: Tim and Emily Stewart, Dave and Hannah Bryant, Josh and Laura Graning, and my brother, Jeff Spencer. Thank you for the time you have sacrificed on behalf of *Reframing the Soul*.

I've been awed and impressed by the many friends who've told me their stories. You are master reframers: Jill Oulman, Erin Doyland, Emily Frei, Russell Smelley, Donna Speer, Sally Peterson, Rachel Parker, James Peel, Kelly Noling, Lisa Siemens, Amy Meyer, Elizabeth Poucher, June Michealsen, Jim Halvorsen, Patrick Steele, Adam Kirkes, Byron and Robyn Beck, and Cici Corrales. All of these folks have kindly granted me permission to tell their tales—some with their real names and others without. I will not report which is which. You've shared the fabric of your lives, sometimes the parts with torn seams and gaping holes. The book and my soul are better for it.

Most of the poems included have been vetted and certified by the wise and careful pens of my poetry group: Ron Alexander, Dan Thomas, Gudren Bortman, John Eliot, and Tessa Flanagan.

A huge thank-you goes to Mark Sargent, Provost of Westmont College. He graciously gave me a gift no one else could provide: time. If you want some, you'll have to ask him how he did it. I'm also grateful to Westmont College for Professional Development Funds to work on this project.

Finally, the Leafwood team of Jason, Rebecka, Duane, Frank, and others has cheerfully and skillfully shepherded this little lamb of a book along. Thank you.

Fifteen Years
Down the Hatch

I am saddened that my tongue cannot live up to my heart.
—St. Augustine

My parents did a lot of things right. They taught me that I could not take credit for my circumstances—for my social class or color of skin or any particular God-given talent. They reminded me that "being funny," no matter how good the joke, did not justify "being mean." In his workshop, my dad showed me how to use power tools without slicing off my fingers (though one time I managed to push my thumb into the band saw). And my mom made me feel great by laughing at my high school escapades, one involving a stolen stop sign, pole and all. Though my parents didn't say it, I knew they loved me.

But my parents also got drunk every night for fifteen years.

Increasingly, from my early adolescence through my early marriage, most of my parents' off-the-job moments involved a beer or some bourbon in their hands. After living through years of glassy-eyed stupors, I couldn't stand to be with them. Every moment in their chemically altered presence ate at me. If I made the mistake of coming home, and my mom saw me tiptoeing into the house with a buddy, she threw her arms around my friend and slurred how happy she was to see him. This did not go over well.

Our household was a mess. Moldy food reeked in the fridge or on the stove. While the TV blared at my parents in the den, the three of us kids fought through our meals alone in the kitchen.

"You are such an idiot."

"You are an idiot plus ten."

"Shut up. I should scream until Dad comes in."

"As if he'd care."

One Christmas Eve, my mom drank until she passed out on the living room floor. My dad staggered from wall to couch. Disgusted, I stormed out and, sobbing, drove slowly around a friend's house until the mom saw my pleading face and let me in—just as they were opening their presents.

———

For years, when I talked about this period in my life, I said that though I knew my parents "deep down" loved me, they abandoned me through their drinking. They made life at home miserable and lonely. For the most part, I was on my own for money, advice, and finding whatever recognition I could. They did not coach me about college or check in about my life. They just weren't "there" as parents for my siblings and me. What did exist at home was often painful. So, the painful truth was that they abandoned me.

Yet, slowly, over about twenty years, without denying the suffering I experienced, I began to talk about my parents in different terms. I *reframed* the situation. After dwelling in the knowledge of forgiveness, after coming more to terms with my own anger and sadness, I could eventually say that they were broken people who needed healing. Though the alcoholism was monstrous, they weren't monsters. They were ordinary people who had made poor choices as they coped with the stresses of work, marriage, and children. My dad had seen terrible things in World War II. My mom did not know how to work through conflict. These circumstances didn't excuse their bad behavior—but I realized that I have my bad behavior too, behavior that I consistently view through the lens of God's grace. We are all wounded souls.

I had framed my story one way and then I reframed it another way. Was the first summary a lie and the second the truth? No, both ways of naming my experience were part of the whole. But until I could articulate the second version—*I could not seem to live out its meaning.* The first frame emphasized my victim status, what had been done *to* me. The second one underscored my parents' wounded condition, something we shared. I began to see that we frame our story—we tell it with certain words that get us to see it in particular ways—and then our story frames us.

Whichever way I labeled my experience, I lived in the story I told. As a language-user, I'm bound to all the audacious capacities and frustrating limits of words. We label, we name, we frame *all* of our experiences, past, present, and future. We give words to our inner and outer worlds. In doing so, we construct a kind of home we carry with us.

"Carrying a home" might conjure up images of turtles lugging around their shells, their homes. But perhaps you could imagine not a turtle-shell-on-our-backs kind of home but a regular house we carry, an extension of our bodies that has walls and doors and windows. The idea is that we live in the "homes" we've made with our words, so we see only whatever the word-windows allow us to see. And that's what we usually do: we look out from *inside* the frame, *through* the pane. I once saw my parents from inside the frame of "reckless deserters," but now I see my parents' broken-ness because I am viewing them through the window of the word "broken."

We are used to looking out through the windows to the world outside. This book refocuses our attention to the windows themselves, to the words we use. Sometimes we notice that the words we use need to be cleaned up or replaced. We realize that last night wasn't "awesome"; it was "pretty ordinary." Sometimes our "houses" need to be remodeled. A significant disappointment such as a death or a divorce might shake our faith to its very foundation. A surprising joy such as a pregnancy or a hike in a rain forest might awaken belief in a Creator.

I believe we all need to reframe our stories, at least parts of them, in order to heal, to discard lies, to move from partial truths to richer, fuller explanations, to see our lives as God sees them.

This kind of review is the purpose of *Reframing the Soul*: to walk through our houses and take a good long look at how they have been made—to examine how our word choice has influenced us and then to decide if we want to make any changes. Do we want to wash some windows, move some pictures around, or do some full-scale remodeling? To some degree, we are architects of our own houses. We decide which frames to use, where to put our windows, what words through which we'll see our lives. There's an art to our word choice. And that art can lead to the trans-formation of our faith.

A key question along the way is: *When we frame our lives, what's in the picture?* Am I a failure or a work in progress? Is life a bowl of cherries or a rotten heap of stinky fruit? Is life a mystery story, a treacherous hike along cliffs, a dance choreographed by a loving God—or all of the above? How we speak—how we frame things—matters. We tend to think that life comes to us just the way it is, but life comes to us, not entirely but significantly, through the way we see it—and we see it as we label it in words.

The reframing of my parents' behavior dramatically transformed my life. For my sake and theirs, I needed to see that my parents were not just *parents* but *persons* who, like all human beings, struggle and fail and need help. Until I could articulate these words, until I could imagine my par-ents more sympathetically because of these words, I struggled to change my relationship with them. Until I changed my habits of speech and spoke of my parents as potential recipients of forgiveness, I was not able to fully forgive them. But once I did forgive them, I began to connect with them more meaningfully and to look honestly at my own bitterness and lack of compassion.

As long as the main story line was *their* cause of *my* pain, my anger endlessly cycled through the same arguments and evidence against them. I was stuck in one vision of things, and getting unstuck took years. Among other habits and choices, I needed to stop talking about my suffering in the same blame-oriented way, to stop—as we all tend to do—looping through the same defensive story in my head. I needed to reframe. As I did so, I saw (more than I wanted to believe at the time) that the house I lived in was one *I* had built with accusing, self-protective words. I told myself over and over that I deserved pity, that my mom was an embarrassment, that my dad cared only for himself. The house that I framed with my words was a dirt-floored shack with thin walls, a rotten foundation, and holes in the roof.

I also moved toward reframing by listening to others' forgiveness stories. Rhonda talked about forgiving her adulterous husband. Virginia forgave God for her son's debilitating disease. New terms, new phrases gave me a richer, more nuanced view. I had never considered that my par-ents felt trapped in their behavior. Although they didn't speak about what they felt, I could see that my mom laughed to cover her insecurities—and drinking helped her laugh. My dad wanted the social status of the cool crowd, the cocktail-consuming Rat Pack of Frank Sinatra and Dean Martin. "Everyone handed you a drink after work," he said years later. "That's just the way it was." He couldn't seem to muster the strength to resist.

Reframing helped my empathy.

All day long, all of us are framing and reframing our lives. We talk about the memory of our adorable but sexist grandpa. We label ourselves as movie critics or introverts or justice-lovers. We say that the future is full of doom and despair—or stocked with opportunities and adventure. Most of us sort out life well enough to keep moving along.

Then something happens—a car accident, a promotion, a cancer scare, an offer of marriage, a terrorist threat, a retirement party—and our world gets turned inside out. Our sense of order bursts with joy or unravels. Our words seem inadequate. They don't say enough or they say too much.

When these kinds of events happen, if we slow down long enough to examine our speech, we may see cracks in our frames and begin to search for ways to reframe. One disruption might lead a person to say, "I thought I trusted God for the future, but my anxiety about my children is so faithless." The way we describe reality matters because, as simple as it sounds, we cannot see through a window unless the window is there. We are stuck in the houses that our words construct. What if my windows are small and barred and leave me in a prison of prejudice? What if I realize that I can make my windows larger—to see more and appreciate the landscape before me? Specific language choices give us access to specific realities.

———

These possibilities raise questions. What happens when we change our habits of language? What work is involved in reframing? How hard is that work? What influences our framing and reframing? Does reframing mean that we just "make up" the truth or reality we want to live in? How can that be? Are some labels better than others? What do our names for things reveal about our basic, life-directing beliefs, about our desires for the good life? When we notice certain words that we consistently use, can we reframe and change the picture? What is the difference between mindless reframing and wise reframing?

These are the kinds of issues I address in this book—and I do so in part by telling dozens of reframing stories, based on extensive interviews with people whose "disruptions" range from a mother discovering her next baby will have Down syndrome to a student becoming physically paralyzed while doing a flip on a lawn. Though our disruptions might be as minor as yet more traffic on the freeway, we all work on *how* to tell our story.

To frame is to put a language boundary around our experience. It is to name what happens in particular ways, to say how we see the world, and to see the world how we say it is. Framing includes telling our personal story, the story of our times, the stories of the ways things are and should be. What do I say about being a good father or a bad son? How do I talk about the car my neighbor has or the prospect of declining health? We do our best to frame truthfully, faithfully, and lovingly—because we know the damage caused by interpreting the world falsely, cynically, and destructively.

But the goal is not to frame everything positively. This book is not about spinning things toward cheerful words. To recast from "I despise life" into "Let's just be happy" is little more than simplistic propagandizing. Are we supposed to put a smiling face on terrorism or suicide or pandemics? Are we meant to "look on the sunnier side"—even when both sides are in a hurricane? As linguist George Lakoff puts it, spin and propaganda are used to "make the embarrassing occurrence sound normal or good, . . . to get the public to adopt a frame that is not true and is known not to be true." Spin and propaganda are not the goals of good framing.

Framing well does not mean pretending to ignore the pain of a broken relationship or the tragic aftermath of an unexpected death in the family. Even the man called the Messiah wept. Jesus didn't say, "Relax, everybody. I'm about to raise Lazarus from the dead" or "Let's see some smiles out there! Don't you believe in God?" Jesus didn't talk just about things that felt good or sounded pleasant.

Though we see through a glass darkly, though our windows are smudged and damaged, if we care about the truth, we will strive for evocative and faithful words. This is a challenging task. In many cases, it is harder to frame *well* than to frame *happily*. But it is also crucial and honest and potentially transformative.

We all have our reframing stories, and we all have more reframing to do. For some time now, I've noticed how my spiritual development depends on it—because *faith*-work is often *frame*-work. Does my life have purpose before a living God or am I merely the product of my genetic code? Does it matter if I *follow* Jesus or *walk alongside* or *trail far behind*?

Reframing is especially relevant for what I call our four essentials of the soul: remembering the past, anticipating the future, dwelling within ourselves, or engaging with others. Although we function during our days as if these aspects just "are the way they are," they are significantly informed by *how* we remember, the *ways* we anticipate, the *names* we call ourselves, and the *terms* we use as we engage with others. How do I remember my adolescence, anticipate my retirement, dwell with my perfectionism, or engage with those who consistently annoy me? These practices are inescapable—and since we cannot avoid them, we would be wise to bring them into whatever light we can.

These four essentials speak to where we live: in the present between the past and the future, in the center between our inner and outer worlds. It's the intersection of time and space. This is the life we are called to reframe well.

But first, a few words about words.[1]

---

[1] For further reflection, I've included a poem of mine at the conclusion of each chapter. Sometimes the connection to the chapter will be obvious, and other times less so. In every case, I have provided some guidance by asking a related question in the Discussion Questions, which are located at the back of the book. One tip: read the poem aloud, slowly, and pause slightly at the end of each line.

The Beginning of the Road of Ice

Remember the time when we first knew?
On that sloppy, wide-eyed ride, the three of us

                        kids in the backseat, no seatbelts
                to keep us tight and safe? We grabbed

the front seat, remember? Leaning in,
leaning hard, we held on as Dad jerked

                the car this way and that, around one blind turn
                and then blinder still on that snake-night road.

"Why are you driving so fast?!" we screamed.
"We can go faster in the dark," he said,

                        "'cause you can see the other guy's
                headlights coming." But the thing is,

we didn't see it coming, this drive,
this beginning of the road of ice

                and bourbon and night after night of near misses
                and hits. Now we know—but, remember this too:

we didn't crash that night. Though we've had our
accidents, our mangled frames and body work,

                we made it home.
                That's what we did.
                We made it home.

CHAPTER ONE

Every Word
Is a Window

What you call "worry" . . . I call "preparation."
—Richard Bandler and John Grinder

In a short story, Jhumpa Lahiri writes about Mr. Kapasi, a man who translates to a city physician what rural Indian people say about their illnesses. When Mr. Kapasi complains to a friend, Mrs. Das, that the job is meaningless, she tells him that his occupation is a significant responsibility, that he is "interpreting people's maladies." Mr. Kapasi is greatly affected by her description. He feels named, enriched, emboldened, a person conveying delicate and dark truths.

For Mr. Kapasi, the words from Mrs. Das opened a window. He had perceived his work as a typical mindless job, but Mrs. Das offered a fresh perspective, a different and beautiful way to frame his work. She fulfilled Walker Percy's rich phrase that one of the noblest roles of a communicator is "to render the unspeakable speakable," to point to qualities others have been unable to articulate.

Most of us have had parents or coaches or teachers change our vision of ourselves by putting one of our characteristics into promising words, naming a previously unvoiced trait, making it "speakable." We may have heard, "You are musically gifted" or "I've always seen you as a leader" or "I love the way you encourage your friends." The expression of these words helped us see what was hidden.

It's true for the words we use as well. Do I say my job is a *necessity* or a *calling*? Is America divided, polarized, or at war? Is God a loving friend or a distant relative? We often don't see what we mean about things until we describe them. Every word is a window onto some vista.

So, if saying something reveals the insights we know, wouldn't it also be true that struggling to describe something can show that we don't quite know it? Sometimes students who receive a low grade on an exam exclaim, "But I *know* it! I just couldn't access it in the moment." Of course, that could be the case. Another explanation is that the feeling that we know something does not usually represent the same depth of knowing as being able to express it meaningfully to someone else. When we put appropriate words to things, we can learn more, others can learn more—and, in our most poetic and holy moments, we render the unspeakable speakable. We frame something so well it comes alive.

After years of emotional ups and downs, ecstatic peace and paralyzing anxieties, Angela asked to be admitted to the psych ward of the hospital. Through therapy and tears, she learned she was clinically depressed, a diagnosis that thoroughly liberated her. She said, "Because I could at times be so joyful, I never thought that my issue was depression—but everything fits together now." She feels more clear-headed and stable than she has for a decade. "It sounds strange," she says, "but I'm so grateful I can say 'I am depressed.' It's the first step toward getting well."

In *Saying Is Believing*, Amanda Hontz Drury makes a strong case that sometimes "we don't know what we really think until we say it out loud. We often talk our way into our beliefs." She doesn't mean that we should try to convince ourselves of what we know isn't true, but that beliefs—including our beliefs about God—move from fuzzy hunches to sharper conclusions when worked on by words. Speaking helps us to see the strengths and weaknesses of our beliefs and moves us from vague thoughts to concrete formulations, from "anxiety issues" to "clinical depression."

All of this may sound logical, helpful, even inspiring. Who doesn't want to say well what needs to be said? And it's simple, right? Just make better choices with words. Yet even if we are gifted at doing so, the activity of framing is, as we have all experienced, far more complicated.

For one thing, we don't begin with a blank slate.

We've Already Been Framed

Be safe.

Treat others as you want to be treated.

You can do whatever you set your mind to.

Don't leave your towel on the floor.

Most of us heard these familiar lines as we grew up. We've had our lives framed for us by voices we could not control—and we've framed our own lives by our own choices, some thoughtful, some not. Sometimes it feels like a crime drama, like we are trapped by evidence that was planted. "It's not my fault, officer! I live in the morally bankrupt twenty-first century!" We can even feel falsely accused, framed by someone out to get us, or by culture or history. When someone from a different culture calls me "an arrogant American," I feel framed by the stereotype. When I find myself parroting some spurious cliché about "needing to stay young" or "how poor I am," I feel framed by consumerism and advertising.

Perhaps we could all learn to be better detectives about the mysteries of what we say. Good detection begins with good questions. Two might be "What frames us that is *not* in our control?" and "What frames us that *is* in our control?"

Frames We Did Not Choose

What lenses have we inherited? Consider these categories. *Heredity*: I could say that my mom and dad gave me certain genes (white, male, "high-strung"). I frame the world the way I do in part because of my physical abilities, height, metabolism, and DNA-driven predispositions. Being the shortest, skinniest kid in every elementary grade influenced how I saw and talked about the world. *Family upbringing*: Since my parents raised me, they encouraged me to see the world in certain ways (do things right the first time, live and let live, be a man, etc.). *National culture*: Growing up in the United States, I learned particular values. Individual freedom is king. We're the best nation in the world. I need to be constantly entertained. *Social class*: As part of the suburban middle class, I accepted the importance of education, hard work, and thrift. I felt safe. I learned prejudices against those unlike me: poorer city dwellers, country "hicks," and rich "snobs." *Media*: From rock music and television, I was told that romance and sex were the highest goods, that if indecision struck, I should "follow my heart" . . . or just go out and buy something . . . on sale. And these examples just begin to tell the story of frames that affected me.

Being a detective of our own influences is tough work, because we don't usually notice our assumptions until we meet someone who doesn't share them. Perhaps cousins from the city come to visit. An immigrant asks about American ways. We go to Thailand and meet locals who seem happier than most of our friends.

Frames We Did Choose

Another investigative question is, "What frames us that *is* in our control, that we have chosen?" Samantha was a good girl. She obeyed the Girl Scout law, rooted for underdog Olympians, competed for good grades, and watched her weight. She *really* watched it. As she looked at magazines and talked with her friends, she decided to accept their definition of "fat"—so she kept working on staying skinny. Though she lived in a beauty-conscious culture, she did more than inherit its labels. She decided which ones to make her own. Food equaled calories. Control meant slimmer thighs. "Slender" was not good enough. She chose these frames.

Of course, no matter how skillful we are as detectives, we can't account for all the reasons we frame the world the way we do, nor can we reframe everything that comes into our awareness. We'd go crazy if we constantly evaluated every observation we made.

Wait. Why did I say "crazy"? How does that frame the event? Do I think people are going mad? Do I have a disorder? Am I being hurtful toward the mentally impaired—I mean, the brain-injured? You see what I mean.

If we constantly thought about *how* we were seeing things, we might never communicate at all—which is, after all, the point of speaking. If I read cookbooks all day long but never ate a meal, I'd starve. At the same time, if I never looked at recipes, my food might end up a mishmash of microwaved slop—which is how some conversations come out. So, it's worth our time to examine the words we use to explain our lives.

Since we've all been framed, we are never a *tabula rasa*, a blank slate. We are embedded in what we inherit and what we choose. Though each word, each phrase, is but a pixel in the image of the world before us, a small part of the whole, we've all framed and reframed in ways that show the difference words make in our experience. Here's why.

We Live inside the Frame

This comic from "Ballard Street" could not be more on target.

Lyle built it himself.

It seems silly for Lyle to have made a wooden box and stepped into it, a typical example of cartoonist Jerry Van Amerongen's off-center humor. But, in fact, we all live *inside* the ways we have been framed and the ways we frame things. We see the world through the windows of our house. What else could we do? How else could we see beyond the walls that separate us from the world?

Consider Mark. When he went to work one morning as an intern in the Capitol in Washington, DC, he slipped by the tourists and went to his office. But not long after he arrived, he was running full speed out of the building, along with everyone else. It was September 11, 2001. Once the announcement came that commercial planes had crashed into the Twin Towers in New York City—and that another attack was on its way to DC— Mark took off. "The weirdest thing," he said, "was that all I could think was 'I'm in a movie.' There I was running down the steps of the Capitol, out onto the lawn, my life in serious danger (or so I thought), and it's like I'm outside of myself watching myself as an action hero in a film." Like many in our media-saturated times, Mark imagines himself as an actor in a drama, focusing on his performance through the camera's lens. He has his movie frame and he lives in it.

We Don't Merely Stand outside Words and "Pick Them Up"
This idea that we live *inside* our frames, our word choice, can seem counterintuitive. Aren't words just tools we use and put down when we are done with them, like a hammer or a wrench? Take the word "mother." We can't use the word neutrally, like some dictionary word without any context. If your mother was kind and generous but controlling, your "mother" has these associations. So, when someone says "mother," your memory of your mother is triggered, however slightly. The word also comes to you with the ways others have talked about their mothers—and a smattering of fictional versions of mothers. You can't use the word "mother" as an unbiased term. It comes with your entire history associated with the word.

For these reasons, some people have problems using certain familial terms for spiritual relationships (father, mother, brother, sister, and so on). If your father had an affair and ran out on the family when you were twelve, can you picture a Father-God who cares for you unconditionally? If your sister tormented you relentlessly, might you struggle to reframe yourself as a happy member of "the family of God"? These kinds of situations sometimes motivate us to work to reframe. We say we are trying to "redeem" a certain word or to recover its original, more positive senses.

We could also say that some aspects of our lives consist almost entirely of words—and part of our existence is lived *in* these aspects. What is our reputation but the words others say about us? Our reputation can change in a second if "word gets around" that we have lied or won a prestigious award. Isn't our identity largely what we say (to others and ourselves) about who we are? If I talk about myself as an active, athletic person, who am I when I get injured? Most of us know retirees who have had difficulty making the transition from the work world, in part because their former labels don't fit anymore. "I used to be *important*," some say.

Here's an example that reinforces the idea that words aren't just tools. When I was in elementary school, textbooks emphasized the story of

Manifest Destiny, of a U.S. sense of purpose in settling the West. Immigrants sacrificed everything for their children. Pioneers bravely fought Indians and built rugged homes on the prairie. I pictured this "sprint" to the Pacific Ocean as a glorious and inevitable victory for my ancestors, even though no one in my lineage ever hitched up to a wagon train. I lived in this view. It affirmed American values of risk-taking and hard work—and superiority to all who oppose true Americans.

Then, in college, I read a few books about this time period told from a Native American perspective: *Bury My Heart at Wounded Knee* and *Custer Died for Your Sins*. Wow. Massacres, broken treaties, relegation to desolate reservations. I realized how one-sided my education had been. It wasn't entirely inaccurate, but I needed to reframe. I was living as an American in an image of our history that was limited, prejudiced, and reinforcing to my sense of special privilege. And this is also true: when I made adjustments to my view by changing my language, I stepped inside *those* frames too. Though we can increase our awareness and do our best to name situations well, we never get completely outside the frames. We can only see what our window-frames, however clear and large, allow us to see.

From inside the Frame, We See Our Image of the World

So far, I have focused largely on words, words that create images in our minds, as did the story about Mark on 9/11. We could say that we live not so much in the world as it is, but in our *image* of the world. Words don't create worlds (we can leave that to God), but they do create visions and versions of worlds. We see ourselves in a particular time and place, with a particular identity, and family and culture. We conform our behavior to our image of the world, an image we might happen to call *exciting* or *depressing, pleasant* or *disagreeable,* perhaps something resembling a *movie* or a *chess game*. If I see America as "a safe and gloriously free place," I might live with more confidence and pride. If I see America as "a violent and greedy place," I might live with more fear and ambition.

Our words select certain parts of the landscape, and that's the landscape we tend to see. Researchers Andrew Newberg and Mark Waldman explain that the brain doesn't put thinking and believing in one area and what we've learned through the senses in another:

If you ruminate on imaginary fears or self-doubt, your brain
presumes that there may be a real threat in the outside world. . . .
So choose your words wisely because they become as real as the
ground on which you stand.

Our framing provides considerable power to see reality in particular ways.

Although our choices are varied and rich, frames are not utterly flexible. We can't talk the world into being whatever it is we desire. Everyone
who looks at you with squinty eyes is not out to get you, nor is the "cute
young thing" next door thinking about you with every dip into the swimming pool. We can't frame things any way we want—especially when there
is too much evidence to the contrary. Or to put it another way, we *can*
frame things any way we want—but if our labeling doesn't sufficiently
mesh with the world around us, we might end up in a mental institution. If
you insist on saying you are Napoleon, I can't stop you from doing so, but
I'm quite glad that you aren't actually a military megalomaniac.

Even so, within the boundaries of that evidence, we have considerable "naming" room. We can call the day a "successful turning point" or
a "tragic step toward destruction." We can say that our twisted ankle is a
"catastrophic accident" about which we are "bitter" or a "forced Sabbath"
for which we are "grateful." We live inside our images of the way life works.
And we are invited by God to do so.

We Are Called to Reframe

During my first few months away from home, I wrote my parents a "college is hell" letter. My roommate chewed tobacco and had a hangover every
weekend, a bodily response that is considerably less pleasant in person
than it appears in the movies. I was too much of a "longhair" for the conservative cowboy crowd and too much of a moral conservative for the
Revolutionary Communist Youth Brigade. I didn't seem to fit anywhere,
not with the churchgoers or the nerds or the beer-guzzlers. I was lonely
and alienated.

One afternoon, when reading through the New Testament for the
first time in my life, I dropped my Bible onto the dorm room bed. I had
just read, "In this world you will have trouble. But take heart. I have overcome the world" (John 16:33). I was stunned by the drama of these words.

Suddenly, in my epiphany, the world changed from "a place of trouble" to "a place where Jesus has overcome the trouble."

Scripture constantly reframes things and challenges its readers to do the same. The world is not random; it's created. It's not just murder that's a problem, it's anger. Your good works and religion don't suffice; you need redemption. On one level, all scriptural assertions say, "It's not THAT (randomness, murder, works), it's THIS (Creation, anger, redemption). Don't talk about your faith like THAT, in spirit-killing legal terms. Talk about it like THIS, in life-enhancing terms of grace."

In fact, *every* conversation is an invitation to reframe, a request to see things from a slightly to significantly different point of view. Bob says, "I don't think the movie was insightful" (THAT). "It was sentimental and dull" (THIS). Or "Life isn't hopeless; it's purposeful." Requests to reframe are not intrusive, objectionable acts. They are unavoidable if you plan to have any contact at any hour with any human being. We are constantly calling others to reframe, and listening to the reframing of others. Reframing is central to human existence—and so it is central in all discourse, including Scripture.

In the Sermon on the Mount, Jesus highlights the importance of framing: "Anyone who says to a brother or sister, 'Raca' [you are contemptible], is answerable to the court. And anyone who says, 'You fool!' will be in danger of the fire of hell" (Matt. 5:22b). And when speaking to the Pharisees later on, he says, "I tell you that everyone will have to give account on the day of judgment for every empty word they have spoken. For by your words you will be acquitted, and by your words you will be condemned" (Matt. 12:36–37). I'm taken aback every time I read these passages. All those careless, hurtful, angry words I've used! In our language-lazy times, these are fearsome words about words. As Eugene Peterson says, "For those . . . who decide to follow Jesus, it only follows that we will not only listen to what he says and attend to what he does, but also learn to use language the way he uses it."

Though Jesus doesn't mean that our words are *all* that matters, he does mean that our words matter. The byword of our day, "whatever," as in "who cares," does not reflect an appreciation for language. I see this language-attentiveness in Jesus' disciple Paul. In the book of Romans, he asks, "What shall we *say*?" (italics mine) seven times. In each instance, he implies, "Should we continue telling ourselves error? No, we should speak the truth. We should live the truth." Romans 6:1 says, "What shall we say, then? Shall we go on sinning so that grace may increase?" Certainly, Paul doesn't want us merely to *say*, "We have decided to stop sinning." He wants us to stop making life-crushing choices—but he also wants us to stop justifying them by the way we frame them. We are more likely to sin if we give sin our verbal blessing.

Since every word is a window, we are all called to examine our speech, our conversation and writing, to ask whether the view out a particular window is worth our gaze, whether our THAT should actually be a THIS.

———

Years ago, astronomer Johannes Kepler inspired scientific work by calling it "thinking God's thoughts after him," encouraging researchers to follow the logic of God's mind. Perhaps the inspired goal of good framing is "speaking God's words after him," encouraging communicators to pattern their language decisions after God's choices. Both can lead to restoration or reformation, even resurrection.

Morning Tapestries

The fabric of this summer day unfolds
in loose bluebird threads and yellow
warbler weavings; it clothes the hill
above my sandstone wall in browned
grass stitches; it blends down and
blurs up into a madras of acorns
and oak leaves and dappled sun. What
a miracle to hold the hem
of God's garment, his earthly covering,
to slip into this billowing, blousy praise.

CHAPTER TWO

There Is No Immaculate Perception

Hamlet: Denmark's a prison. . . .

Rosencrantz: We think not so, my lord.

Hamlet: Why, then, 'tis none to you,
for there is nothing either good or bad,
but thinking makes it so. To me it is a prison.

—William Shakespeare, *Hamlet*, 2.2.11

Above my head, I hold a book. Strolling toward a student in the front row, I ask, "What is this?"

She smiles and says, "A book."

Gently, I bop her on the shoulder with the book. I move to the student behind her. "What is this?"

Sporting a nervous grin, he replies, "A bunch of ideas."

A little harder, I tap the book on his head and move up the line. This student cowers, hesitates, and squeaks out, "A . . . *good* book?"

Bop.

I step to the next and see the pseudo-fear in his eyes. I raise the book high above my head. "What is this?" I say.

He mumbles something.

Through my smirky grin, I bellow now. I bring the book down as if I will hit him smack on his noggin. "What is this?!"

Hands raised to protect himself, he says, "Something I don't want?"

"Yes! But what *is* it?"

Sheepishly, he squirts out, "A weapon?"

In triumph, I pull the book away and shout gleefully, "A weapon! It's a weapon! You see: there is no immaculate perception!"

Besides showing you my teasingly abusive teaching methods, this story points toward a central problem in communication: the difficulties we have in achieving mutual understanding. One person says, "Why did you call me a dork?" The other person says, "I didn't. I asked for a fork." Sometimes we don't have enough context to understand what is going on, and sometimes we just get things wrong—in small or significant ways.

Paul echoes these concerns in 1 Corinthians 13:12, "We don't yet see things clearly. We're squinting in a fog, peering through a mist" (*The Message*). To state Dominic LaRusso's phrase, "there is no immaculate perception," is to admit that we don't see everything about anything. Our perceptions of things aren't complete or perfect. We just see parts of events, however crucial or trivial our perception. As Madeleine L'Engle puts it, "I have a point of view. . . . You have a point of view. But God has view." To say we *fully* understand even one simple experience would be a kind of blasphemy because it would be a claim to omniscience.

"There is no immaculate perception" reminds us how easily we over-state what we actually know or how we partially misread an event. We frame our perceptions one way, but we also constantly reframe them as new perceptions arrive, including the possibility that we have been framing in error or in a self-serving way. Sometimes we are *sure* someone is mad at us—then we discover that this someone had received bad news that day, or we learn that his or her typical facial expression just looks grumpy. Jeremy hated how his father felt disappointed in his performance as a son. Then his older brother said, "He's not truly critical of you. That's just the way *he* is." And most of us are surprised when we learn that eyewitness reports in court can be alarmingly unreliable (see endnote). Seeing through a glass dimly means that we can't see everything—and it also means that we may be mistaken in what we think we see.

Our overconfidence about what we know is one reason plot twists work. As audience members, we've been following a story just fine. Everything makes sense. Then some revelation tells us what *really* happened: the compassionate executive actually cheated, or the cheerleader was the murderer, or the heartwarming parents were the arsonists who set their own house ablaze so they could get an insurance settlement. We think we have perceived things fairly well, but then learn we haven't accounted for all the details.

Not only does no one frame things perfectly, truth is not impossible to misunderstand. It's not just that *we* can't see clearly; the truth itself can be obscure. Just because something is true doesn't mean that it is unmistakable. Sometimes we think, "What's the matter with you? Can't you see [the obvious truth of] what I'm saying?" Not all truth is sitting on some sort of pedestal that everyone sees in the same way.

For this reason, I've always found the complaint that "the Bible can be interpreted in a thousand ways" to be an empty criticism. *Everything* can be interpreted in a thousand ways. Welcome to life! A brilliant student can say she is stupid. Some say the Holocaust never happened. Yes, anyone *can* make an outlandish assertion about a mind or a massacre or a biblical passage, but the real issue is if the contention can be solidly supported.

Our purpose in many conversations is to sort through the diversity of views. We talk, in part, because perceptions aren't immaculate. Since you don't see what I see, I offer my outlook, and vice versa. We explain, listen, argue, question, and inform. After I drove two hours to see Vanessa, I was glad the conversation turned to her relationship with her father. As I encouraged her to reconcile with him before he died, she wept openly. I thought I'd struck just the right tone. A year later, Vanessa lashed out at me about how hurtful the conversation was, that I had no business telling her how to run her life.

Though we can be discouraged by how widely perceptions vary, we might also be encouraged by how the need for clarity can motivate us to connect with others to enrich our view—and how much we enjoy speaking with others about these different views. In fact, almost every time we speak, we imply, "Please add my perspectives to the mix" or "Please reframe this situation as I do." Of course, we don't always say please—but far from being coercively intrusive, this sharing and persuading can be a beautiful aspect of community life.

We all require assistance to see what we've missed. If my grandpa hadn't told me about his trip to the Philippines in 1906 and how he arrived in San Francisco not long after the big earthquake, I might have a different sense of adventure. If Reggie hadn't told me about getting harassed because of his skin color, I might not be as sensitive to racial issues. If it weren't for my wife's gentle commentary about love, I might still be stuck in my more junior high versions of it. When we participate in these conversations, we engage in the acts of framing and reframing—and there's no immaculate view of that metaphor either.

The Framing Metaphor Dismantled and Reassembled

So, what's this framing metaphor about? We use the comparison copiously. We refer to:

> framing events with words
> frames of a painting or photograph
> framing a scene when pointing a camera
> frames in sports: a baseball inning or a turn in bowling
> the human skeleton as a frame
> framing as a step in constructing a house

Although I have already introduced the metaphor, I want to extend the discussion.

Inside a room, we see frames around windows. One is clear, another translucent, another broken and smudged with fingerprints. Through the window, we see what's "on the other side," the backyard and the fence with an alley behind it. There's a bluebird making a nest in the white birdhouse. From the far side of the room, all we can see is the bluebird and the birdhouse, but when we walk right up to the window, we see trees, trashcans, and a broken swing set.

The frame is not the same thing as the object it frames—but the frame has a lot to do with whether or how we *see* the object, even if that object is just our little bluebird. And that points to the central question of this book: *When we frame our lives, what's in the picture?* In particular, when we frame our memories, our future, our inner lives, and our relationships to others, what ends up in those pictures? How have we labeled events in our past? What terms do we use as we imagine the future? How do we name our own strengths and weaknesses? How do we describe our relationships with friends?

Each frame creates a window through which we look—and we invite others to look through our frames too. Because no description leads to a perfect perception, three parts of the framing metaphor are especially relevant.

Frames Create Boundaries

When artists look at a blank canvas, they appreciate that they have a space to work within, an area for the eye to linger over, a place for the meaning of the piece to flourish. The same is true with our lives. We need frames to manage our existence, to give us our bearings, to create a space within which we can focus and explore.

A local public relations director explains his job by drawing a smattering of Xs all over a giant whiteboard. He says, "Let's suppose each X is one aspect of my client's company: the office staff, their product, the product's usefulness, its liabilities, the product's packaging, the dartboard in the work room, the waiting room décor, etc." Then he draws a square (a frame) around a couple of the Xs (the product and its usefulness) and says, "Here's my job: to ask the public to focus on a few Xs. I say, 'Look here!' Look at *these* Xs, not the other ones. I don't say that the dartboard and the administrators don't exist. I ask the public to pay attention to the aspects I highlight."

Just as he can't represent everything about his client's company, we have to decide which words we'll use to provide listeners a place to focus. *We never merely report* what we think or experience. We always say, "Look here." Notice the vibrant sunset. Think about the chocolate gelato. Gasp at the violence in the news. Every time we frame a picture with a camera, we have chosen what we want future viewers to see: most likely the nesting bluebird, not the trash. This works with words as well. For example, "I thought Keisha was snippy and aloof, but I recently discovered that [Look here!] she is a generous and thoughtful person."

By limiting and focusing the topic at hand, the borders of a frame encourage listeners to look *for* something. By calling Keisha "generous," her friend alerted others to be on the lookout, to have their antennae up, for evidence to support that description. When my summer job was blacktopping driveways, I "saw" dull, cracked driveways all over town. If I frame the world as terrifying, causes for fear abound. All frames say "look here." See THAT part of the world, not THIS part. Words frame events and provide windows.

Windows Always Reveal and Conceal Something about Us

As visitors come into our living spaces or visit our social media connections, they see what we have chosen to say about ourselves. Here's a photo of me climbing some mountain (I'm adventurous!). Here are my children looking as cute as can be (Ain't I a good parent?). Here I am holding my umpteenth beer (I'm a party animal!). I don't mean these statements in a sarcastic way. I mean that our descriptions reveal our interpretations of events. Each word choice seems to say both more and less than we might wish.

Every frame opens onto a certain view and, by doing so, also tends to conceal other views. When, on the first page of this chapter, Hamlet named Denmark a prison, he did not call it a refuge. We often forget that we tend to miss what *isn't* said, what isn't pointed out. Tiffany typically frames her experience as "God is punishing me." Her relationships with men "blow up." Her family persecutes her, and her dreams are consistently dashed. No matter what happens, she fits everything inside the "punishment" frame. But when she sees this, she admits that her frame misses what is good in her life—and the things she is grateful for. We might say, "We see what we see because we say what we say." Words always both reveal and conceal.

The Sizes and Shapes of Frames Affect What Is Pictured

If you have taken a painting or a photograph to an art store to be framed, you were probably amazed at how different the image looked with each possible frame: a huge golden frame vs. a narrow black one, a grainy wooden frame vs. shiny chrome. Whether we are skilled choosers or not, we search for a frame that "fits" what's inside it. Sometimes we don't search very hard to find apt words—and keep using the same tired phrases. Other times we find a word that almost feels magical in its ability to express the mysteries we think and feel.

And some words create real problems, such as when we choose a frame that accentuates only a small part of the whole picture. Not only is there no immaculate perception, but some perceptions are significantly twisted. Stereotyping is a small frame that forces all of reality into a tiny space. French people are rude. Kenyans can run forever. Poor people deserve their poverty. "My husband is so stupid. He can't even take out the garbage right." When our kids were learning about drugs and alcohol in a grade school program, they spoke as if anyone who smoked a cigarette had committed the most heinous crime on earth. Stereotyping says, "This person is *only* this small thing."

Another part of the metaphor is that some frames are ornate, while others are plain. Do the frames we choose correspond to the pictures inside? I once heard someone refer to a stunning sunset as "nice as hell." Why did he put an ugly frame around something beautiful? Some frames just don't fit, like when our children throw a tantrum over an inconsequential event. One mom says to her boy, "Hmm. If you cry like this over a little scratch, what will you do when you break your leg?" We expect words to represent reality well.

Sometimes no frames seem to match what we think or feel inside. We say we "don't have the words" to adequately tell the story of a life-changing conversation. Or we don't know how to talk about a car crash that took the life of a friend, or describe the moon rising behind the silhouette of oak trees. Likewise, in the hymn "Crown Him with Many Crowns," Matthew Bridges called God "ineffably sublime." God is so good, so rapturously magnificent that our best description is that God is indescribable. When we say that "words fail us," we hope to find writers who help us say, "That's it! That's just what I haven't been able to express." In Edmond Rostand's play, Cyrano's big nose kept him from romance—but not from expressing romance on behalf of a tongue-twisted lover.

"No Immaculate Perception" Is No Excuse for a Messy Window
When the Tea Fire of 2008 swept through Santa Barbara, 211 homes and nine structures at Westmont College (where I work) burned to the ground in about twelve hours. In our immediate neighborhood, one-third of the houses went "down"—and most everyone's landscaping fried in the heat or the sizzling flames. The night of the fire, rumors flew, yes, like wildfire.

We heard that the prayer chapel at Westmont had burned and that our house was "toast." Neither was true. We didn't know what to believe until a good friend—whose house had succumbed to the blaze—called us from our street to confirm that our house was still standing.

Though our walls endured, we felt traumatized. Our neighborhood looked as if tanks had blasted their way through it. There were ashes, ashes, everywhere, and it didn't help that just a month earlier, the Great Recession's stock market tumbled hard and a donor for the college had withdrawn a huge pledge for buildings that were already started.

Most of us spent many days climbing up and down the ladder of anxiety. In the midst of these struggles, I read an article in the local newspaper written by a woman whose house had burned in a previous Santa Barbara fire. She said our first task was to see ourselves as "survivors," not only as "victims." Even indisputable events like a fire can be framed unclearly or inaccurately, with or without the tone we hope to represent.

The idea that "there is no immaculate perception" is no reason to give up attempting to explain things well; it's no excuse for leaving our windows smudged and broken. Since every word focuses our attention in some directions and not in others, our recognition of the potential "messiness" of our windows leads to two different commitments: truth-telling and attitude-making.

Framing Matters Because Truth-telling Is at Stake

Though some of our framing is on-task but incomplete, we can also, intentionally or unintentionally, get things wrong. Yet some people hesitate to make any truth claim at all. They say it's arrogant, presumptive, a claim to a God's-eye view. Isn't everything we say a function of our upbringing, such that nothing can be said with confidence? It's true; we can't help but see the world through our own eyes, but that does not mean we see poorly or that we can't work at being empathetic—nor does it mean that all visions are equal.

Truth exists: truth about physical reality, moral choices, and the meaning of life. We don't have to be arrogant about this, but we don't have to be ashamed either, even though we don't perceive the truth perfectly.

Unless we believe that some perceptions are more faithful to the truth than others, we won't care much about the precision of words.

G. K. Chesterton said that people may not want to quarrel about words but, "If you called a woman a chimpanzee instead of an angel, wouldn't there be a quarrel about a word?" Precision of meaning matters. Students in my classes have, without intending to be humorous, written about "Jesus and the leopards" (instead of "lepers") and "The Sermon on the Amount" (instead of "Mount"). One Public Speaking student summed up his presentations by saying that he had communicated his "points and views in a manure understandable to all." When a commitment to accuracy is weak, professors tend to get going with red ink.

Grossly embellishing and falsifying our own stories or the stories of others are also issues of faithful reporting. Based upon his study of adolescent behavior, researcher Chap Clark says that one of the key differences between current young people and previous generations is the way they talk about and practice lying. "Nearly every student [that he interviewed] admitted to lying regularly, without remorse. Yet these same students actually believed that they were highly moral, ethical, and honest people!" During summer conferences, when he spoke to nearly three thousand students about this trend, not a single high school student protested his findings.

Though immaculate mutual understanding isn't possible, usually a good-enough measure of it is. If that weren't true, we wouldn't bother communicating at all. You wouldn't be reading this book, because the difference between what I think and what you perceive would be too significant.

Since truth-telling matters, we need to commit to *faithful reporting,* as faithful a framing of events as we can muster. If I call Rachel "bossy" without also mentioning her "compassion," my lack of faithful reporting has consequences. If I go on and on about one rose blooming in my front yard after the Tea Fire, without mentioning the charred ground cover everywhere else, I would mislead my listeners. We can't "get it perfectly right," but we can be committed to framing situations well.

Framing Matters Because Attitude-making Is at Stake

Is today an encouraging day or a discouraging day? Are you grateful you were the oldest child or are you bitter? Are you tired of either/or questions or are you fine with them? Some aspects of our experience are mostly subjective. An old story is told of three masons working on a wall. Each one was asked, "What are you doing?" The first one said, "I am making money."

The second one said, "I am laying brick." The third one said, "I am building a cathedral." Each way of framing reports faithfully, but each evaluates the situation quite differently.

Consider Ellen and Denay. Ellen is an above-average sales exec. She surpasses her quota much of the time and calls herself a "success." Though she doesn't get a lot of praise from her supervisor, she sees progress in her work and looks forward to a position with more responsibility. Denay is also an above-average sales exec. She surpasses her quota much of the time, but calls herself a "failure." The lack of praise from her supervisor confirms her incompetence—and depression about her future marks her life.

Many times, what matters is less about an accurate rendering and more about helpful attitude-making, not so much faithful *reporting* as faithful *valuing*. In the first case, we bear truthful witness to the situation at hand, exercising care not to willfully misrepresent events. In the second, we bear faithful witness to what is good or how we desire to live, taking care not to misapply true values. Since hope is better than despair, Ellen chose hopeful words. Since compassion is better than complaint, I can choose to describe my difficult neighbor as persistent rather than annoying. "No Immaculate Perception" sometimes means that we get to choose our perception.

One of my favorite stories along these lines comes from Victor Hugo's *Les Misérables*. When the ex-convict Jean Valjean is refused a bed at a half dozen places, he knocks on the door of an abbey. The bishop, whom Valjean takes for a lowly priest, welcomes the weary man to a warm meal and a bed. Because he had told the bishop about his life in prison, Valjean is astonished by this hospitality. The bishop then says,

> "This is not my house; it is the house of Christ. I tell you, who
> are a traveler, that you are more at home here than I; whatever
> is here is yours. What need have I to know your name? Besides,
> before you told me, I knew it."
>
> "Really? You knew my name?"
>
> "Yes," answered the bishop, "your name is my brother."

Everything changed for Valjean because of how the bishop framed the situation. Jean Valjean began to see himself not as a shameful ex-con but as a meaningful member of God's extended family.

Attitudes grow from our choices—and other behaviors often follow attitudes. During a banquet celebrating remarkable advances made by children with motor-skill issues, the speaker said, "The problem begins with names. If we call these children 'brain-injured' rather than 'mentally deficient' or 'retarded,' we will approach our work differently, with hope, not resignation." Those who foster "positive thinking" have understood this aspect of framing—and much research confirms the worth of these choices (see Mirivel, etc., in endnote).

Our moral attitudes grow out of our framing too. One might say that the road to hell is paved not so much with good intentions as with euphemisms. I'm not enraged; I'm expressing myself fully. It's not gossip; it's being more informed about my community. Our culture often changes moral language in an attempt to avoid criticizing any personal choice, associating "evil" with only the most terrible crimes. Jesus seemed to do the opposite, pointing toward our intentions as immoral: our anger, not just our physical violence; our lust, not just our physical sexual transgressions. We have misconstrued "maintaining a positive attitude" to mean never saying anything that might be perceived as unpleasant.

But our attitudes (our perceptions) about unpleasant experiences, even death, are also influenced by framing. Knowing this, a friend dying of ALS told the pastor who would speak at her memorial service that she didn't want the service to be only about "rising" in her resurrected state. She wanted her last years with the disease represented as dark hours during which God was present. It mattered deeply to her that those at the service knew her attitudes in the broader truth about her years of suffering.

———

Because there is no immaculate perception, no one perfect way of seeing or conveying an event, our framing is central to how we live. If we see that truth-telling is at stake, we will care enough to report events as faithfully as we can. If we see that attitude-making is at stake, we will seek ways to project our desires, values, and beliefs as faithfully as we can. Our word choice may seem insignificant, but it can be the difference between looking out at life through a small, broken basement window and looking out through a clear picture window through which one can watch both a raging storm and the soft colors of the dawn.

Another way to worship is to praise a lake

Buttery soft, Lake Almanor smooths over the wrinkles
rippling out from the night's churning. On an old dock perched
in the morning sun, I see a grebe dip
through the creamy surface, bobbing for breakfast.

Binoculars in hand, I scan and wait for an osprey
to swoop and snatch a trout, turn it straight into the wind
—head facing the nest—and fly there for a feast.

So I start my push-up routine. An arched-back
stretch, then twenty slow ones, my breathing paced
with the gently lapping waves. I sit up.

I don't hear that hook-beaked predator
screeching, so I do my second set, thirty-two,

but who's counting? A squirrel squeaks birdlike,
scattering cone-scraps near my feet. Then I grind out forty,
my stomach taut, my shoulders straining—
but the lake will have none of it, reminding me

that the day's first duty is due. After set four,
I rise, warmer now, holding solid at the end,
another plank on the dock. In the distance I hear

a motor revving into wakefulness, but I lean
away and listen in for the pealing of the lake, the bobbing,
the lapping, its rhythmic glory pushing up into my ears.

Watching an osprey feed is not the only way
to feel the face of God.

CHAPTER THREE

Order, Order, Everywhere

The answer, Mr. Perkowitz said . . . is to
reframe the issue using different language.

—John M. Broder, "Seeking to Save the Planet, with a Thesaurus"

I remember the exact moment I became a true athlete. It was when, like all legitimate competitors, I had arthroscopic surgery on my knee. One day, during my weekly basketball game, "George the Rock" smashed into "Greg the Breakable," and the result was a cartilage tear. In pre-op, the anesthesiologist gave me two options. He said he could put me completely under anesthesia or he could put me out from the waist down. One advantage of the waist-down option, he said, was that I could watch what was happening inside my knee on a TV monitor during the surgery. "Don't worry," he said, "all you will see is the monitor. A curtain will block your sight from anything happening below the waist."

Feeling brave and masochistic that day, I chose the waist-down option. I liked it. With my head slightly raised, I watched the instruments at work inside my knee. A little pincher tool nibbled off the torn cartilage like a video game muncher. Amazing! Then a tiny vacuum cleaned things up. Fascinating! Then, a nurse bumped the curtain. Whoa! I looked down at the bottom half of my body and saw a side of beef held up by the nurses.

What the heck is that? Oh my gosh. It's attached to my hip! Help! That can't be my leg. I *know* where my leg is. It's flat on the operating table!

When I saw my leg hanging in the air, I broke into a full-body anxiety sweat that drenched me until my paralysis vanished in the recovery room. The sense of order I had about my body, where my legs and arms should be, flew into disorder. I was a mess until that order was restored.

In one of his case studies, neurologist Oliver Sacks writes a riveting story about a patient, Christina, a woman whose reaction to a drug left her unable to control her limbs—unless she looked at them. She had difficulty walking or sitting, and even her face became unusually blank. After much analysis, the attending physicians concluded that Christina had lost her *proprioception*, her intuitive sense of the location of her muscles, tendons, and joints.

Proprioception has been called our sixth sense. It's how we know where our body parts are—without actually touching or seeing them. We don't have to physically feel our left ear or our right hamstring to know where each is. Proprioception is our body's sense of itself, its sense of order. Though we take it for granted, a little bump of a surgery curtain can help us see how important it is.

When telling his story about Christina, Sacks says that proprioception is "the fundamental, organic mooring of identity." Our sense of our bodies anchors us physically, tethers us to reality. We know we are a person, in part, because we know where we are, where the different parts of us are. Proprioception gives the body its orientation in space, a way to understand how things fit together. Might words do the same thing for our mind?

Our Mind's Sense of Order

If you ask me about my writing habits, I might say, "I like to sit in my 'inspirational' chair on my front porch." If you confide in me about your spouse, I might say, "All marriages have their secret struggles." Not only do we have a special physical sense of order, thanks to our proprioception, but we also have a special cognitive sense of order, thanks largely to our language choices. Our framing moors us to our place in the world. We are "docked" in whatever "harbor" our framing creates. For better or worse, I "drop anchor" by the weight of my word choices, some of which are thoughtful reflections and some of which are matters of habit.

We talk about how our experiences fit into the scheme of things. My wife Janet comes from a large extended family. She has sixty-five *first* cousins. Her father's family were Mennonites who fled from Ukraine during the Russian Revolution. Her mother's side immigrated from Holland during great poverty, and became farmers in the Yakima Valley of Washington. Many, many stories create a sense of order for Janet: How one grandfather traveled the country in 1940 to tell FDR about the coming Japanese attack. How the other grandfather met his bride on the boat sailing to Ellis Island. Stories of faith and hope. Stories of struggle and tragedy.

Our words secure us in time. They number our days in sequences of weeks and years. They tell the arc of our lives in a way that "makes sense," narratives that have believable characters, plot lines, and compelling emotion. In *The Call of Stories*, psychologist Robert Coles explains how he felt he wasn't being successful as a young therapist. He'd ask a client a question about symptoms, only to be greeted by silence. Everything changed when he began simply to ask his clients to talk about their own stories. Coles realized that when his clients explained themselves, they could become their own "appreciative and comprehending critics," stitching together the loose threads of their lives. Not only did he engage with his clients through stories, he also suggested that their central therapeutic goal was good analysis of their own descriptions of events. We frame our lives—and sometimes need to reframe them.

My friend Kaylee talks about how she loves being in control. She went to college, did well, got her master's degree, got married. She framed her circumstances as "manageable." Every obstacle was something to be overcome. Her go-to line was, "I've got this." Then she had twins. Prematurely. Then her husband had a stroke, an event induced by an automobile accident that occurred the day after the delivery. Kaylee was in the hospital for six weeks after the birth—and her husband and the twins had issues too. Suddenly Kaylee's framing didn't work. She didn't "have this." She was anything but "in control." When we cannot fit ourselves into the story unfolding before us—when a severe storm comes—our mooring slips. We feel adrift. Gradually, Kaylee reframed with less confidence in her ability to manage her circumstances, and more trust in God.

Without our physical proprioception, we would be "lost in space," struggling to negotiate every step, unsure of how to grasp a glass, bewildered by distance and the weight of things. Without our rhetorical proprioception (through language), we would be "lost in time," unconnected to a meaningful story, perplexed by sequences of events in our day, uncertain of how to proceed into the future.

Framing and reframing are ways of talking about the sense of order that we achieve through language choices. I tell myself that I live in beautiful, privileged Santa Barbara (a reference to space) at the beginning of the globally challenged twenty-first century (a reference to time). This gives me a sense of order that is different from saying that I live in drought-stricken, elitist Santa Barbara, at the dawn of the end of the world as we know it. Of course, there are limits to the labels I bring to space and time. If I say "Relax! Slow down!" to firefighters on their way to douse a blaze, I'd likely get some disgruntled looks. More absurdly, if I say I live on the Planet Zippie-doo, on the cusp of the Age of Buttered Toast, I will most likely find myself labeled mentally ill. Our words can anchor us well or leave us floating about aimlessly.

Order, Randomness, and Framing

This phrase I've been using, "a sense of order," might seem a little too pat. Isn't life pretty random? One minute life is predictable and the next minute there's a flash flood or some random shooting. We hear the word random a lot. "Mary and I both like kale in our smoothies. How random!" Or, "I randomly ran into a friend on the steps of St. Peter's in Rome." Life seems so random at times, so meaningless and chaotic, it's a wonder we ever meet people at agreed-upon places or have conversations in which we have a high degree of understanding or find ourselves experiencing the same weather as others standing next to us.

But, of course, we do. Though accidents happen and events befuddle us, order is the norm from which randomness is measured. Most days, most everything about our bodies, our schedules, and our activities is fairly reliable. We notice accidents because, most of the time, traffic flows just fine. Most people obey the law, objects fall when dropped, and sometimes people even stay on topic in conversation. The world is so astoundingly consistent that we are stunned when events break the pattern. The sense of order we create through framing is not wishful thinking or a wavering candle in the darkness. More than we might notice, things are remarkably dependable.

I don't mean to dismiss the terrible pain caused by pointless accidents or unthinkable crimes. I can't fit everything I learn into a neat system of thought. But I also want to say that, to grasp the role of language in our sense of order, it is important to see that "it's random" is a way to frame events. Although we may feel out of place, have crushing anxiety about our relationships, and tense up with the insecurities that lurk around every corner, that doesn't make the world undecipherable. "It's random" is a way to explain difficult and catastrophic events. Some things may be random, but "it's random" is not a statement of fact.

Whatever our attitudes toward randomness, we might try, for the sake of thinking through framing, to put on a lens of "order" to see what we might see. Each of our daughters went through an "I see patterns" phase. Everywhere we went, we heard "Look! Three triangles! It's a pattern!" or "Both ducks are green. It's a pattern!" As we put on a lens of order, we may not be as irrepressibly cute as my daughters were, but we could be on the lookout for structure, principles, predictabilities, and effects that follow causes.

We do our best to make meaning by picking and choosing what needs to be said. Framing is what we humans do. Language choice is our chief proprioception-making faculty.

Our Sense of Order and Things "Out There"

We see order out there in the world we observe. How could we not? In *The Believing Brain*, Michael Shermer says that "The brain is a belief engine," that "patternicity" is wired into our brains. On the lookout for order, we organize what we observe through the senses. At least we try. When we see a moving shape in the distance, we compare it to other shapes we know until it conforms to a previously known form. As a conditioned Californian, when I smell something burning, I wonder how close the wildfire is. We may get things wrong. And, of course, mysteries remain. After we seek resolution, we may end up with confusion or tension or paradox—settling into the anxiety of meaninglessness or the peace of acceptance. But we are driven to interpret, to explain, to understand.

Some people are "over-explainers," feeling compelled to have some clear, clean principle that answers every question. Some apologists are like this, listing every possible argument against faith and offering every possible counterargument, turning the Bible into an indexed answer book or a you-never-need-to-be-unsure-of-anything book. It wasn't when *all* my questions were answered that I came to faith. It was when I realized there really was a Savior who could rescue me from my sin, a God who loved me.

Others are "under-explainers," avoiding hard questions and intimacy. If you asked my mom how she was doing, she would always say fine. Even in her years with cirrhosis, she (according to my dad) "never complained." While admirable in some respects, I believe her lack of vulnerability led her to mask her fears and struggles with alcohol. Others seem intent on not seeking answers, covering their doubt with busyness or superficiality. They don't want to be troubled with meaning and mystery and the difficulties of analysis. It interferes with having fun. But, without becoming obsessive, we can do our best to comprehend and then try to figure out how to carry what is burdensome to grasp, what continually upsets our proprioception.

Despite over-explainers and under-explainers, order seems everywhere: the cause-and-effect reliability of most things, laws of physics, principles of heredity, even in our moral sensibilities. Paul says in Romans 1:20: "For since the creation of the world God's invisible qualities—his eternal power and divine nature—have been clearly seen, being understood from what has been made, so that people are without excuse." Some kinds of order are built into the way we are made. We "know" God exists. We "know" this means certain things about how to live. We can't offer the justification that we had no idea that love is preferable to hate or that life is good and should be protected.

For the most part, we expect our experience to "follow form," and we frame things accordingly. Sometimes, when life doesn't fit, we try to make it fit. Two quick daughter stories. One: When one daughter was eight, she said, "Do people in Oklahoma shoot each other a lot?" I said, "Not more than anywhere else, I suppose." She paused, then said, "So why is it shaped like a gun?" Two: When driving home from a Christmas service one day, one of our daughters sang, "God and sinners, recon-smiled." At her age of eight, "reconciled" meant nothing, so she impressed some meaning onto these syllables. Shermer says, "Although true pattern recognition helps us survive, false pattern recognition does not necessarily get us killed." Good thing for our girls!

Our Sense of Order and Things "In Here"

Not only do we see order outside of ourselves, we see it and seek it inside ourselves. We want our inner world to make sense, to have our internal proprioception secure. We ask:

Who am I?
Why was I made this way?
Why I can't I stop my vices?
What is my significance? Where do I fit?
Why am I still bothered by something that happened so long ago?

So much anxiety, so little time. I have a psychologist friend who is one of the best conversationalists I know. He is interested in just about anything anyone brings up and asks important, provocative questions. I guess it's part of why he became a psychologist. He also keeps a messy house, has trouble staying on top of his billing, and struggles to make progress on his writing projects. He says, "I need more anxiety, like you." We talk a lot about our inner sense of order, the way we frame the values that drive us and how we respond when these values have not been satisfied. Is he complacent or is he content? Am I driven or am I disciplined? We both want to achieve our vocational, familial, and spiritual goals—and live peacefully in the inevitable distance from complete success.

As language-makers, Kenneth Burke says, we cannot avoid seeking order because of the fundamental human act of searching for the perfect word. We can't help ourselves. Because we are language-choosers, always striving for the best way to capture something, we want to "do it right"— whatever it is: Be a good mom. Be the coolest, hippest person around. Be the most stellar employee. When we don't fulfill our frame, we feel out of sorts, disordered. Sometimes, we get new ways of framing—like "introvert" or "extrovert"—and we feel more resolved.

We frame the world in certain terms and we have to talk our way through the aspects of life that don't match our framing. Perhaps strangely, this seems to be the plan of the gospel. Jesus upsets our sense of order on a regular basis, asking us to see things *this* way, not *that* way, as he did when he raised Lazarus. In John 11, the story is reported. Here's a sketch of Mary and Martha's constant need to reframe:

> Mary and Martha: Our friend is sick.
> Jesus: The sickness won't end in death.
> Disciples: Don't go to Judea. They'll stone you.
> Jesus: I won't stumble. I'm in the light.
> Disciples: Lazarus is sleeping. He'll be okay.
> Jesus: Lazarus is dead.
> Martha: If you had been here, he wouldn't be dead.
> Jesus: Your brother will rise.
> A Jew: Couldn't Jesus have kept this man from dying?
> Jesus: If you believe, you will see the glory of God.
>   Lazarus, come out!

At every turn, Jesus upsets the proprioception of those around him. He says that what you think of as dead is alive, what you think of as danger is safe, what you think of as life is death, what you think of as important—physical healing—does not begin to compare with spiritual healing. He wants his followers to see the order "out there" as God's order, and to have the Spirit's sense of order "in here." Ultimately, he wants his disciples to trust his way of framing the world.

Order, order, everywhere; we see it when we think. Without my bodily proprioception, I couldn't grasp that the leg before my eyes was mine. With poor rhetorical proprioception, I might fail to see how God used my knee surgery to transform my spiritual perspectives. Our sense of order must adjust to shifting circumstances. Life is not stationary, and if we intend to live by faith, our frames will need to move as well.

Dementia Road

My mother-in-law is accidentally
driving us down the street called
Weeds in the Garden of Sanity Avenue.

It's tough enough to wind down
these lombardian, obstacled roads
at our best. But now, with Connie

at the wheel, we're reeling, banging
against the armrests, grasping
for seatbelts or any tightening thing. We're afraid

we'll fly out. We feel that one more
turn and the wheels will come off,
the axles grinding through the asphalt

like cartoon plows. And why? She planted and
watered well over the years, and now this harvest
of careening loss is what we reap.

She used to drive with both hands and cautious
eyes, as predictable as corn or beets,
and we've always known that she will eventually

run out of gas. But so will we
—and we wonder, whose emptiness
will find the narrow shoulder first?

CHAPTER FOUR

When You Frame Your Life, What's in the Picture?

To change your language, you must change your life.
—Derek Walcott

I begin this next story where I must—several years ago, on that fateful day when we bought our first (and only) new car. We'd done the necessary research and ended up getting the car in Los Angeles, two hours from our town. After nervously signing papers, I slipped behind the wheel for the drive home.

A few miles into the trip, the small of my back began to ache, so I shifted my weight. It still hurt. I tried adjusting the seat. The sharp pain continued. No matter what I did, my lower back screamed out to me—I mean really hurt—and I started screaming in my head. "What have we done? Why am I in so much pain?" Buyer's remorse rushed into every crack in my psyche.

By the time we made it to Santa Barbara, I was in a full-bodied agony. I grabbed my phone and called the dealer. "Can we return the car? I can't believe how much pain I'm in, serious pain!" He was not sympathetic. "Once you drive it off the lot, it's a used car. That's the law." I was crushed. Sweaty, panicked, and crushed.

What could we do? I investigated trading the economy seat for a better one. When that failed, I asked an auto upholsterer to change out the padding in the seat-back. No go.

A frightful prospect loomed. We had planned to drive the new car twelve hundred miles to Vancouver, British Columbia, to greet our first grandchild. Graciously, Janet suggested that we rent a car and leave this one home. We could figure out what to do about the whole mess after the trip. "No," I said. "This is why we bought the car. We aren't going to waste money on a rental." This is what men do, right? We don't let a little pain interfere with an irrational choice. So, I "bucked up" and buckled up.

I hated every mile. I squirmed in my seat. I tested every pillow and lumbar support ever made. Whatever our progress each day, I could not wait to get out. My back hurt. My ribs ached. My cheekbones throbbed. Everything hurt.

And yet sometimes—sometimes—after hours of walking around and stretching, I felt okay. I managed as best I could. I knew that when we made it home after the trip, I'd heal up in a few weeks. Things would be fine.

But things would not be fine.

A year and a half after the trip, my back pain was about the same. But other things got worse. Six months into my struggle, my neck tightened up and remained so for a year. I spent parts of every day in the fetal position on the floor. Because I couldn't sit for more than about ten minutes, I lost twelve pounds off my already thin frame. The Back Pain Diet, I called it. It's guaranteed! Curiously, no one seemed interested in learning my method.

To Janet, and just about anyone who would listen, I talked a lot about my pain, my enormous regret over buying the car, and the ridiculous amount of money we were spending on trying to get me better—without me getting better. Here are some of my common lines:

No one has any idea what is wrong with me.
All I think about is the pain. I'm never going to get better.
My body is broken. It won't heal.
God has deserted me. Why doesn't my faith make a difference?

I became so depressed, my wife later said, "I thought I might lose you." I wasn't suicidal, but if I squinted, I could see the rope out there in the distance. The pain itself felt like a rope, pulling on everything from my neck to my hamstrings. When the rope went slack, I would forget about my pain altogether, instantly. But it never lasted. I felt strung out, strung up, hopelessly tethered.

My point is not to work on your sympathy. My point is that I started this story by saying: "I begin this next story where I must—several years ago, on that fateful day when we bought our first (and only) new car."

But this isn't so.

I don't *have to* start the story here. *I chose* this way of framing the event. "Must" says that there are no alternatives. And look at two other key words in this sentence: begin and fateful. My story, even a story about my back, doesn't begin the day we bought the car. It's part of the whole story of my life and my ways of experiencing and dealing with pain. And "fateful." What makes this day full of fate? Did this date have more fate than other days? Is fate the operative cause?

So, there's a backstory to my back pain. For a year and a half, I framed the cause of my pain as the anti-ergonomic car seat, a devilish design destined to destroy me. But then I learned there were other ways I could frame the car and my experience. That's when things began to change.

Much of the time we talk as if we are merely reporting the obvious, recording life "how it is" or "how it was." To reexamine the assumptions housed in our frames can be the beginning of healing.

The title of this chapter is "When you frame your life, what's in the picture?" I said in the introduction that this line is one of the driving questions of the book—and I believe it is one of the most important questions we can ask about our lives. In the case of my back pain, the question helps me see that my framing of these events matters and that my framing creates a picture of my experience, an image that might look quite different if framed in other ways.

I tell this story at length because it is such a clear example of what I have reviewed so far about our sense of order and what I will develop in this chapter about four essentials of the soul and how they are central to our framing and to a transformation of our souls.

When Faith Is in the Picture

So, where have we come? We have a sense of order that is, largely, created and managed by the ways we frame things, by our "rhetorical proprioception."

Framing matters, because truth-telling and attitude-making are at stake. We are often oblivious to the power of our words, but then *something happens*—a significant event like a car ride and back pain, a new relationship or a collapsing one, a disease or a healing—and our sense of order is dramatically disrupted, leading us to realize that certain ways we've been framing our experience are inadequate, including our beliefs about God.

Most of the messages we receive have little to no effect on our image of the world, but sometimes something rocks our world. I had my way of thinking about my body. It usually served me pretty well. I eat okay. I exercise. I'm healthy. Then I developed acute, enduring pain that disrupted my way of living and my view of the world. It changed the way I talked about my body. It changed the way I talked about my faith, because I grieved that my faith did not provide more solace for me. Was it me? Was I a lousy believer? If I was honest with myself, I needed to recalibrate, re-center, reframe.

When something significant challenges our routine, our first question is, "What is going on?" How does this new event fit with what we already know, with the frames that have, to this point, worked fairly well for us? Though we expect that a simple explanation will clear up the mystery, sometimes it doesn't—and we feel doubt or anxiety. I called it *dread*. I wasn't used to sitting on the edge of my bed at night and wondering how I could keep this up for the rest of my life. My former conceptions weren't working.

In many ways, this revelation is a good thing. It arrives like an inspector who sheds light on some flaws in the house we've built. Maybe we just need to reframe the picture of Jesus over the mantel—but maybe some windows need to be enlarged, or the framework for our house needs major repair. It's better to know there are cracks in the structure.

Of course, all frames have flaws. They can never say everything about any particular thing. We do our best to describe, to be compelling, to represent our beliefs well, but there is always something elusive that stays outside the frame. We say, "Homosexuality is wrong," and then a son declares he is gay, or "My life is one disaster after another," and then we discover we are loved by God.

When our frames get shaky, it can be unnerving to face what we've always known deep down—that our explanations leave a lot unexplained.

And more than that: some of our ways of naming things have led us astray. They are skewed or flat-out wrong. "My body is dependable" is a frame that denies certain daily or periodic failures, and will eventually collapse as we age and our body declines.

The real frame-shifter for me was reading about a new way to think (and talk) about what was going on in my back—that perhaps one cause of my pain wasn't structurally physical but emotional. One writer convinced me that the rope didn't go just from hamstrings to neck; it went all the way to my brain. I needed to deal with my stresses, including some anger in my past. How I dealt with stress brought me to spiritual issues of trust. Did I really believe God cared for me?

The cycle of reframing often implies something fundamental about faith, that faith is dynamic. Faith is not something that is set at conversion and that never changes. Certain beliefs might remain static (the Apostles' Creed), but our day-to-day faith is always adjusting to new circumstances, new discoveries about ourselves and God. Sometimes we worry that if our faith is changing, if it isn't unwaveringly rock solid, something must be wrong. We must be wobbly believers. But a dynamic faith is one that is alive and taking new knowledge seriously. In *My Bright Abyss*, Christian Wiman transparently chronicles his spiritual journey. It's okay to be wobbly, because life circumstances carry us "forward to a place where the faith we'd fought so hard to articulate to ourselves must now be reformulated." Our words transform our faith and our faith transforms our words.

Doctrines may endure in stone, but our relationship to those doctrines is more like the vines curling around the stones. They grow and attach in different ways over time. God is who God is, but my faith gets modified by what I learn about life and God. I may learn that I have articulated my faith falsely. All this to say that reframing is inevitable and therefore central to our lives and our lives of faith.

After I started counseling, my back began to improve. In fact, during my first session I talked about one of the earliest bouts of back pain I endured—when I was about twelve years of age. Besides thinking "Who has back pain at age twelve?" I suddenly remembered that my parents started their serious drinking about that time. The insight stunned me. I went out to the car and just sat there taking it all in. I wondered and prayed if this event could mean anything about my present ordeal. Then, suddenly, for the first time in a year and a half, I had no pain in my back and neck. For about thirty-six hours, I was free. That felt like a miracle.

When *something happens*, we respond to the uncertainty with our primary understandings about how the world works. We look to our past for answers. We wonder what the future holds. We examine our labels for ourselves and we think about our relationships to others. These actions point toward four central aspects of our very being.

Framing and Four Essentials of the Soul

One way to sort out our framing and reframing work is to explore what I call four essentials of the soul, ideas inspired by Eugen Rosenstock-Huessy's "Cross of Reality." He says our lives can be seen in how we talk about the past and the future (the horizontal line of his cross) and how we discuss our inner and outer worlds (the vertical line). In all four areas, he says word choice is vital: "Our words must strike a balance; language distributes and organizes the universe, in every moment, anew."

I have translated and expanded Rosenstock-Huessy's Cross into four "soul essentials": remembering the past with gratitude, anticipating the future with hope, dwelling within ourselves in peace, and engaging with others in love. Each essential is crucial to our sense of order.

To say that we live at the intersection of time and space sounds complex, but it is simply a way to describe our everyday experience. We all live *in time*. In the present moment, we carry memories of the past and conceptions of the future. How we live in the present has a lot to do with the way we frame our memories and how we anticipate what's ahead. We also all live *in space*. We have inner worlds (our sense of self) and outer worlds (our relationships with others). How we walk in the world has a lot to do with what we say as we dwell within ourselves and how we engage with others.

Because these categories are so common in everyday experience, we can see how our framing in each area is central as well. Hence, they are four *essentials* of our being, of our soul. We all have particular experiences in each area—but our framing in each area matters. Remembering: How do I remember my childhood? Dwelling: Who do I say that I am? Anticipating: Where do I say the future will take me? Engaging: What should my interaction with others be like? For example, I might call my past "idyllic," but later reframe it to "superficial." I might call the future "destined for disaster," but reframe it to "cautiously optimistic"—and so on with the others.

These four parts of daily life could be pictured in a frame. I'll explain how the virtues fit a little later.

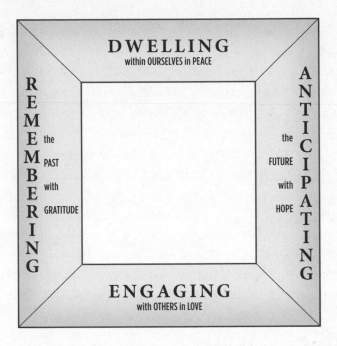

DWELLING
within OURSELVES in PEACE

REMEMBERING the PAST with GRATITUDE

ANTICIPATING the FUTURE with HOPE

ENGAGING
with OTHERS in LOVE

When I lived through my two years of back pain, I framed and reframed each of these essentials constantly. Initially, *anticipating* was my key focus. Will this pain mark me for the rest of my life? Will I ever be able to walk freely again? Would a good God give a person a future so bleak? Mainly because of my relationship with my wife, *engaging* loomed large: I talked about the guilt I felt for disrupting her life, for being such a constant downer. How can I be a loving person when I feel so cranky? As time went on, the pain got into my *dwelling* within: Who am I if I can no longer be an active person? Will I still be "me"? What parts of my identity are wrapped up in labels that may no longer fit, such as tennis player, hiker, hard worker, or gardener? My *remembering* was activated too: Would this event be a marker between the previous me and the present me? What did my past experiences with pain teach me? What could I do to keep from ruminating on earlier painful events?

As I've reflected on this experience, I've wondered, why do we frame things the way we do? Do we have a kind of default perspective that gets expressed? Is it because of our personality or upbringing? Is it because of beliefs we hold, rules we think we need to follow, or desires that drive our choices?

Staying with the house metaphor I've been using, I'd say we have the window frames we see through (the words we say that affect our sense of order), and below these frames is a foundation for the whole house (a framework that supports everything above it). To understand framing, we need to examine our *frames* and our *frameworks*.

Framing and Framework

From my journal during the two years after the drive to Vancouver:

> I don't feel loved by Jesus. And because I can't do so many things, I feel less worthy, less lovable.

> There is always something to feel glum about—and always something to feel grateful for. Much of my life is wasted time. I need to give up my rights to perfect health, perfect productivity, perfect perfection!

> Reading John Sarno's *Healing Back Pain*. He says much of our pain comes from emotional stress that squeezes our blood vessels in the neck and back, and that we need to deal with the sources of this pain. Can I believe this?

Undergirding our various word choices might be many different frameworks, from beliefs we are trying to implement to commitments so deep that we cannot begin to unravel them. My journal tapped into foundational beliefs about "deserving to be loved," "the need to be perfect," and "the nature of the human body." We can see the relationship between frames and frameworks with Dominic LaRusso's phrase "we say what we say because we are who we are." The line argues that our words are not just invented in the moment; they come from our person: our character (or lack thereof), our knowledge, cultural background, family history, and so on. The phrase also implies that if you want to change what you say, you need to work on who you are. Frames come out of frameworks.

In *You Are What You Love*, James K. A. Smith makes two points that connect well to the issue of frameworks. First, he says we are far more influenced by what we desire than what we believe. For belief-oriented Christians, this sounds counterintuitive, if not downright wrong. But Smith argues that, at our core, we are not mainly thinking beings but desirers. Because we are fundamentally worshiping beings, what matters most is what we love. When Jesus says we should believe in him, he is talking about living out a loving commitment, not merely reciting "I believe in you."

Who we are comes out of our basic desires. If we love nature or power or contemplation, these desires will direct our choices—including our word choices. Smith says, "You are what you love because you live toward what you *want*." So, we need to ask: How is framing related to the frameworks of our loves?

Second, Smith says that we learn about our loves by looking at our habits. What do the ordinary rituals of our lives say about our desires? If we love having stuff, we will habitually stop at garage sales; we'll spend a lot of time on product websites. Our speech habits will reflect these desires. We'll regularly talk about the deals we got and how our next purchases will influence our lives. The frame about "my amazing new wardrobe" probably derives from the framework "I love the status of having things." When we frame our lives, what is in the picture? We say what we say because we are who we are.

A blogger recently reflected on her parenting, realizing that she and her husband often say, "Have fun!" to their kids as they leave for an activity—and they also say, "Did you have fun?" when they return. The parents became aware that this framing reinforced a framework of the good life that said, "Everything we do should be entertaining and highly pleasurable. The most important 'good' is to have fun." Not only did they not want to be communicating this message to their children, but they also wanted to change *their* frameworks and the framing based on it. They wanted a new craving, a desire for greater breadth of appreciation of all that God has to offer us, not all of which will be "fun." They talked about the idea among themselves, encouraging and inspiring each other to hope that a change could be made. And they worked on their speech habits by saying not just "Have fun!" but "Be good to your friends" and "Hope you learn a lot." When their children returned, they asked, "How did things go with your friends?" and "What did you learn?"

———

Whatever frames we use, we'd be wise to ask about the frameworks that support those terms. As I review the four soul essentials in the next chapters, part of the discussion will be about these foundational desires. How does my framing of the past derive from commitments (desires and beliefs) I have concerning bitterness and forgiveness? In what ways do my "anticipation" statements bubble up from the simmering I've done in fear or with courage?

Thankfully, I am in less pain these days. It's hard to write a book when you can't sit or stand for more than ten minutes at a time. It's hard to write a book no matter what! Though my body has improved, I've worked at new habits in keeping with my rekindled desires. I do my physical exercises and I do my verbal exercises. I keep reminding myself that I need to attend to my emotional issues that need healing too—and which may be the root cause of stress-induced pain. I try to frame faith as a gift, and say with the writer of Hebrews, "Like Abraham, I am looking for a city which has foundations, whose architect and builder is God" (Heb. 11:10). That's the framework I want for my framing.

And, yes, we sold the car, the one I called "Satan" every time I saw it in the garage.

Bracing Back

I can't seem to get perpendicular enough
to stop the pain. I want to bolster

>   my back,
>   to freeze it
>   like the icepack
>   I daily strap
>   to my vertebrae.
>   It the only way to be these
>   days, to deaden or be dead.

"Sit tall and straight!" My mother said.
She doesn't need to say it anymore.

>   It's all
>   I can do.
>   She used to
>   complain about
>   my roundedness.
>   "I'm going to put you in a back brace!"
>   And I'd imagine some medieval strait-

jacket, an iron genius of immobility. She'd
zip her thumb along my spine and I'd stiffen,

>   flattening out
>   as she desired,
>   making myself
>   rigid and grim—
>   till she turned her back
> and I hunched over
>   and cupped my hands
>   to catch imagined water
>   swirling   curling   flowing
>   down the rivers of my unbraced mind.

Remembering the Past with Gratitude

CHAPTER FIVE

Remembering

What was hard to bear is sweet to remember.
—Portuguese Proverb

When I was in eighth grade, I was four foot ten. I loved basketball and a blonde beauty who was five foot six. Let's just say that fulfilling my dreams was challenging. Though my big chance never came in basketball, it did arrive on the dance floor one magical Saturday night. Somehow, I mustered the courage to ask The Beauty to dance and somehow she mustered the humility to say yes. Since it was a "fast dance," we were pretty much in our own worlds of awkward kicks and flailing elbows—but after the music stopped, I walked her back to the "female side" of the room. As she turned to her girlfriends she said, "Don't ever dance with Greg. He's so short!"

Our memories resurface in many different ways. Some memories, like the one above, hurt in the moment but prompt laughter now. Though many difficult memories fade, others linger like monsters under the bed, reaching up a gnarled hand or growling in a way that keeps us from "going there." A friend of mine, Sarah, discovered in her thirties that her father had engaged in a series of affairs for many years. Of course, the revelation sent Sarah's sense of order, her proprioception, reeling. What was she to do with her memories of good family times? What did it mean to say the word "Dad"? Initially, in the moment of hurt, she concluded, "Now I know that *anyone* could betray me. If my father did, maybe even my own husband could. The only way I can see myself through this is to make sure that no one gets close enough to touch me." That's a monster of a memory.

Remembering is a significant aspect of our lives. It's how we keep the past in the present. Memories can inspire, destroy, and direct our choices for good or for ill. Often, when I sit down to write, I hear voices from my past, critical voices of those who have said my work is not worthy of their time or it's overblown or angry or silly, that somehow it just doesn't measure up. To get to the point of being liberated enough to write, I have to "send the demons away." I have to tell these memories that they will not have power over me, at least that morning. Sometimes the demons win. As we know, the past is not just in the past; it is with us. We live *in* it, in how we've framed it.

Many scriptures speak to the influence of remembering. Note the variety of emphasis below (italics mine):

> Only be careful, and watch yourselves closely so that you *do not forget* the things your eyes have seen or let them fade from your heart as long as you live. Teach them to your children and to their children after them (Deut. 4:9).

> [The Lord said] "I will forgive their wickedness and will *remember their sins no more*" (Jer. 31:34b).

> [And Jesus said] "All this I have spoken while still with you. But the Advocate, the Holy Spirit, whom the Father will send in my name, will teach you all things and *will remind you of everything I have said* to you" (John 14:25–26).

> [The thief on the cross says] "Jesus, *remember me* when you come into your kingdom" (Luke 23:42).

In just these four verses, we see references to the importance of remembering what God has done, the reality of having sins forgotten, the Holy Spirit's role as a reminder of Jesus' teaching, and an impassioned plea to be remembered by God. These compelling categories speak to the importance of examining the nature of recollection.

It's no surprise that remembering well is an essential of the soul. We live in time, and time lives in us. Occasionally, we hear the refrain that we should just live in the present. To this, G. K. Chesterton offers: "To live in the present is like proposing to sit on a pin." Though we can dwell too much on the past or the future, we can't simply decide *not* to be influenced by our memories. Rather inevitably, they *remind* us. All of this we know intuitively, but we may not sufficiently recognize the "houses" we have built as we have framed and reframed our experiences. How have we "recorded events in our brains"? What do we play up and what do we play down, emphasize and neglect? How do we retell our stories to others and ourselves?

Remembering is a significant part of who we are, and reframing is a significant part of remembering. If this is the case, *how* we frame the very act of remembering might influence how we *recall* and *forget*. What is the memory like and what is it not like?

Remembering *Is Not* like Storing Data in a Computer or in a Container

As I mentioned in the chapter on "no immaculate perception," eyewitness reports are often less reliable than we think they should be. Sometimes lawyers try to get a trial postponed, knowing that testimonies tend to shift over time. Of course, we can't remember everything. We can't *perceive* everything. Sometimes what we remember is true as far as it goes, and it might be considerably more accurate than what others remember. Sometimes we embellish events to serve our own needs, and sometimes we are mistaken. Our memory is never separated from our view of the event. How *could* it be? We are the ones selecting what to remember.

Our memory is not an exact record of the way things were because (though we use this metaphor all the time) our brains are not computers. We don't have a digital hard drive. What goes in is not a copy of what happened, and what goes in is not usually what comes out. Our brains, fantastic though they are, move things around, misplace things, and can even mash up several events together. All we have to do to be reminded of this is to have a conversation about a memory we've shared with someone else. "You remember WHAT? Dad actually said that?" or "Oh my gosh. I'd entirely forgotten that you got sick in the cabin."

Our memory does not work like a computer; neither is it a container, a silo in the farmland of our brains, awaiting the harvest of knowledge. This metaphor implies that the memory is something that gets filled up and emptied repeatedly. Students often think this way about taking exams: "I can't fit anything else into my brain!" and "Once I regurgitate all this information on the test, it's gone"—as if knowledge comes out of our "containers," flows down our arms, into our pens, and onto the page, never to be heard from again. At least, we teachers hope not.

Whatever it is we manage to remember, we remember it selectively—and with what researcher Elizabeth Loftus calls a "superiority complex." After our first trip to Italy, my wife and I loved showing pictures and telling stories about the wonderful bridges in Venice. One day it dawned on me that I had conveniently forgotten that (oops!) we really didn't enjoy Venice on that trip. It was blazing hot, trashy, stinky, and full of rude tour groups with their umbrella-popping tour guides. After a while, I realized that I wanted to tell a story that was better than our actual experience. The crazy thing is that I had begun to believe my own story! "Oh, Venice, it was so lovely and charming. Oh, wait . . . that's not quite right." Was I forgetting or embellishing or just neglecting to tell the whole truth? Though we'll never sort out all these decisions precisely, the situation reminds us that our memories are always made up of conscious and unconscious decisions about how to frame our experiences.

In addition, all memories suffer from certain problems, what Harvard psychologist Daniel Schacter calls memory "sins," such as forgetting what we'd like to remember, not being able to forget what we don't want to remember, editing our memories in ways that favor ourselves, etc. No wonder family reunions are so often enlightening and contentious—as we hear different versions of stories. Sometimes I think that telling the truth is a bit like typing; you only have to be a little off on the keys to end up with a lot of nonsense.

So, what do we make of all this? Do we throw up our hands and say that since we can't be wholly accurate, we don't need to bother? At the very least, these characteristics ought to inspire some humility about what we remember. Instead of saying, "This is exactly what happened!" we might say, "This is how I remember what happened." When we make this shift, we acknowledge the role of framing. We know we have remembered the story with certain descriptors—and we may have missed or skewed something.

Remembering Is like Leaving Lunch in a Stomach or like Sitting in a Room

Don't get me wrong. The memory is a marvelous thing, a gift from God that enriches our lives beyond measure and for which we are to be faithful stewards. It's terrific lumber, useful for constructing towering ancestral and national edifices—but the wood is usually splintered and sometimes warped. Or maybe the human memory is more like a stomach, something that changes what it "digests." This gastric image resists the digital deceptions in the computer metaphor. When our stomachs work well, we use the best parts of what enters and get rid of the waste. Although many truths wind through the intestines of this metaphor, you can see where it's going. So, maybe we should move on to a different comparison.

Frederick Buechner says we could think of remembering as "the room where with patience, with charity, with quietness of heart, we remember consciously to remember the lives we have lived . . . taking time to remember on purpose." Buechner sees remembering as a room, as a place we can return to—and one that serves us if we do important contemplative work in it. Our memory isn't just a storage facility from which we collect information; it's a capability that can lead us to greater wisdom and greater hope.

Before moving on to more precise ways of thinking about remembering and how reframing relates to this essential of the soul, I'd like to digress for a few pages to discuss a language issue that has a bearing on all four essentials: metaphor.[2]

— Excursion into Metaphor —

In the two paragraphs before this excursion, I referred to computer, container, construction, stomach, and room metaphors, and those are only the obvious ones. In just the second sentence alone, I made comparisons to gifts, riches, measuring, and stewarding. (The hunt is on to find them

---

[2] Each of the "Essentials" chapters will at some point take a short trip down a side road to visit a language subject that significantly directs our framing efforts in all four essentials of the soul: metaphor, questions, advertising, and clichés.

all! Oh, wait, "hunt" is a metaphor too!) If you aren't interested in the relationship between metaphors and framing, you can skip this excursion and
track down the next sections on personal and social memory. But before
you do, you might ask yourself how you could "skip" this section or "track
down" the next one without thinking a bit about metaphor.

Though we tend to see metaphors as artistic flourishes (and they often
are), we would be wise to also see every metaphor as a framing of ideas,
an argument that says that one thing is very much like another thing. We
speak about talking *down* to someone, or going *up the ladder* to success.
We refer to our lives as *a rat race* or *a roller coaster,* or *a dream*. Do any of
these metaphors really matter?

In *Metaphors We Live By*, linguists George Lakoff and Mark Johnson
claim that all metaphors matter, that we live our lives in keeping with them.
If I say that life is a beach, I'm saying that the most important aspects of
life are the vacation and fun parts: sun, sand, relaxation. In addition, with
every metaphor, we state a comparison directly and imply other connections. If life is a journey, what happens when you get lost? If romance is
craziness, what happens when you need to be rational and work hard?
Like all frames, more than we realize, metaphors have power to shape
our experience.

We tend to get into habits of metaphor that frame our lives in unin-
tended ways. For example, we often use financial terms to explain "dealings"
with other people. We say, "I'm investing in you"—and we mean this positively, even endearingly. But what does this imply about our "balance sheet,"
"cutting our losses," and "maximizing gain"? If I invest time in you, do you
need to "pay dividends"? Using the investment metaphor might lead us to
"account for profit and loss," to measure what I did for you and what you
did or didn't do for me.

This metaphor contrasts sharply with Jesus telling us that we won't save
our lives until we lose them (Matt. 16:25). He says we are to forgive others
just as we have been forgiven (Col. 3:13). How can we do this if we attempt
to balance every relational transaction? Many biblical metaphors speak to
relationships that are more cooperative than the way investors watch their
investments: we are to be neighbors to all others, members of a body working together, apprentices looking to the journeyman Jesus.

All metaphors point listeners in some directions and away from others. Sometimes reframing a metaphor can change our lives dramatically. If you saw life as a giant chess game in which you were a powerless pawn, what might it mean for you to reframe yourself as an adopted child of the King?

And these issues of metaphor apply to all four essentials of the soul. Is our future "bright" or "dark"? Do we dwell within ourselves as a princess (prince) or a mama (papa) bear? Do we engage with others in a "battle for survival" or regard others as "solid" or "flaky"? You might try to discern the more common metaphors you use to frame in each soul essential.

In the spirit of metaphor reframing, Andy Clark contends that our memory is less like a container and more like scaffolding (the kind used for repairing a building, not for hanging a horse thief). The metaphor implies that, like scaffolding, our memory can grow to accommodate what we are learning. We can keep adding new planks and supports that help us to access our memory—rather than merely pouring knowledge into a container that at some point gets filled up. I like how this expands our notion of memory. When it comes to remembering the past as a soul essential, metaphors matter.

—— End of Excursion ——

The Memory Matrix

Whatever image or metaphor we use for remembering, we could also think of our memory in terms of the matrix below: we have short-term and long-term memories, and we have personal and social memories.[3]

	Personal	Social
Short-term		
Long-term		

Short-term and long-term are self-explanatory terms—but they are not self-explanatory in practice. Why do some things stick and others

---

[3] Oh, the irony: As a testimony to the undependability of our memories, I have a confession. I've been using this matrix for so long that I can't remember if I put together these classic aspects of memory or if I learned the matrix from someone else—and who that someone else might be. If someone else, I hereby acknowledge you, whoever you are.

don't? Why can't I remember a crucial detail that happened five minutes ago (how an argument escalated) but I can't forget a meaningless detail that happened forty years ago (like these actual lyrics: "Yummy, yummy, yummy, I've got love in my tummy")? The most straightforward and technically accurate answer to this question is "How should I know?"

But I do know that how we frame our memories has a lot to do with our short- and long-term relationships to them. Some memories, as the epigraph at the beginning of the chapter states, are "hard to bear" but "sweet to remember." When Sarah grew past the pain of her father's affairs, she realized the "sweetness" of growing in empathy for others in their suffering. Other memories seem to harden our hearts and pollute our ability to trust. Some women who have been sexually abused never feel entirely comfortable around men again.

So far in this chapter, I have been discussing our *personal* memory almost exclusively. But each person also carries a *social* memory, a sense of history. We know about U.S. history and church history—and something about the history of race relations, language, transportation, and gender. We frame each of these histories too—and adjust our social memory as we learn new ideas, some of which displace certain "facts" we used to be certain were true. I grew up believing that George Washington threw a silver dollar across the Potomac. Then I traveled back east and saw the width of the Potomac. Washington was a great man, but he was not Superman.

For Christians who reframe, examining social memory provides the opportunity to learn from the saints of the past, to compare our memories of living with Christ with the memories of earlier disciples. As a young believer in a college Western Civilization course, I was inspired by the devoted lives of many Christian "greats," from Augustine to Martin Luther, from Charles Finney to Mother Teresa. I began to see my life rooted in a rich history. 1 Peter 2:10 came alive to me: "Once you were not a people, but now you are the people of God; once you had not received mercy, but now you have received mercy." I had joined the people of God by seeing all previous believers as my ancestors.

How we talk about the past matters. Because our personal memory includes our own story—our own accounting for our place in time—it contributes significantly to our sense of order (and mystery). Inevitably, we place our personal history in the larger context of time, in social memory.

Remembering and Reframing

As established in the previous chapter, when it comes to our memory, we have a sense of order, our proprioception supplied by our language. We have some go-to stories that present the past as we want it displayed. How we survived falling into a mud hole. What happened when Mom and Dad split up. In part, we are making sense—we are creating order—out of the mystery of our lives. When we frame our past, what's in the picture?

Sometimes we go to Buechner's "Room Called Remember" because we know we have some reframing to do. We've become aware of some destructive or problematic ways we talk about our past. We hear a speaker. We read a book. We talk with a friend—and we come undone. Our sense of order is disrupted. We might have a personal revelation. One friend realized, "I've used my past to build in myself a house of suspicion, and I wish I didn't have to live in it." To move on, he must go back and examine what led him to be so untrusting.

Other times we are taken by surprise. In a conversation on campus one day, Lauren made an offhand comment about how she did not like to be touched. Given a few other comments she had made about the way she distanced herself from others, her friend Oliver said a prayer, gathered his courage, and said, "Were you abused as a child?" Lauren's eyes widened. She teared-up and whispered the beginnings of a terrible hidden story. As they were leaving, she leaned toward Oliver and said, "I've never told anyone anything about this." Lauren's work with her memories began with admitting the truth—and included lots of therapy.

Our mental sense of order can be challenged by good news, bad news, or just news. When we feel disrupted by the news, we work at reframing. This is good though sometimes painful work.

———

Years ago, I was asked to speak to high school seniors at the spectacular and remote Young Life Malibu Camp in British Columbia. When the campers met in their cabins with their counselors, we adult guests also met together. Over the course of the week, we discovered some remarkable commonalities. The physician had entered his profession to work at a CARE unit at a hospital because of his alcoholic mother. The yacht hostess (so named because many boaters stopped and wanted a tour) had been significantly abused by her often-drunk father. Two others, an artist and a writer, were working on a series of books about family problems told from a child's perspective. They had written a book about divorce; now they were working on one about alcoholism. And then there was me. At the time, my mother was dying of cirrhosis.

This convergence of wounds stunned me. I couldn't help but think, "Who put this group together?" It was one of the most powerful experiences of God's orchestration I had known. Early in the week, the artist and writer asked the rest of us to tell our stories—so they would have images and events as material. Many difficult memories flooded in: the smell of my mother's unwashed clothes, the stumbling of my dad down the hall, the shame and anger, the loneliness of many nights looking for something to do, someone to be with.

Sharing those memories in that safe place has become a kind of Exodus remembrance for me. Just as the psalmists did, I look back and remind myself what God did for me in Malibu. By God's grace (and this is crucial), I *verbalized* my past. I paid attention to the ways I spoke about it, and heard ways to reframe these times.

As I framed these memories, I let go of some of the slavery of my bitterness. I began to better understand my parents as wounded people and myself as someone still carrying deep wounds. It sounds almost absurd now, but I was scandalized to learn from the physician how much of a classic "adult child of an alcoholic" I was.

I wanted to think I was unique, that I was "saved" in the sense that I had come through the experience relatively unscathed. Instead of accepting my memories at face value, I tried to deny that they had had much of an effect on me. I was ashamed to admit that I hadn't triumphed over my past, that it continued to haunt me, that it had shaped some destructive choices I was making and continue to make. All this to say that a better direction for me was to speak the truth about my experience, as best as I could. I needed to remember well and to practice remembering as an essential of the soul.

Diamond Mercies

Oh, Charlie Hammer, in eighth grade
you had enough acne to embarrass
us all. Those purple mountain
travesties, always rising, erupting—
and your pigeoned toes, shuffling
toward some calamitous end. We'd
whisper, "Retard!" Did it matter?
The best you could do was stutter back.

Then on the last day of school, during the softball game, we *had* to let
everyone hit, so Charlie came to bat. No Babe Ruth, he swung and missed, as
he did every day. And we said, "There goes Charlie Hammer, nowhere, as usual."
Strike three left the pitcher and we were already snickering when Charlie's bat,
its good wood, found the ball and carried it over Steve Cobb's straining glove
at first. Charlie and his smiling pimples lumbered up the line, as open-mouthed
as we were. Then, more shocking still, Gary Quinn, from right field,

grabbed the ball and flung it and—I know you won't believe this—he threw
it over the second baseman's head, on purpose, or so it seemed. Charlie
chugged along, the little engine who couldn't. He stepped on first, then
second base. At third, Mike Shima spied Charlie pounding toward him, so he
set one knee down to block the ball, just as he'd been taught, but somehow
the ball hit the heel of his glove. You would have thought he'd meant it—and
now Charlie rounded third, his tongue in the breeze, his eyes bugged out.

The miracle donned its rally cap now.
From left field, Jeff Benesch, backing up
third base, bare-handed the ball and cocked
his wicked arm. The ball zoomed,
a sidearm soaring precisely on target,
twenty feet over the base. Charlie crossed the plate.
Charlie came home. We ran to him and held him high,
each of us carrying Charlie on our errors,
screaming "Charlie Hammer hit a homer! Charlie Hammer
hit a homer!"—till the whole world knew.

CHAPTER SIX

Remembering Well

Four things come not back:
The spoken word; the sped arrow;
The past life; the neglected opportunity.
—Arabian proverb

I couldn't believe it. I had gone to the motel to pick up my graduate school mentor and take him to the airport. Before we left the room,
Dominic handed me a $100 bill and said, "You have to promise me one
thing. You will spend all of this on Janet." His generous gesture grew even
larger to me because of his sensitivity to my wife. And what a night we
had! Dinner at the Palace Café and musical theater afterwards. I cherish
that memory.

What does it look like to remember well? We know that our memory
is not just a mindless record of what happened. It is a *mindful selection*
of what happened—and what we wish had happened. How we remember matters.

The Old Testament says that Joseph, after being sold into slavery by his
brothers, tells his "bitter" story in a surprising way. When his brothers come
to him, fearful that Joseph will exact revenge for all the wrongs they did to

him, Joseph says, "Don't be afraid. . . . You intended to harm me, but God intended it for good" (Gen. 50:19–20). Joseph remembers redemptively.

But perhaps this example is unfair. Since Joseph's story turned out well, of course he could reframe his experience positively.

What about these next stories? Todd's wife of twenty-five years gets cancer. She goes through years of the ups and downs of remission and resurgence, and finally dies. After a few years, he marries a woman who is diagnosed with ALS just after they announce their engagement. Less than two years of debilitating diminishment later, she is gone. Or Russell: his teenage daughter dies of brain cancer. Two years later, his house burns to the ground.

For these sufferers—and for ourselves, since all of us suffer in various ways—what does it mean to remember well? Is the phrase itself a slap in the face, another layer of pain? When our wounds are raw, remembering well might feel too tidy, even inauthentic.

But what is the alternative to remembering well? Remembering poorly? Remembering falsely? Remembering angrily? We all have easy and hard stories that we keep retelling. As I walk through aspects of remembering well, I encourage you to hold a particular memory in mind, a memory that continues to challenge you.

Remembering Well Is Essential

Remembering is not just some inevitable thing we do; it is a crucial part of being human. Dogs don't dream away the afternoon thinking about the cat that got away. They don't feel guilty for how they barked at Mrs. Johnson and scared her half to death. But we humans spend a lot of the present in the past. Simply being human means, in part, working over our memories. Most of us, eventually, want to remember well; that is, to remember wisely, truthfully, bravely, gratefully. Our remembering relates to at least four basic human needs.

We Remember Because We Need to Feel Rooted in Stories

There's something about feeling rooted that provides the security from which to branch out. Our memories tell us where we've been; they give us a story in which we are the main character. Our life should have an arc, a meaningful narrative, a plot that came out of somewhere and is going somewhere. If it doesn't, we can feel adrift—and untethered people can cause themselves and others a lot of pain.

On my first day of English Composition in college, my professor asked us to write a short response to the question, "Who are you and why are you here?" I wrote, "You got me, pal." Partly I was just being my sassy self—but partly I was admitting my inability to answer the question in a meaningful way. I had not yet found the soil into which I could sink my roots, soil I later found in the garden of the church.

Our history contributes to our sense of order, where we fit in time. Do I belong anywhere? In large part, I answer that question with the framing of my memories.

We Remember Because if We Forget, "We" Aren't There

More than we realize, we actively resist amnesia. Of course, in the extreme, literal sense, losing memory is devastating—if not eradicating—to a sense of self, and to our sense of the selves of others.

When Janet's mother was in her later Alzheimer's years, we lost contact with the Connie that we knew. We did our best to help her retain her memory, and to help each other remember her pre-Alzheimer's personality. As she slipped further away from us, we worried that we would get stuck in memories of the last five years of her life, the sad, angry, diminished years. In some mysterious way, her death gave us permission to go back, to recall her cheerful, loving days as mother and grandmother.

We work at holding on to what's dear. In *Lament for a Son,* Nicholas Wolterstorff writes poignantly about the year following the death of his mid-twenties son from a mountaineering accident. He said that living faithfully and authentically with Eric gone "means not forgetting him. It means speaking of him. . . . We are to . . . resist amnesia, to renounce oblivion." We guard our relationship with those who have passed, to honor the living they did in our midst.

But we resist amnesia in simpler ways too. Just look around your house or office. We have all reminded ourselves of certain people or events by memorializing them in photos or souvenirs, through social media. The romance. The hike. The grandkids. The vacation. By telling ourselves to remember certain events more than others, we remind ourselves of the values we associate with those images, those events: that we are loved, that we care about God and our neighbors, that we can be brave and joyful. Many have tattooed their body to memorialize an event. About so many things, we *decide* what to remember and how.

When Janet and I were engaged, we lived two thousand miles apart. Not infrequently, I stared at her picture on my dresser. One night, oddball that I am, I had a bit of premarital anxiety because I couldn't imagine Janet's face from any other angle. I felt limited to her photograph. I thought, "How could I be sure about marrying someone I couldn't *remember* beyond the printed image?" Thankfully, I got past this nervous moment—but it speaks to the work we do to remember and the standards to which we hold our ability to remember.

We Remember Because as We Frame Things, the Past Influences the Present

We don't need much convincing here. Surely, we do what we do and we are who we are because of what has happened to us in the past. We studied law, so now we practice law. Our parents taught us follow God, and so we have remained in the church. But it's not that simple. We talk about events in *particular* ways:

> Losing that job was a *crushing blow*.
> When I was forgiven, I was *forever changed*.
> After the accident, my life *utterly collapsed*.

The past provides the context for our current existence—physical and verbal contexts that influence our present behavior. It also calls out voices that repeatedly speak to us:

> Forget the choir. You can't carry a tune in a bucket.
> Can't you do anything right? I'm not sure you're going to make it.
> I've noticed you are a consistently generous and other-
> centered person.

We might struggle to account for much of anything we do outside of the words others have spoken to us, the words we loop round and round in our heads. When we change the way we talk about the past, it doesn't change the past. It changes our present and our future. It changes how we live now.

*We Remember Because as We Frame Things, the Present Influences
the Past*

This idea is more curious. Think for a moment how our present experiences create lenses through which we view the past. If I've just learned about the effects of gossip, I might look back on my life and for the first time "name" instances in which I have both spread rumors and been damaged by unfounded comments. Or after hearing someone speak about gratitude, I might consider how to be grateful for things I've taken for granted in my past.

We may resist this idea at first. We don't like to think that "the past" is so flexible. But research shows that if we are currently experiencing a lot of physical pain, we will "remember" physical pain in our past *as stronger than it actually was*. After reading this chapter, you might take the ideas new to you (in the present) and examine your past differently.

Remembering is an essential part of being human. We need to feel rooted in our stories, to hold on to who we are by resisting amnesia. To be human means that the past informs the present and the present informs the past. When our human faculties are working well, we can't avoid remembering in these four ways. When we aren't able to remember well, we fear our very humanity is slipping—or perhaps we are fading such that we don't recognize the slippage but others do.

Yet remembering well is not just necessary, it is part of our soul practice.

Remembering Well Is an Essential of the Soul

When I decided that I did not want a secular life but a spiritual one, I gained a future and a past. In an instant, the history of the Bible and of the worldwide church become my history. I also gained new ways of relating to the past.

Living under God, striving to see the world truthfully, and growing in virtue—all of these pursuits depend on what we learn from and how we view the past. In fact, our soul depends on how we remember. As a starting point, if we seriously consider the past, we will find it hard to maintain our self-importance. How many of us will be remembered in history books? In family stories? For how long? These questions sound like good places for soul-work to begin. How is remembering well an essential of the soul?

Remembering God Fully

In Scripture, we are told to remember the Sabbath (Exod. 20:8), God's words (Deut. 4:9–13), God himself (Deut. 8:19), and to "forget not his benefits" (Ps. 103:2). Psalmists often model soul-nurturing remembering: "Therefore I will remember you [God] from the land of the Jordan" (Ps. 42:6). We are told to remember Jesus (2 Tim. 2:8).

Jesus himself, during the Last Supper, "took bread, gave thanks and broke it, and gave it to them, saying, 'This is my body given for you; do this in remembrance of me'" (Luke 22:19). This passage invites believers to participate in Communion (see Paul's instructions in 1 Cor. 11:17–34)—but in it Jesus asks his followers to:

1) remember *some things in particular* (Jesus' death),
2) *do* some things as an act of remembrance (take and eat), and
3) use these choices to *draw close to Jesus* himself (in remembrance).

In addition to the spiritual practice of Communion, this pattern makes connections to other choices in our lives. When on a retreat, for example, we often go on a spiritual pilgrimage of memory. We:

1) remember *some things in particular* (former times of faithfulness),
2) *do* some things as an act of remembrance (write in a journal), and
3) use these choices to *draw close to Jesus* (renew our commitments).

Teaching and Healing the Soul

In Lois Lowry's profound young adult novel, *The Giver*, a society has "relieved" its members from the burden of memories by loading them all into one person. When this person is in the process of passing on all memory to the next Receiver, the two of them discuss the benefits of someone knowing these memories. "It is how wisdom comes. And how we shape our future." Without knowledge of the past, the rest of the town only experiences the present—and is stuck in a repeating sameness. Lowry reminds us that the past can warn, encourage, and teach—if we are willing to engage with it.

I struggle with insomnia. At times, I struggle in the framing of my insomnia. Recently, after two difficult nights, I said I'd had my second *terrible* night in a row. This is how I told myself to remember my insomnia. Is this frame faithful to the event? Insomnia *is* difficult, frustrating, and anxiety-producing, but shouldn't *terrible* be reserved for child abduction, terminal disease, famine, or some such truly awful thing?

Not only do I need to consider how I frame my sleep-interrupted nights, I also need to *remember* previous patterns. When I have these debilitating times, what are the memory markers to which I can return for solace and hope? Two rough nights do not ensure a third. I remind myself that sleep itself is a miracle, a gift, a behavior that no striving can achieve. I am no more abandoned by God than, as a father, I abandoned my own children when they repeatedly struggled with any besetting thing. For the past to teach and heal, we need to have our framing "at the ready." This work is an essential of the soul.

Not all of our struggles submit to clear and healing reframing. Some people are stuck in consistent pain and fading health in ways that seem to make lists of memory markers irrelevant. The past may haunt us because of something we did or didn't do, or because of something that happened to us, something beyond our decision-making.

Yet, no matter how severe our circumstances, we have choices about how we frame things. Even after experiencing psychological torture for months in the Yugoslav military, Miroslav Volf says, "To remember a wrongdoing is to struggle against it. . . . How should I remember abuse as a person committed to loving the wrongdoer and overcoming evil with good?" The way we remember, Volf says, can move a debilitating memory from the center of our identity to the periphery, and can give us hope.

Being a "Reminder" to Others

When we think about what we say, we like to believe we say important and original things, influencing our friends with new insights—and we may. But much of the time, we only remind others of what they already know, in part because, in the circumstances, there is no need to be original, and in part because what others usually need to hear is a reminder of some sort. Yes, you are loved. No, you can't earn it. Yes, you've received grace. No, you can't bargain for it. Over and over; it's a lot of what we say. Reminding is central to our speaking and listening lives.

In *The Living Reminder*, a book about the role of memory in a believer's life, Henri Nouwen says we can be healing, sustaining, and guiding reminders to others. "To be a living memory of Jesus Christ," he says, "means to reveal the connections between our small sufferings and the great story of God's suffering in Jesus Christ." All of us remind others of something, of someone. Nouwen asks, "Who am I as a living memory of God?"

When I frame my story, about what do I remind others? Does my framing of the past remind others that the human story is a search for the good life, a longing for home that can be realized in God, or does my retelling speak only of the grand tragedy of human suffering? Do I remind others that they need to be more concerned about their appearance, their stuff, and that they must earn my favor? Do I remind others that beauty of soul is more important and that love is unconditional? When we frame the past, we remind others of what we think truly matters.

Discerning What to Remember and What to Forget

Sometimes people say that we should "never forget." Sometimes we hear that forgetting is healing. We have all experienced how remembering brings life. And we all know people who go to certain memories with a mental fingernail that keeps picking the scabs of their wounds. There are those who want to forget and can't. Sometimes (especially as we age!) we need to remember, and nothing comes to the surface. We might say that the memory is a fickle companion—and so remembering well involves studying our relationship with our memories and sorting out what's life-nurturing from what's death-making.

Beneficial remembering. Of course, we *should* remember, right? It's what we've heard since grade school. Unless we remember, we're doomed to repeat the Alamo, the Holocaust, Vietnam. We will suffer from our denial, our naiveté, our unwillingness to study what we needed to know.

Every year, on the anniversary of their daughter's death from brain cancer, my neighbors Russell and Allison ask friends to come to the local park to tell stories about Allysa, to release balloons in her favorite colors (orange and blue), and to share a meal together. This event honors the memory of Allysa—and frames how her qualities should remind us to live with curiosity and love, and in the confidence that God will ultimately make things right. Russell says, among other things, that this experience taught him to "be kind to yourself and to others."

Of course, remembering isn't just about sorrow. We frame the present in light of our ancestors' brave choices, according to the heritage made possible by them. We choose the parts of our experience to pass down to our children, both cautionary tales and heroic adventures. Good remembering means working at knowing the bitter and savory flavors of the truth, not just the sugar-coated stories.

Destructive remembering. Years ago, in a rural community, a young man's first child died at the age of five. As if that wasn't a difficult enough burden to bear, the pastor at the memorial service said that because the boy wasn't baptized as an infant, he was not going to be in heaven. The father screamed inside—and he never forgave the preacher for his incredibly insensitive and arrogant remark. He never forgave God either. This was the story he told, and retold and retold. It *was* awful, stupendously stupid, and a wound that one could not expect anyone to easily "get over."

Without denying the horrific pain of these events, might we wonder if this father's remembering, his way of framing this story, his pattern of repetitively cycling over the offense, marked his life with a bitterness always boiling just below the surface? Some memories are destructive not just because of the original wound but because of our compulsive resistance to healing.

In a book about Communist China's Cultural Revolution (just a little light reading to give me sweet dreams), I learned that in 1963, Mao orchestrated what he termed "Recalling Bitterness" sessions, meetings in which "elderly workers and peasants came to tell of the harsh and miserable days before liberation." He wanted to instill hatred.

As absurd as these meetings sound, sometimes we do the same. We wage our own campaigns of regret—as did the young father—angrily remembering what was done to us. If we just hated harder, we think, our oppressor would feel our pain. But, of course, the one feeling the pain is the one who stays bitter.

Beneficial forgetting. Though remembering has its benefits, forgetting is no slouch either. When *should* we forget? When is forgetting the best choice? For one thing, remembering can perpetuate the pain, not only in ourselves, but in whole communities and nations. Red and blue states, the Irish Protestants and Catholics, the Rwandan Hutus and Tutsis—the list goes on and on: groups that keep fighting over things that happened long ago, even centuries earlier.

Although my mom was one of nine children, I only met one of her siblings because an early rift over money divided the family. The oldest brother became rich, and all the other siblings expected a piece of the pie. Because they would not forget this decades-old issue, the family remained split until my mother, near the end of her life, reached out to a sister she had not seen in forty years.

One of the problems with forgetting is that it is difficult to achieve through our willpower. Forgetting is like falling asleep. The harder we try, the further we are from our goal. That's why reframing is so crucial. It's a lot easier to start saying, "I will look for what I can appreciate" than it is to stop saying, "You have committed an unforgivable offense." The best we can do is set up conditions for forgetting, to stop holding mental meetings for our bitterness campaigns. Good forgetting calls us to reframe.

Destructive forgetting. One of my good friends from high school could never remember Janet's name. This pained her. *Really*, she thought, *you can't remember the name of your best friend's fiancée—after being introduced repeatedly?* Some forgetting makes us feel invisible, and other forgetting may deny us access to a "good word" or the appropriate resources in a conversation.

Sometimes we try to forget what we still need to remember. Bella recently told me she'd had a surprisingly wonderful talk with her parents about the difficult past. Bella's now sober father expressed regret that he had pushed her around when she was a teen, that he had threatened her and told her she was less than nothing, worthless. Relieved, Bella told me, "So that's done. I just want to move past this, to put it behind me and move on." But it seemed clear to me that Bella was not ready to do so, that forgetting would be pretending that she was not still greatly affected, tormented even, by the events in her past. Forgetting may be in Bella's future, but she has more inner work to do before her forgetting is good forgetting.

As we weigh good and destructive remembering, good and destructive forgetting, we are reviewing whether to retain a particular way of describing an event or to reframe that event. Discerning what is wisest isn't simple, but we can say with confidence that some choices are wiser than others and that some choices are truly wise.

———

Remembering well is an essential of the soul. We see this in our calling to remember well, in the ways reframing can teach us, even heal us, in how our life among others serves as a reminder, and in our need to discern what to remember and what to forget. Framing matters because truth-telling matters and attitude-making matters. All of us can cite examples of times when we remembered poorly, inaccurately, or with a warped lens. We all have memories we would like to frame differently, memories we know we keep retelling in self-serving or self-crushing ways. Some memories have created a slow leak in our soul, draining out any spirit of appreciation. Ultimately, good remembering involves a commitment to gratitude.

Isaiah says

some things we should not remember.

Which things? I wonder.
The former things,
he says—but aren't they all?

How can we know
which things of old
we shouldn't know?

Some wounds I keep reinjuring.
Some pain I like
to recount. Some drama

I won't reimagine
with newer stories,
fresher greens for aging browns.

Isaiah says to wait
for another thing and see
if we can perceive it.

If there's a river in the desert,
if jackals and ostriches dance
in holy time, look and listen,

dare and drink.

Isaiah 43:16–21

CHAPTER SEVEN

Remembering with Gratitude

*When someone remarked in his hearing that he had
lost an eye in the Civil War, he said, "I prefer to
remember that I have kept one."*

—Marilynne Robinson, *Gilead*

When I was traveling in Italy with a group of students, we arrived at our first hotel, accommodations that my colleague and I had selected online. The place was a first-class dump. It smelled. It was dirty. There was one shower for every six rooms—and the shower ran out of hot water in about two minutes. After I stepped on a cockroach in my room, I called a team meeting with everyone so we could apologize for the awful conditions. We did—and a long pause followed. Then one student said, "Dr. Spencer, Dr. Taylor, do you realize we are in Rome? We are in Rome! We're going to have a great time!"

It's a good goal, thankfulness. Who wants to be an ungrateful wretch, stingy with praise, cynically bitter, untrusting of whomever reminds us of our wounded past? I make it sound so attractive! As an essential of the soul, remembering well is lived out through the virtue of gratefulness.

Our situation is like this: On one level or another, my struggles with the past boil down to seeing myself as a victim. I can't change the past. When I reframe the past, I don't change the past; I change my present, my future. I may have actually been a victim—or I may have mistakenly framed my life as a victim. No matter what happened to me or what terrible choice I made, I'd like the past *not* to control me. I'd like the past to be redeemed, to be a teacher, to be a place I can visit without being oppressed and from which I can see what it means to live a heavenly life. To get to this place, I need to frame the past with gratitude. As I listen to what I say, what do I hear?

Gratefulness is the appreciation for whatever can be appreciated. We turn from a focus on ourselves as the receiver of what has happened and toward someone or something else, to the giver of what we have received. Those who are grateful recognize, among other things, that it is only polite to say thank you. Over time, we learn that it is not only polite, it is life-changing. It's important that we name all blessings as blessings.

Too often, we miss this. Our problem is not that we can't figure out what might be appreciated—but that we don't express our appreciation, even to ourselves. When our lives are 95 percent blessing and 5 percent curse, we can manage to see only the tragedy. And some people do the reverse. They seem unnaturally peppy when circumstances are catastrophic, like one friend who said immediately after a death in the family, "I'm glad she avoided all that future teenage suffering." It seemed like she skipped mourning altogether.

Curiously, our losses can drive us in a good way to gratitude. Deprived of safety, beauty, our senses, affirmation, we see more fully what we took for granted: good roads, roses, the delight of spices, and the joy of kind words. But—can we remember to be grateful when the deprivation fades? When I used to travel away from my children, I looked with sweet sadness at every toddler I saw in the airport. But ten minutes after I was back in their arms, I might be sighing about the chaos that ensued as we walked to the car.

When it comes to framing our memories well, gratefulness is the characteristic virtue, because when we remember just how extraordinary ordinary memories are, we are transformed. At one of our Thanksgiving gatherings, each of the guests was asked to tell a story of gratitude drawn from a particular time period from their past. We heard grateful memories about raising rabbits during the Depression, surviving the streets of New York in the '50s, and parenting children in the '90s. At the table, because these ordinary memories were honored, they felt extraordinary to the rest of us. We were blessed.

Gratefulness also guides remembering well because it resists the ways we frame ourselves as "fundamentally" a casualty of circumstances. In his workbook on anxiety, Edmund Bourne suggests four types of problematic self-talk. The type that fits the soul essential of remembering is *the Victim*, "that part of you which . . . generates anxiety by telling you that you're not making any progress, that your condition is incurable, or that the road is too long and steep for you to have a real chance at recovering." When we practice destructive remembering or destructive forgetting, we almost always reaffirm our victim status. Gratitude directly challenges our stories with a series of questions.

> In the story that I tell, what can be appreciated?
> Through the event, what good came out of evil?
> What did I learn that I might not have learned otherwise?
> How might the situation have been much worse?
> When I tell my story, am I sensitive to truth-telling and
>   attitude-making?

Robert Emmons connects his research on gratitude to the processing of memories: "Gratitude maximizes happiness . . . [by helping] us reframe memories of unpleasant events in a way that decreases their unpleasant emotional impact." When I talk about my parents' drinking, sometimes I make them out to be ogres. I paint the image bleaker than it was. Don't get me wrong, it was plenty bleak at times. But I have much to be grateful for during those years: that we never had a drunk-driving accident, that my parents eventually stopped drinking, that my siblings and I have had some important conversations—and that, because I went searching, I found my way to faith in Christ.

Gratitude isn't about lying to make things better than they were. It's about appreciating whatever can be appreciated—and most things can. Sometimes it's about finding what, in the circumstances, leads to a surprisingly good end, what Emmons calls the "redemptive twist," the mercy that arises out of the curse or the way our character has grown through suffering. Until we find or develop this way of seeing, I wonder if we can ever be free from the pain of the past. The redemptive twist that leads to greater freedom always involves how we frame our experience.

One misunderstanding about gratitude is that we need to be grateful for everything. Being grateful is not pretending that things did not hurt, and it is not pretending that things don't bother us. As I work on this chapter in a coffee shop, a guy two tables over is speaking so loudly that everyone can hear him. In fact, it's impossible *not* to hear him. Should I be grateful that he is loud? I suppose I could be. He is forcing me to a higher level of concentration. And he has contributed an example for my chapter! But even if I can't be grateful *for* the situation, I can be grateful *in* the situation. I'm grateful to be here, to be in a position to have these First World problems. I can put my wounds in perspective.

None of this is to say that gratitude is easy. When the hummingbirds crowd the feeder and the kids tell us they love us and our work is rewarding, life feels full and rich. It seems, as I said, almost impolite not to say "thanks." But when the sorrow is deep, when the bad news of our illness gets worse, when the kids spurn us for vulgar friends, when we get fired, life weighs heavy on us—and expressing gratitude can be difficult. It can almost feel offensive or sappy. Yet gratitude is a virtue; it is a character quality practiced in better times so that it might be depended upon during more stressful times.

When we frame our lives, our tendency is to put on a lens and wear that lens exclusively. We slip on blue glasses because we've been blinded by some difficulty—and they capture our blue feeling. It should not surprise us then that everything looks blue. But when the lens is coloring the events more than the circumstances warrant, we need to take off the glasses. The trouble is that, usually, we've forgotten we had put them on.

What would it look like to talk about our past with gratitude? For starters, we could listen to what we say. Might I change "The past is set in stone. It is what it is. I'll be forever ruined" to "My past is under construction. It is, in part, how I frame it. My memories can be redeemed"? As we speak new words, as we tell new stories, not just to ourselves but to others, we can learn to be grateful.

Here's Amanda's reframing story.

In 2008, our two-year-old son Jack had open-heart surgery. At some point, his pulmonary artery detached, and his left lung overcompensated and pushed his heart to the other side of his chest. The surgeon did not know what he was going to do until he opened Jack up. But, praise God, the surgery was a huge success. Afterward, my husband asked me. "If we had lost our son, would you have blamed me?" "No," I said, "I'd have blamed God." Somehow that gave me permission to enter depression and cry out. I was angry, confused, upset. Then our business struggled, our house flooded, and a car got totaled. I decided to get up at 6:00 A.M. (thank you, coffee!) to seek God. I discovered God. Was. There. Not that everything would be fine. Not that Jack would survive this—because God doesn't promise these things. He promises to *be there*. And he was. It was a shift for me, a reframing. I know God will be there for me every step. No matter what.

She learned to be grateful by articulating her understanding of the presence of God.

Frameworks of Bitterness and Forgiveness

As I said in Chapter Four, the virtue that guides each essential of the soul is built upon a foundation. Our frames have frameworks. If the framework supporting the frame is weak, the frame will wobble. In the house metaphor, if the framework was poorly constructed (made of cracked lumber or built with an insufficient number of two-by-fours), the frame won't survive the "shaking" that regular life sends our way. If the framework has dry rot or mold, it may crumble from within or make us sick. We might be able to fake on the outside what we don't believe on the inside—for a while— but eventually the phony edifice we're attempting to construct will show its true foundation. As Jesus says, "The things that come out of a person's mouth come from the heart" (Matt. 15:18).

If gratitude is *the virtue* that guides our framing in the "remembering" essential of the soul, bitterness and forgiveness form the *framework*. That's a complicated sentence for a fairly simple idea. Our approach to memories, our ability to be grateful, is determined by how bitter or forgiving we are.

You might ask yourself, do I *tend* toward regret, accusation, and a pit in my soul—or do I *lean* toward resolution, compassion, and a freedom born from letting go of remorse? Our tendencies, our leanings, make all the difference in our ability to exercise gratefulness. How can we be grateful if we are trapped in a *habit* of resentment? How do we actually talk about the past? Do we say things like:

> I don't want to talk about my father, the jerk.
> I still can't believe what my co-worker said about me.
> I live every day in the pain of what happened twenty years ago.

Or do we lean toward:

> My father was wrong, but I've forgiven him.
> A co-worker hurt me. Now I see that she had her own issues.
> I'm still affected by my past, but I've learned through
> that experience.

Desires matter here. Do you *want* to hold on to bad memories or to be healed? It may sound strange to say that we desire to be bitter, but sometimes we have an investment in our bitterness. We have a lot to lose if we let go.

Holding on to Bitterness

When we keep grinding through a memory, when we play the hateful tape over and over again, when we enjoy pushing the imaginary knife into our oppressor (which may be ourselves)—one of two things is occurring. Either we *feel* stuck in some memory gunk and don't know how to get out, or we *are* stuck and have decided that we have something to gain from staying stuck.

When we hold on to a memory in bitterness, we are often taking a ledger-keeping view of life. We are keeping accounts. Not only do we see our past as a balance sheet of gains and losses, but we also keep our eyes focused on the debit side. "See my losses!" we seem to be saying. "See my disappointment!" Bitterness reminds us and others of what we *haven't* received. But what good is that?

Someone in the depths of bitterness-reframing is Corinne. She writes,

I was lounging in my backyard and I received a phone call that my four-month-old nephew, Sam, was in the hospital. Over the next five days the source and extent of his injuries became clear. His injuries were catastrophic and not accidental, and there was no hope of recovery. We learned that someone had been intentionally harming him for months, and this person had attempted to end his life. For four days he denied it, but on the fifth day my adopted brother, Alex, Sam's father, confessed. He was arrested, pled guilty, and received a life sentence with possibility for parole after 15 years. My mind cried out against the unfairness of the situation. The unanswered questions. The sheer lack of any silver lining. Witnessing the fatal suffering of the innocent can sear your brain and brand you for life. I recognize that if left to my own devices, I will construct a scaffolding of regret, fear, bitterness, and distrust. It's hard to rush these things, so for now I wait, hope, and ask Jesus— someone who knows a thing or two about reframing—to give me the right tools to rebuild.

I like how Corinne is aware of the dangers of bitterness and is working on reframing.

Unlike Corinne, some of us think (though we would never say it quite like this) that bitterness has its benefits. Recounting our suffering can elicit pity from others and self-pity from ourselves. At least we get attention! When I come home from work, I make sure to tell Janet all the difficulties of the day, because if I frame my experiences this way, I might elicit some of her sympathy. Of course, much of the time, this is just fine—we have to have someone with whom we can share our struggles—but sometimes I am just staring down the debit side of the ledger. I talk about my losses because I don't seem to gain as much by talking about the gains.

We keep accounts in part because our primary frame is that life is supposed to be fair and that we deserve a larger share of fairness. We focus not on our responsibilities or our character but on our rights.

A friend of mine typically frames his experiences in terms of how he's been wronged. Others stereotype him. His peers do not respect him. One day I asked him if there were any other possible interpretations to his view of a conversation he was recounting. "No!" he shouted. "I am right!" That I suggested the possibility of other perceptions just reaffirmed to him that I "just don't get it," like everyone else. He was marginalized and mistreated all the time, and that was that. When we aren't willing to listen to other stories—and there are always other stories—we can become prisoners of our own framing. We live in the shadow side of the light of day.

Significant consequences can follow. When we lean toward bitterness, when we hold on and dig our fingers in, resentment takes a toll. For one thing, it takes effort. In M. L. Stedman's novel, *The Light Between Oceans*, Frank tells his bitter wife, Hannah, "You only have to forgive once. To resent, you have to do it all day, every day. You have to keep remembering all the bad things." I'm not sure I entirely agree with this statement—but it is worth pondering how much energy we put into resentment, and how we can use resentment as a reason for not maturing.

Hate can become a habit, a verbal habit. Disappointment, complaint, and regret can become a way of life. We say, "Look at what happened to me. I'm damaged goods." We see our memories as determining our present lives. "Don't you see the pattern of my life? It's just one hardship after another." I wonder if this is part of what the Bible means by hard-heartedness, refusing the soft vulnerabilities of humility. If I *should* be treated well, why should I bother saying thank you? I'm entitled to these things.

One strategy for ridding ourselves of bitterness is to switch our framing from the debit side to the asset side. It's a good strategy. A better strategy is to throw the ledger out the window altogether—to be less interested in how things measure up. This is what forgiveness does.

Healing Up through Forgiveness

We can't change the past, but we can change our resentment. I like how Lewis Smedes puts this: "Forgiving is love's revolution against life's unfairness." Letting go of bitterness opens our hands to receive. And opening our hands requires the humility to say that we might not know or remember the *whole* story or that—at the very least—we don't know what we don't know; that is, we don't know what might have happened if the bitter memory hadn't occurred.

We tend to assume our lives would have otherwise been ideal. If I hadn't driven that stupid car for three thousand miles, I wouldn't have had back pain for two years. Maybe. But maybe I would have been in a head-on collision, or maybe . . . well, I just don't know. If I weren't still single, I would be so much happier. Maybe. Or maybe your spouse would have had an affair and you would have divorced. We just don't know. Admitting this is helpful. It's part of what it means to trust God for our lives.

We need to get to the point where we can say, "I am willing to give up the benefits of bitterness" and to let go of the power we feel by maintaining our anger at ourselves or our oppressor. But doesn't this mean I let the offender off the hook? Isn't my resentment some sort of justice, some appropriate punishment? Here's where we see that the first advantage of forgiveness is the advantage to ourselves. When Tanya says, "I'll never forgive that man," *that man* isn't the one harmed by her anger. She is.

For most of us, we become ready to forgive others when we realize how often we ourselves need to be forgiven. Instead of seeing only the *other's* gossip or lust or lying, we see *our own*. We know, though we might not have committed as grievous an act as our oppressor, we have the same foibles. We need redemption no less than the next person. When I saw what a deeply wounded person I was, in need of healing, I could then begin to see my parents in the same way. They had gone through the Great Depression and World War II. My mom delivered a stillborn child. I could forgive, couldn't I?

And what is forgiveness? Smedes helps us here too. Among other things, he says that "Forgiveness has begun when you recall those who hurt you and feel the power to wish them well." I like this, because we know when we have made this step. I recently heard another view, that forgiveness has occurred when I no longer believe that the other person owes me something. These are great interpretive markers.

When Ken's wife, Kim, died of cancer, Ken realized he would need to forgive God. He thought God owed him a better life, that serving God for all these years should have gained him more than this measure of suffering. After much anguish, he concluded, "Do I want to spend the rest of my life resenting God that Kim died or being grateful for what we had?" By forgiving God for "taking her," he helped build the framework for gratitude.

Forgiveness liberates us for gratefulness. It's the best we can hope for from our memories. When we frame our past, what stories are we telling? Are we holding on resentfully? Are we invested in our wounds? Or are we healing, moving toward greater freedom? Are we willing to hear the truth related to the past?

A memory is not a resource to us until it is redeemed, until it is reframed. Ultimately, we'd like to say with Richard Rohr, "Everything belongs. God uses everything. There are no dead-ends. There is no wasted energy. Everything is recycled. Sin history and salvation history are two sides of one coin. I believe with all my heart that the Gospel is all about the mystery of forgiveness."

I'm grateful for days

They start over.

Just about the time
one runs out

there's another one
and they each come
with a morning.

In the dying afternoons
it's good to know

there'll be a rising.

Anticipating the Future with Hope

CHAPTER EIGHT

Anticipating

"If you come at four in the afternoon,
I'll begin to be happy by three."
—Antoine de Saint-Exupéry, *The Little Prince*

When Jill went to see her OB/GYN to get her twelve-week ultra-sound, she was thrilled. She loved her doctor—and the ultrasound tech was a kick. As the instrument glided over her belly, Jill joked about this and that, until the tech suddenly grew quiet. The baby, the tech told her, had a thicker than typical NT (nuchal translucency), which could be a sign of Down syndrome. Instantly, Jill started to cry. What about all her hopes for her baby and family?

After blood was drawn, Jill kept telling herself that this diagnosis just could not be true and that the test would come back negative. It didn't. Jill's doctor discussed the situation with great sensitivity and then asked her if she wanted to terminate the pregnancy. Jill said no. As an oppressive darkness filled her, Jill simply could not believe that this reality was now her life, her new normal.

Three months later, at the end of her second trimester, she had made some emotional progress. She no longer cried every day. Though she had not reached a state of "acceptance," she and her husband could say they were preparing to meet their son—and "that was a pretty good place to be."

When we think about the future, we imagine its glorious and terrifying possibilities, and we talk about it accordingly. The long-anticipated baby. The long-anticipated baby arriving with limitations. Our new job. The prospect of losing our job. Sometimes things go as planned or even better than planned. Nothing quite says "grace" more than unforeseen joy. But at other times, what we look forward to becomes something we dread, and we feel abandoned on some confusing and lonely island of disappointment, with treacherous terrain and no supply boats—and then it starts to rain. We have a sense of order, our way of framing the future, but then life happens. Circumstances come and disturb the relative serenity of our frame, and we are moved to reframe.

Like remembering, anticipating is an inevitable part of being human. Living in time (as we do) means that we don't just live in the present. We live with our sense of the past and our sense of the future. We can't help but look forward to things, to anticipate. The question is, how do we do so? How do we frame the future? Do we see it as a constant ascent: an expectation of gradual improvement—in financial security, physical and mental skill, wisdom, and maturity? Or is the future collapsing before our eyes: rising temperatures, rising political chaos, rising vulgarity?

No matter how we verbalize the future, we do so in certain ways. As Ralph Waldo Emerson said, "Always the seer is a sayer." Every forecaster (every anticipator, forward-looker) is a speaker (a framer, an articulator, a word-maker). We publish our dreams in the book of our speech.

God is also concerned about how we talk about the future, as these scriptures reveal (italics mine):

> "For I know the plans I have for you," declares the Lord, "plans to prosper you and not to harm you, plans to give you hope and a *future*" (Jer. 29:11).

> I pray that the eyes of your heart may be enlightened in order that you may know the *hope* to which he has called you, the riches of his glorious *inheritance* in his holy people (Eph. 1:18).

Forgetting what is behind and straining toward what is ahead,
I press on toward *the goal* to win the prize for which God has
called me heavenward in Christ Jesus (Phil. 3:13b–14).

Not only do these scriptures recognize the importance of the future, they also state how we are to think about the future, our hopes, our inheritance, and our goals. Anticipating is a major part of our lives. How we frame the future is part of what it means to live before God.

Although we live between the past and the future, what we frame about the past actually happened (a lot of it anyway) and what we frame about the future has not yet happened. Though the past is remarkable and our framing of it is consequential for our lives, *our framing of the future, our work in anticipation, has greater power—the power of imagination and hope.* Each vision of the future (whether positive or negative) creates a road that leads toward it. If we say we want more authenticity in our friendships, or more intimacy with God, these framings point the way. We can't change the actual past, but we can change the future. Whatever we say about it leads us in that direction.

Our work reframing our past is work we do for the sake of framing our future. Though some people are significantly "stuck in the past," endlessly looping over some regret, all of us are stuck in some way. By recognizing this problem, we energize the power of hope. Ultimately, we want to discard the loop and be a part of a more meaningful story. We want to be in a position to truly look forward. It may begin with a simple step. Jill and her husband did not hope for a Down syndrome baby—but they also did not stay stuck in the memory of that revelation. They anticipated. They framed the future as "preparing to meet our son."

Anticipating the Good Life

When we frame our future, we do at least two things: we reveal how we are anticipating—what our attitudes are through our expectations, worries, hopes, anxieties, planning, etc.—and we reveal what we desire for the future. This second part can be heard in our answer to one of the most important questions we can ask: What is the Good Life? What is our vision for the future that we hope to live into? Romantic comedies have an image of the good life. Perfect lovey-doveyness. Utopian fantasies (*Star Wars*) have their ideas, the triumph of good over evil. So do dystopian thrillers (*The Hunger Games*), freedom from the oppression we can't escape. The framing of our answer is crucial, because we adjust our behavior to conform to our words.

Though we might not be eloquent as we answer questions about the Good Life, we all have an answer—and our answers often reveal current cultural values and current cultural worries. Here are four framings of the Good Life. You can probably think of others.

The Good Life Is an Everlasting Party

Let's have a good time, all the time! Who doesn't want to enjoy every minute? Well, losers for one. Grab a drink and let's go! Here, the Good Life is seen as a dawn-to-dusk-to-dawn vacation from responsibility. No one works. Everyone gets smashed or loaded (note how neither phrase, taken literally, sounds appealing). What's a few hangovers between friends? Or trashed condos or major embarrassments? It's hilarious!

Another way we define the "Party" in Everlasting Party is with material stuff, an endless celebration of purchased goods: fancier houses, bigger TVs, more bling, shiny times and shiny things, the Happy Hangover or the Perfect Picket Fence. This focus on personal enjoyment can lead to the neglect of other good goals. As we dance in our decadence, we only care about the present, and we don't feel responsible enough about the future to anticipate what the next generation needs to learn.

Framing the Good Life as an everlasting party attempts to dodge the troubling question, *How can I avoid death?* How can I have some sort of tangible, temporary happiness and put off the issues of mortality? If I medicate myself with alcohol and sex, or a cool car and chic accessories, maybe I won't hear the voice in my bones reminding me that even they will let me down someday.

Must we talk about death? Atul Gawande makes a superb case for such a conversation in *Being Mortal*. No matter how loud our Party is, it can't drown out our decline forever. He says, "We regard living in the downhill stretches with a kind of embarrassment. We need help, often for long periods of time, and regard that as a weakness rather than as the new normal and expected state of affairs." Because we pretend we will never die, Gawande says, we have created costly and harmful medical policies that prioritize safety and survival—instead of the real need of the elderly, which is to have a reason to live beyond themselves. A good party is a good thing, but an everlasting party does not make for a good life.

The Good Life Is What I Deserve

Not too far down the street from the Everlasting Party is the Good Life as "getting what I have coming to me." The Good Life is my life now. Pay attention! Things should go my way.

Jade and Derek pull their fifth grader, Sierra, out of school for a week-long ski trip, giving the teacher one day to assemble all of Sierra's work for the week. When they return, they complain that the teacher should not require that Sierra take exams at the same time as the other students—because, after all, Sierra was in ski lessons all day every day. "While I have your attention," Derek tells the teacher, "you assign too much homework. Sierra can't do it plus her three after-school activities." Entitlement creates a future in which all roads lead to meeting my needs.

Those who see the Good Life as their entitlement attempt to manage the persistent question, *How can I avoid anxiety?* If I'm spoiled and don't know how to fend for myself, I'm nervous about the future. Maybe, if I *demand* the Good Life, I can suppress my worries and get the measure of happiness that I deserve.

We are an anxious lot, so perhaps it isn't surprising that we are an entitled lot. How can we *not* be anxious—given financial pressures, the pace of life, constant comparison with my friends, and the thirty-two texts I need to answer immediately? And this is to say nothing about terrorism, climate change, and race conflict. There are a lot of reasons why we might not get what we want, what we are entitled to.

Anxiety is more a mark of our culture than ever. In his book *Anxious*, researcher Joseph LeDoux says, "Anxiety is . . . about the self. . . . [It's] a contemplation of what that future self will be like if bad things happen—not just to it but also to those the self cares about." Anxiety seems to go hand in hand with the Good-Life-as-Entitlement.

The Good Life Is Technological Control

Some say, "The future is what we make of it." And we're making it. We can power through storms, over great distances, around boredom, and into any slice of information we want. Technology may cause problems, but there's a technological solution for that—and for the problem caused by the solution. The Good Life means being in control of my life, my time, my energy, my resources—and for First World folks, that means technology.

Sometimes we look out and see only unmanaged chaos. Nothing seems meaningful. This is the issue this version of the Good Life addresses: *How do I cope with the random nature of existence?* The answer technology promises is that our purpose is achieved by being in control, even though, ironically, we are giving up our control—to Big Data, social media, driverless cars, and artificial intelligence. In Ariana's loneliness, she checks her phone constantly. During every break, when she might be making personal connections with those in her presence, she is on her phone, hoping desperately that someone texted her, sometimes pretending to be "doing something" on her phone just so that she looks like she has friends. She's trying to find the Good Life she thinks can be had by controlling everything.

The promise of technological control does not resolve our struggles with randomness. Technology can accomplish great things, but it cannot supply true meaning.

The Good Life Is Peace on Earth

Where I teach, in just one semester, outside speakers came to chapel to tell their stories about racial reconciliation in Africa, inner-city ministry in Houston, sustainable development, religious diversity, relational evangelism, climate change, spiritual formation, economic causes of terrorism, faith in the work world, or reaching those disenfranchised from the church. Most of these speeches ended with a plea for students to use their education to make a difference in the world, to seek their calling to bring love to the poor, to apply their faith personally and socially. I'm inspired nearly every time. And I usually feel guilty.

The Peace on Earth version of the Good Life has a lot going for it. It works at the question, *How can I avoid injustice?* It seeks to understand the ways of love in communities all over the world. As far as Good Life perspectives go, it ranks pretty high. But if we think we will actually achieve paradise, if we anticipate dramatic and permanent change, if we expect we will eradicate hatred and violence and poverty, we will be disappointed. Working toward a more sustainable planet is worthy. Believing that if you just get it right, it will happen, is futile.

Of course, we should be mercy-minded—and sometimes it even feels good and right and beautiful to act this way. But our tasks won't lead to a perfect life. We have to be careful with the Peace on Earth version of the Good Life because it can lead us to live in denial of the realities of a broken world.

Each of these ways of framing the Good Life has its appeal (enjoyment, peace, meaning, and love) and each one attempts to keep at bay some troubling force (death, anxiety, randomness, and injustice). Since we cannot not pursue some version of the Good Life, which Good Life do we most desire—and how does that framing of the future drive our expectations and behaviors?

Anticipation and Reframing

As Jill continues her pregnancy with David, her Down syndrome baby, she touches on the primary issues raised in this chapter, about how living in time means that anticipating builds on remembering—but with greater potential—and how our desires for the Good Life drive what we say and do. She had a working sense of order, her way of talking about the future. But all of that was turned around by the diagnosis of David. She writes:

The thoughts and questions that have gone through my mind as we've processed our new reality are not necessarily ones I'm proud of. Today I am in a ranting mood. I want to process hopes vs. reality and the disappointments that come with both. I am jealous when I see other pregnant women. It's ridiculous because I'm STILL pregnant. I shouldn't be jealous! But I assume they are having a "normal" pregnancy and expecting a "typical" baby and I envy their carefree experience. It was my "plan" to enjoy having a second baby, but morning sickness completely took over in the first trimester and I fell into a depression. At the start of the second trimester we received our positive diagnosis, so just when I should have been feeling physically better, I began to feel emotionally worse.

*This will most likely be the last time I am pregnant, and I feel
I should be relishing all of the things that I will likely never experience again. I should feel giddy when he kicks and ecstatic that
people treat me delicately. I should enjoy eating whatever I want
and having people tell me how cute my belly is. I'm experiencing
a lot of "should" during this pregnancy. Trying to manage reality with expectations has turned this pregnancy into something I
wasn't mentally prepared for.*

Jill writes with deep authenticity and love—and her story will continue as
my next chapters unfold. Because of her past with her family and her first
pregnancy, she anticipates a "normal" pregnancy. She talks of how the past
lays a foundation for a predictable future—and how it influences what she
"should" have. Once her proprioception was disturbed, she wrestled with
expectations based on the Good Life she imagined, one with a lot of fun,
one perhaps she felt entitled to, something partly within her control, something approaching a measure of peace on earth—or at least in her home.
She worked at reframing, and she has a long journey ahead.

She wants to anticipate well.

Terra Squeaka

I awake every morning
at the creak of dawn.

Some think it's a crack, but
the technical term, I believe,
is "eeerk," a grinding, rusty screech
loud enough to get me

to get up and find some oil,
some good grease, and go
to the axis of the earth and
give it a lube. It's been turning
and turning, so I'm not surprised

it scrapes and groans
under the weight of all
these centuries. They say
day breaks, but it doesn't have to,

not if we give it a little
routine maintenance.

CHAPTER NINE

Anticipating Well

In order to make sense of a book's words and phrases we must think ahead when we read—we must anticipate. . . . We are picturing what we are told to see, but also we are picturing what we imagine we will be told to see, farther down the page.

—Peter Mendelsund

Not long after David's birth with Down syndrome, Jill's husband Jason had a revelation. He remembered that when he was young, he always wanted to be on the team that wasn't expected to win. He loved being the underdog. Now he had a son who was an underdog—not just in sports, but in life. David was among the five percent of Down syndrome fetuses that survived to birth. When Jason compared his child to the biblical David, he wrote, "I believe David can defeat Goliath. I believe in my boy."

In this framing of his son and his son's life, Jason points to David's future, a life of overcoming. Does Jason's framing of David guarantee David's inherent Davidness (defeating Goliath)? No. Does it make a difference? Yes.

In the last chapter, I discussed ways we live in time and ways we might envision the Good Life. Now it is "time" to move toward what it looks like to anticipate well. Framing the future is as natural and ordinary as reading.

What do we say about what we see farther down the page? When we frame the future, what's in the picture?

In the New Testament, Paul tells us to anticipate spiritual maturity. He says that "he who began a good work in you will carry it on to completion until the day of Christ Jesus" (Phil. 1:6). Peter says so as well. After discussing the coming "day of the Lord," Peter says, "What kind of people ought you to be? You ought to live holy and godly lives as you look forward . . . to a new heaven and a new earth, where righteousness dwells" (2 Pet. 3:11b–13). We might say that God expects us to anticipate—and the scripture provides help toward anticipating well.

One way to anticipate is to predict the future—a perilous task, as many would-be prophets have realized. Is the world coming to an end? Well, yes—but probably not today. Futurist Kevin Kelly says: "Massive copying is here to stay. Massive tracking and total surveillance is here to stay. . . . We can't stop artificial intelligences and robots from improving, creating new businesses, and taking our current jobs. . . . Only by working with these technologies, rather than trying to thwart them, can we gain the best of what they have to offer." He argues for a "vigilant acceptance" regarding changing technologies.

Some prophets tell us what we should do: "Hurry! Invest in Iraqi currency. You'll make a fortune!" Famed physicist Stephen Hawking says we only have one hundred more years to find another planet to live on because this one will be toast, literally. Some prophets remind me of the line: "He's always certain but never right."

Many contemporary voices predict doom, doom, and more doom. While these projections may come true, what's certainly true is that these prophecies attract large audiences. A few voices are utopian—and are often called naïve. "Don't be ridiculous. A happy ending is just a Disney fantasy." Kevin Kelly says that doomsayers so dominate our thinking that we have become "future-blind," stuck in a present that refuses to imagine what a slightly better future might actually look like.

Whether or not we take our cues from technological change or technological prophets, we would be wise to pay attention to the future. Not that we can help it. We are hopeless predictors, announcing everything from how much we will get accomplished today to what professions our children will enter. "Look at Eric throw the ball. He'll be a major league pitcher one day!" How do we frame the future? Why do we frame it that way?

Anticipating Well Matters

Framing the future is not only inevitable, it is crucial. Is tomorrow worrisome or exciting, an opportunity or a problem, another stupid day on the job or a major test of spiritual and moral commitments? Anticipating well is important because our framing reveals our motivating purposes, because our framing of the future influences our lives in the present, because our framing in the present influences where we are headed in the future, and because our framing of an event's likelihood is one measure of our wisdom.

Framing and Our Motivating Purposes

Before his accident, Aiden liked to say, "I just want to party and get rich, to have fun with life." His speech revealed his sense of purpose. Then he fell off a high cliff above a beach in Santa Barbara. After being discovered the next day miraculously alive, and after a long and not entirely complete recovery, he spoke differently. He reframed his future. "I don't have to be that cool party person anymore. Now I'm grateful for all the little things: to be able to see color, to be in the present. I don't say, 'I'm having a tough time' but 'I'm choosing this.' I am so much stronger now."

Framing the future is inseparably tied to the fundamental human need for purpose in life. On a basic level, we can see how *everything* we do has purpose. All of our actions are motivated by particular reasons, from saying "hello" to writing our will. These reasons may not be wise and good reasons, but we always have some intention, even if our intention is to sit on the couch and do nothing. This purposeful orientation is built into us. We act according to our (stated) purposes—and our sense of well-being is tied to our sense of purpose. Given the every-second-of-our-lives intentionality, it should come as no surprise that we have a purpose-driven life (sounds like the title of a best-selling book!).

Not only do we constantly frame our immediate futures in terms of our purposes ("I want to look good for my date tonight"), we also frame our ultimate purposes ("I want to leave an impact on my city"). We all search for something beyond ourselves, for significance. We might talk about being famous or rich or "calling the shots someday." We frame our future in terms of legacy, vocation, and destiny.

We probably don't need to be convinced about the role of purpose in our lives—but how does this matter for our framing, for our anticipating of the future?

Framing and Our Lives in the Present

Years ago, I had a former gang member as a student. I learned many things from him, including what his homies meant by the phrase 24/7. It meant that their plan was to be drunk or loaded 24 hours a day, 7 days a week. When I asked him why they would want to make that choice, he said that no one expected to live to age thirty, so why not? Their way of framing the future affected their present.

In *Mind over Mind*, Chris Berdik writes about "the complex interplay between what we assume will be and what is." In a fascinating review of how professional athletes are better "anticipators," he says that this superior anticipation can easily be undone by anxiety, such as when athletes begin to worry about the outcome or pay attention to the crowd. Summarizing research in this area, Berdik says that "beginners and chokers focus on technique. Experts focus on what's next."

This seems true for our verbal anticipating also. If I speak of my future workload of phone calls and data entry as drudgery, I'll drag through the present. If I say that my future workload is challenging, I might focus my present energies on meeting that challenge. Berdik reports that athletes who were told they had an advantage performed better, whether they had an advantage or not.

Framing and Our Lives in the Future

The language gets a little tricky here—but imagine the difference between 1) feeling more peaceful now because you frame the future as "something I can get through" (the previous point) and 2) taking many significant steps in the direction of a more peaceful life *in the future* because you framed it as "a tranquil state I'd like to grow into" (this current idea).

By calling his son an underdog, Jason will see David as an underdog and take steps that are consistent with the vision that David is an underdog who will beat Goliath someday. By calling ourselves a failure, we stay on failure's path. In *Think Forward to Thrive*, psychologist Jennice Vilhauer says that the future motivates our actions more than the past—so much so that the "key to thriving is learning to harness the mind's natural tendency to anticipate the future so that you can focus most of your attention on what you would like to achieve." Vilhauer works out the details of the simple premise that we will move toward whatever goal we set.

Framing of an Event's Likelihood and Our Wisdom

Growing up, I was told that the "smart people" were better predictors of what time it was. I have no idea if time-consciousness is a true indicator of intelligence, but I sure was proud when I was spot-on. Another way to see this idea is to compare whether we say something is possible, plausible, probable, or certain—and whether in fact it is. If someone who gets along with just about everyone says no one likes her, we might question her ability to anticipate her relational future.

Today, we are often told we can be whatever we want to be. I'd like to play in the NBA, but I think my window is closing. What do I think is possible? What do I think is probable? In the church, some argue for possibility no matter what the circumstance. Since Jesus said "with God all things are possible" (Matt. 19:26), we feel we are "of little faith" if we doubt. I object. While it seems good to pray for someone with a terminal illness, we are not faithless if we suggest that death is imminent.

I don't like the idea that faith always argues for possibility, because part of being wise means that our projections are relatively reliable. We could use the possibility argument to justify greatly overextending ourselves financially or foolishly ignoring the role of compatibility in marriage. Shouldn't faith and wisdom work together? Perhaps anticipating well here means having wisdom guide our choices while we pray for exceptions to the rule. Jason and Jill prayed for a negative test result of what the ultrasound showed, but they understood the likelihood of a positive fulfillment. The probability that David would be born with Down syndrome became a certainty. This doesn't mean they lacked faith.

Anticipating Well as an Essential of the Soul

What does it mean to frame the future in keeping with a gospel vision, to choose our words as Jesus might have us choose them, emphasizing THIS way of framing, not THAT way? Reframing this essential of the soul has to do with paradise, trouble, time frames, and discernment.

Practicing Paradise

What is your image of heavenly life? Will we be in an everlasting choir? Will we be walking streets of gold, chatting it up in the mansion that was prepared for us, playing golf without ever hitting into the rough, or dancing at a perpetual wedding feast? Though Scripture doesn't give us tremendous detail about the future, I believe that our image of it has a lot to do with good spiritual anticipation.

Where we think we're headed is the path we are pursuing, so our framing influences the steps we take. Too many images of heaven seem passive. Why would God save us for an eternal life of sitting around? I've had some outlandish visions—like heaven will be boot camp for the next spiritual adventure God has in mind, maybe training angels for service on another planet. I also like the idea of conversing around a campfire with all the literary greats who have blessed me—and then they suggest we plan to write a new book together. How fun!

Before you dismiss me as a wacko, consider this: the major appeal of fantasy literature is that it gives us a working vision of paradise. We love living for a time in Narnia or Hogwarts (or the land in my own novels, Welken) because, unlike here, good consistently triumphs, love makes the difference, and everyone has something important to do. J. R. R. Tolkien calls good fantasy a story of *eucatastrophe*, a good catastrophe, a story with "a sudden and miraculous grace . . . ; it denies (in the face of much evidence, if you will) universal final defeat and . . . [gives] a fleeting glimpse of Joy, Joy beyond the walls of the world, poignant as grief."

Don't we all get glimpses of heaven at times, golden moments when our conversation is pure and rich and deep, when the vista is beyond description, when circumstances are infused with the noticeable work and mystery of God? As Elizabeth Barrett Browning puts it, "Earth's crammed with heaven, and every common bush afire with God." If only we have eyes to see and ears to hear!

Practicing paradise means comparing our current decisions and relationships with what we imagine heaven will be like. If we are anticipating well, we get closer and closer to that heavenly life. "How should I proceed in this conversation?" means "What would this conversation look like in heaven?"

Is this presumptuous blasphemy? Can we really do this now? I would suggest that this is exactly what Jesus means when he, repeatedly, says, "The kingdom of heaven is like . . ." In each case, he explains to his disciples how to practice heavenly values in the present. The kingdom of God is the place where God is and where we live as God would have us live. This kingdom is not something we must wait to enter at death. It begins now and continues into eternity. When Jesus prayed "your kingdom come, your will be done, on earth as it is in heaven" (Matt. 6:10), he affirmed the current status of the kingdom. All our loving acts are part of our eternal life.

In other words, at our best, by God's grace, we are living the kingdom of God now, which we will keep on living in the future kingdom, a life that will be rich with creativity and love and (maybe even!) innovation. We're moving toward a new heaven and a new earth, and there will be plenty to do. Although I don't know the details, I'm confident (it's probable) that one purpose of the gift of imagination is to use it toward practicing paradise. We try to do this every day, don't we? We imagine our tasks being done well, with holiness and grace. And then we will walk toward the paradise we imagine.

Recognizing "You Will Have Trouble"

After speaking at length, though indirectly, about his death and resurrection, Jesus says, "I have told you these things, so that in me you may have peace. In this world you will have trouble. But take heart! I have overcome the world" (John 16:33). The first part of his statement, the part about trouble, is most pertinent here. Those who anticipate as a soul essential understand that we live in a broken world that will not be made right just because we say it will. We'll experience suffering and disappointment, frustration and failed expectations. The road of life will have potholes, washed-out bridges, and repairs.

We should not be fooled by claims that this politician will set things right or that this church will bring us into spiritual superiority. We know that life is difficult. If we remember that this world will bring us trouble, we will keep our expectations lower, more moderate. We may protest that love conquers all; but love has a lot to conquer.

Does this make us dour-faced pessimists? Should we look to Eeyore or Puddleglum as the model for our perspective? No. Though life is not always a tragedy, it is not a romantic comedy. If you haven't had much trouble in this world, you will. The question for us is "How will we respond?" Recently a friend's toddler fell into a swimming pool and died. There's no way to "pretty this up." It's the kind of trouble that happens in the world— but this sentiment is not all that Jesus said. I'll get to "take heart" in the next chapter.

Having the Proper "Time Frame"

In *Being Mortal*, Gawande reviews some research that tracked the lives of nearly two hundred people over many years. The conclusion was that, regardless of age, "how we seek to spend our time may depend on how much time we perceive ourselves to have." Contrary to our intuition, we don't gradually change our values as we age. It's not that the young value learning and adventure and the old value community and everyday pleasures. We invest more in the future when we think we have more future ahead of us, whether we are young or old. Our "time frame," the way we see ourselves in relationship to the future, is what affects our choices.

How might this influence the role of anticipation as a soul essential? If I think I'm going to live forever, I might learn a new language, dive deeply into a friendship, or change jobs for greater fulfillment later. If I consider the fragility of life when I'm young, I might more likely say what needs to be heard and more likely count my blessings. The young tend to forget that they will die. They should remember so they will cherish relationships and be grateful. The old tend to forget that death has lost its sting. They should remember so they will continue to learn and take risks.

The question "What is my time frame?" gets us inquiring about our current season of life. It also takes the longer view and recognizes that we all have an eternal life through which to view this present one. As my friend June neared later middle age, when many of her peers were "retiring to an easier life of golf and restaurants," she was asked to get involved with Lithuanian Christian College. Her thinking at the time was that her life was full enough, that God was using her. She told me, "I wasn't seeking anything." When, reluctantly, she said yes, one of the biggest surprises of her life greeted her almost immediately after landing in Lithuania. She loved the people. She loved working with the college. To accomplish new goals, she and her husband had to change plans, constantly host visitors, rework finances, and pray in new ways. June learned that God's first value (even in retirement) is not safety. As a consequence, today she feels more fully alive and has less anxiety about the future. She discovered her time frame.

Discerning the Future Well

Anticipation that supports the soul is not just a matter of "Yes, I need to anticipate" or "No, I don't." Some say we should live in the present. Some say we should plan and save. Still others focus on being spontaneous—no matter how much we have developed our lists of things to do. What kind of anticipating brings life? When is our framing of the future detrimental? Like remembering, anticipating requires discernment—and I'll use categories similar to those in the section on memory.

Beneficial anticipation. When my wife and I were first married, we had $600 in the bank—with no job and no car. After we bought a somewhat functional car for $400, we spent most of the remaining $200 on reupholstering the front seats in Tijuana and . . . you get the picture. Despite how it sounds, we weren't mindlessly moving ahead. We had arranged to house-sit for a month. We were frugal to a fault. And while Janet finished her last semester of student teaching, I set out to find a job. I prayed, but I planned. I had hope, but I had a list of open jobs. Beneficial anticipation does not mean being in absolute control. It means hard work in the context of trusting God. As the old saying goes, "Pray—but don't forget to row."

Destructive anticipation. It took me just two weeks to find a job, a high-pressure, commission-only, competition-inspiring sales job at a well-known furniture store. Today, I tell my students that we all need a terrible job experience to motivate us away from lines of work that suck the life out of us. But that's not my point. During the two weeks of looking for work, I was miserable. All I could think about was that I did not have a job. I imagined us going on welfare or begging from relatives. Constantly anxious, I did not enjoy the beautiful house we were caring for. I paced and fretted and fumed. When I got the job, just as our house-sitting time was over, I instantly regretted the way I had been living in the future. My destructive anticipating robbed me of enjoying the present.

Some of us live almost entirely in the future. We frame our lives in "as soon as I" terms. We say, "As soon as I graduate, I'll be fine." But then we graduate and say, "As soon as I get a good job, I'll be fine." And then it's marriage and children, and on and on. In fact, we can treat everything as if it is scarce: money, accomplishments, time, happiness—and end up always grasping after it, and the next thing, and the next. Perhaps this is one reason Jesus argues against living too much in the future, saying, "Do not worry about tomorrow, for tomorrow will worry about itself" (Matt. 6:34).

Beneficial "being in the present." Of course, the flip side of future-driven anxiety is present-dwelling harmony. Janet and I have fond memories of our first-year-of-marriage Saturday excursions. Since we had no money (I know, an exaggeration. We had $50!), we sought out a free experience every weekend. We drove to the apple orchards of Julian, hiked local mountains, relaxed in La Jolla, and picnicked in Balboa Park. San Diego was a "rich" place if you were poor. We just picked a spot and were open to what developed.

"Being in the present" connects to the centuries-old conversation about being and doing. We are so achievement-driven in our culture that we don't have much margin in our lives to "just be," to sit and take things in. Some say that Sabbath-keeping includes the gift of not needing to accomplish anything. Sounds good to me. A focus on the present reminds me of one of my standard vacation jokes. While walking in a new town, one of my daughters invariably asked, "Where are we?" I answered, "Here." And then I hopped ahead and said, "Where are we now? Here." I hopped again. "And here." Hop. "And here." That's where we were—and are.

Destructive "being in the present." Just when you think something is thoroughly acceptable, I go and nuance it. Oh, well, that's what writers are for. When we discern our framing of the future, we can also overstate the importance of the present moment. In San Diego, we sometimes did a bit too much lollygagging on Saturdays and not enough good labor or service. Though this was not a common vice of ours, it is for some. We can put off all kinds of important tasks (hard conversations, faucet repair, volunteer work), claiming that we just want to play a bit right now or the kids need more attention or the timing isn't right to confront that difficult situation. We can use the present as a way to procrastinate about the future such that we never seem to get around to the mess in the garage, the mess in our friendships.

Living only for today is foolish, a topic addressed in the book of Proverbs, where "fools" are addressed seventy-two times: how they despise wisdom and instruction (1:7), find pleasure in wicked schemes (10:23), show their annoyance at once (12:16), have wandering eyes (17:24), and exalt themselves (30:32). Foolish people do not think ahead or listen to those who have gone before them. Foolish couples hastily decide for marriage because their relationship feels good in the moment, which "must" mean that God is blessing them forever. But the wise couple considers more than this: their compatibility, values, and desires. It's not all about the present journey. The destination matters too.

———

As Jill framed her future, she wrestled with what it meant to anticipate well, as an essential of the soul. She knew her framing would affect her relationship with David and with Jason. It would affect her daily living before God.

> *In truth, this has been the worst year of my life. My marriage*
> *has been tested, I've checked out frequently, I've questioned my*
> *faith—and there are times when I've been jealous and angry. . . .*
> *There are many days when I'm in the hospital in sweats and my*
> *chin is breaking out in stress pimples and I'm not speaking to*
> *Jason because he didn't unload the dishwasher. There are days*
> *when I snap at nurses and yell at Ella and get in fights with my*
> *mom. How does this all culminate in being a good mom to David?*
> *Sometimes it doesn't. Sometimes I'm just barely hanging on. The*
> *best I can do is to call the nurse to check on him before I go to sleep.*

Jill knew she had "trouble in this world." She needed to "take heart," to anticipate with hope.

The Summer of My Gathering Mortality

Things add up. That's what they say. Do the math.
First Alex, at thirty-one, of an errant
blood clot. Then Connie and Phe, sisters of the heavenly
departure. Two friends get cancer. There's the anniversary
of my frozen back—and Mocha, at fifteen, panting her way out.
Maybe it's not an unusual problem
set. Maybe it's just that I'm coming of age.

But when the bluebird
died, the one I found
on the ground by the soft
pink climbing rose, the Cecile Brunner,
I was done. I had had it
with death, with the turning, the fading, and the blotting out
of all things, with the way that wave flashes over me
and rises up my shoulders and pools in my neck.

So I have decided to wait
for spring, for the next sticks-and-string gathering
toward a nest, for the healing green,
the breezy blueness, and the rolling
goodness of the resurrection.

CHAPTER TEN

Anticipating with Hope

Anyone who is among the living has hope—even a live dog is better off than a dead lion!
—Ecclesiastes 9:4

I play a lot of tennis. Most of the time, I'm willing to run around like a madman, chasing down every ball. Sometimes, when I get tired or lazy, I stop and watch a ball that looks like it might sail long. If, instead, it falls inside the court, I say to myself, "Hope is not a good strategy"—because, of course, the best strategy is to move your feet and get into a position to hit the ball. Lazily watching the ball just gives you a terrific view of your opponent's winner.

No extra charge for the tennis advice.

Though hope is not always wise, we know it is most of the time. It's a virtue, we say—even if we aren't sure how to define it. We know what it feels like to have hope, and most of the time this is enough for us. But what is hope and how does it modify and inspire our "anticipations," our ways of framing the future? When is hope just a lie we tell ourselves so we can go on? When is it evidence of a more developed faith, or something else entirely?

The Nature of Hope

In the church, many of our conversations about hope develop into debates about heaven. Though the Christian perspective of the afterlife is crucial here, I'd like to begin with a broader discussion of hope. Heaven matters—but hope matters whether you believe in heaven or not.

Unpredictability and Hope

Whatever we do might be "highly likely," but it is never entirely predictable. To me, this is such a hopeful assertion. Everything we say, we say in hope. We hope for some sort of effect. Even a simple "hello" sometimes yields a surprising reaction. Every question we ask, we ask in hope. Every statement we make is spoken in the hope that someone hears and cares and might respond. We could even say that every act of communication is an assertion of possible future human goodness. We anticipate a worthwhile answer to our contribution.

The old adage (noted in Ecclesiastes above) that "where there's life, there's hope" is usually our default framing. At times, we feel hopeless, but we are not utterly hopeless unless we have decided that life is not worth living. To live is to have some measure of hope. This is good news about the soul essential of anticipation. God has made us with some built-in movement toward the virtue we need.

When we have little hope, we stereotype; we destructively label and limit. Since we have diminished others to some less-than-fully-alive status, we think, "What's the point of interaction?" We treat them without hope. All (fill in the blank) are (fill in the blank). Everyone who voted for so-and-so is blah-blah-blah. All immigrants are blah-blah-blah. All Christians or non-Christians are blah-blah and blah-blah. That's a lot of blahhing—and no one likes to be blahhed about. When we stereotype, we erroneously assume that human action is predictable. When we talk about "those people," we no longer treat them as if they have life; we've lost hope in them.

And when we totally "lose hope" ourselves, we stop talking—quite literally. In my adult life, I have had two friends commit suicide. Both decided that actions they set in motion gave them no alternative. Their family, work, and friends would be better off without them, and they believed that their pain, regret, and fear of the future would not go away unless they went away. They were wrong, but they framed their life in hopeless terms and they acted out their lost hope.

The wife of one of these men shared with me how she went through a reframing after the suicide. She said that her marriage had problems, and that her way of dealing with those problems was to be in control of whatever she thought she could control—the home, the kids, the garden. After the suicide, one of her consuming worries was, "Which family member is going to commit suicide next?" Her kids told her, "We think *you* will." That answer shocked her into confronting herself. She saw her life as foreshortened, and said, "I thought I would be dead in five years. That experience taught me to be less tied to the earth. It's less important to 'get things right,' to be in control. I'm different." The tragedy of her husband's hopelessness led to a change in the way she anticipated the future.

As I said in the last chapter, wisdom is related to our ability to accurately judge what is possible, plausible, and probable. Though this idea might seem to contradict the unpredictability of human affairs, it does not. It may be probable that we will receive a certain response to a question we ask, but the answer is not guaranteed. We need to maintain an openness to surprise, to the mystery and grace of another human being. We certainly hope others will do this for us. Here is human communication's glory (and agony). With hope, we speak in anticipation. When we "lose hope," we stop talking.

What Hope Is

When I was giving my students a pep talk one day, trying to encourage them about what they could achieve, a guy in the back row raised his hand and said, "Do you really believe we can get better?" He was not being sarcastic; he was beautifully, innocently sincere. I smiled. "If I didn't believe that," I said, "I couldn't be a teacher. Hope is the fundamental assumption in education." I think learning explains so much about hope. We point to the splendor of where we are headed. We work together to get there. We are inspired to wait, trusting in the transformation that will happen along the way.

Of course, hope is about more than education. *Hope is the confidence that God has done something that empowers us to wonder, to work, and to wait*. Jesus concludes his line "In the world you will have trouble" with

"But take heart! I have overcome the world" (John 16:33). As I slip on the trouble of the first half of this phrase, the second half feels like a big, fleshy, muscular hand pulling me to safety.

Let's take a look at each aspect in my statement about hope.

Confidence about what God has done. Jesus says he has overcome the world. He's overcome tricky religious questions, political temptations, mistaken views of himself, centuries of life-choking tradition, persecution, stubbornness, and, of course, death. He's the one we are following—and he's overcome the world. It's not that science, government, medicine, business, environmental stewardship and all the rest mean nothing. They can do their own level of overcoming—but they don't deserve the level of trust that we give to a God who is supremely creative, sacrificially loving, insightfully truthful, consistently moral, and possesses the power of resurrection. Repeatedly, Scripture teaches that our hope is in God. There are about thirty statements like this in the Psalms alone.

The object of hope matters—and because God is the object of our hope, we can have confidence that, *ultimately*, "all manner of things shall be well" and, in the meantime, God will walk with us. In a world as continually "on the brink" as ours, this confidence feels countercultural. But it's not a false hope, a lie we tell ourselves, a silly story to put our minds at rest. It's the best we know, the best we can discern: God lives, loves, redeems, and oversees with parental care. Our confidence is not in our circumstances (which might not improve) but in God (who will redeem the circumstances). Romans 5:3–5 reminds us that, contrary to our intuition, our own suffering can lead to perseverance, our perseverance to character, and our character to hope. If, in the midst of suffering, someone tells us, "Don't worry, this will lead to hope," we shake our heads and protest. But when we walk through the stages, we know things work this way. We can reframe our experience, no matter how bleak or brinkish.

The road toward hope was long for Jill. She said,

> *Throughout this experience, I've been holding my breath for the*
> *ultimate silver lining. I'm trying to wrap my head around the*
> *fact that this may just be a horrible year for us and there won't*
> *be a positive, that nothing intrinsically good will come out of*

having to live without our son for the first months of his life. This sucks. Period. But, we have been blown away by kindness. I am overwhelmed by the people who have reached out to us, brought meals, contributed to our crushing medical costs and tirelessly prayed for us. In the most trying season of our lives, people who love us have stepped up in ways we could never have imagined. That's it, that's the silver lining. We are loved.

Inspiration to wonder. Jill shows an outsized confidence that ultimately things will be resolved, that an "expectant eventuality" can mark our framing of the future. Hope always seems to function with some sense of amazement. It's the wonder that, despite our flaws, we are cared for, that regardless of the unlikelihood of something good raising its graceful head, some undeserving mercy comes.

Sometimes this wonder bubbles up naturally from the hot springs of life we're soaking in. God is good, we say. Life is beautiful right now. The body, the mind, relationships, our world is going well. Hope swells from within.

Sometimes it comes through a view from the heights. As Oliver Sacks said when he was dying of cancer, "Over the last few days, I have been able to see my life as from a great altitude, as a sort of landscape, and with a deepening sense of the connection of all its parts." We don't need to be on death's door to see things from higher up. We anticipate, for example, the fuller story of our own infant's life. She won't always scream at 2:00 A.M. Or, when we keep making the same moral mistake, we locate where we are in the larger arc of redemption. This anger, this lust, this jealousy will one day be healed. From an eternal perspective, we know the lion will lie down with the lamb. Inner and outer peace will reign.

Sometimes we assert wonder as a matter of truth. We believe in God's goodness though we don't seem to be able to discern it now. We might be so far down in the pit with physical or emotional pain that we can't see the light at the top. Even so, even so, we remind ourselves, we will yet again praise God (Ps. 42). In this way, hope can feel like good effort, an anticipation we assert toward the light we know is there. Hope also encourages us to get to work.

Motivation to work. When teachers set up an inspirational standard—content worth knowing, skill worth learning, or excellence worth achieving—many students set to work toward those goals. Their hope of true understanding leads to their participation. They'd better not "hope to improve" by doing nothing. Instead, their hope motivates them to take steps toward the vision of becoming knowledgeable enough to be a physician or skilled enough to write revelatory fiction, or whatever kingdom task they see before them. When we catch a vision for some ideal (compassion or patience or purity), we hope to achieve it and we move forward toward that goal.

Willingness to wait. As my family well knows, I am not particularly good at waiting. I've been champing at the bit for so long that my teeth are worn to the gums. Though hope motivates me to work, to find my way toward the vision I see, waiting is something else altogether. Perhaps it's the rare person who works well and waits well—but maybe it is exactly here that hope can teach us how to frame both kinds of anticipation.

One of the ways hope has not transformed me enough yet is that I've twisted it into thinking it should mean constant victory. The word *victory* betrays a perversion of hope—that it has to do with winning a competition: on the tennis court, with my productivity during the next four hours, over my sins, and on and on. Though hope is built on confidence in eventual victory, it is not built on the certainty of *present circumstantial* victory. If hope means we expect to win all the challenges set before us (beating the traffic across town, finding a spouse on the Internet, resolving ongoing conflict with our kids), we are doomed to disappointment—and we will probably become annoying to those around us.

Some in our midst are not hopeful. They are cynical. Weary from repeated unfulfilled hopes, they retreat into sullen defeat. Those who feel their marriage is dry and "hopeless" might say: "He'll always be an idiot" or "She'll never stop whining." Cynical jealousy will lead some to avoid people in happier states, saying, "I can't bear to be around couples who seem to 'have it together.'" Perhaps there used to be hope—but it hasn't been able to endure the waiting.

I don't have a magic wand here (or anywhere, for that matter), but I will offer two comments about the relationship between hope and waiting. My own plan is to keep reading these ideas until I learn to implement them!

Waiting, as a manifestation of hope, comes from a promise of inheritance. When my dad died recently, he had just enough money left in his bank account for my brother and me to go to dinner. Woohoo! Because we've always known we would receive little financial inheritance, Janet and I have had considerable insecurity about our financial future. It's forced us to be good savers, which is not a bad thing. But Paul tells us that our true hope is in "the riches of his glorious *inheritance* in his holy people" (Eph. 1:18b, italics mine). God promises us a rich future, one lived in his presence with a resurrected body and soul. That security could cultivate in us now an attitude of "waiting in hope." We could interpret our experience through the lens of God's promises. Instead of saying, "We are doomed to a retirement of poverty" (just a slight overstatement!), we could say, "We trust God will be at work in our lives at that time—just as he is now." Waiting in hope involves reframing the ordinary as the extraordinary work of God.

As we think about our hopes, our frames regarding the future, a host of clichés come to mind, habits of speech that say something about where we are headed and what we should desire. Clichés are worth a short excursion into their repetitive "highways and byways." Remember, though these detours are reviewed in connection with just one of the soul essentials, they can be applied to all four. (For example, the previous detour into metaphor relates to anticipating the future: Are we pawns in some cosmic game, travelers on a grand journey, characters in a story with no determined ending, or are we headed for a city with gold streets and many mansions?) Likewise, clichés abound in our framing of memory, the self, and others.

Excursion into Clichés

Clichés have really taken a beating in our times. Everyone and their dog criticizes them. Personally, I avoid them like the plague. But sometimes, under pressure, when I can't think of anything to say, a cliché tickles the ivories of my brain and I think, "A bird in the hand is worth two in the bush." Not that I've ever hunted for pheasants or anything.

In an earlier chapter, I suggested that frames could be seen as word habits. We can't be entirely inventive all the time, so we rely on patterns of speech that we have used in the past, repeated tried-and-true combinations of words. If we have been thoughtful about these habits, they serve us well. If they reinforce our core beliefs and help to keep us pointed where we want to go, word habits are frames that give life. But a mindless word habit is a frame we repeat to ourselves and others about what we do not truly hope to embody. If we stopped to examine our clichés, we would often say, "Wait, do I really believe that?"

Many clichés speak of the future. Even something innocuous like "Good luck!" says that "fortune" is what we hope "smiles on us." We say we have to "play the cards we are dealt" and "let the chips fall where they may," but I want to know, what's poker luck got to do with it? Is chance our guiding paradigm? If it isn't, might we think of something else to say about the future? How about "Godspeed"? A little archaic, maybe, but its heart is in the right place. Here are some other common future-oriented sayings:

Follow your dreams.
You can do whatever you want to do.
The future is what you make of it.
You have your whole life ahead of you.

All these lines are more hopeful than despairing, which is, well, hopeful. They seek to empower a person to act rather than doom a person to an unchangeable destiny. They sound rather American, full of self-determination, and they all imagine the future in fairly self-centered terms. Whatever *I* want is good—and I can get what I want. But maybe the future isn't mine. Maybe it's yours. Maybe it's better thought of in communal terms, as in, "The future is ours." Maybe it's (another cliché) in God's hands. What sort of a difference would that make?

Sometimes saying a cliché is the best we can manage. In difficult times, clichés can, as Randall VanderMey says, "grease the hinges" when we don't know what to say. But he also says that stock phrases signal "a dulling of vision, and such dulling is in no one's best interest." When we speak thoughtlessly, we are probably thinking thoughtlessly—and how we frame our thinking matters. Christians have their clichés too: We can be "on fire for God," or a "prayer warrior" who "loves on people." These sentiments aren't immoral or even misguided—but they are usually unexamined. When we take a closer look, we might realize that our language choices are misguided, or that they are misguiding us.

When chastising the pious-tongued religious leaders of his day, Jesus said that the "mouth speaks what the heart is full of" (Matt. 12:34b). What do our clichés say about what's in our heart? Faith in good fortune? Self-centered fantasies? Grabbing for gusto because tomorrow we die? If we reframe the way we speak about the future (and the other soul essentials), we can live in the hope of a transformed life and a restored community. Jesus is frighteningly direct about our framing: "But I tell you that everyone will have to give account on the day of judgment for every empty word they have spoken. For by your words you will be acquitted, and by your words you will be condemned" (Matt. 12:36–37).

It would be wise to take our words into account *before* the day of judgment.

—— **End of Excursion** ——

My definition again: *Hope is the confidence that God has done something that empowers us to wonder, to work, and to wait.* If our hope is mature, we can express our anticipation confidently, saying that because of what God has done, we have an "elevated" sense of wonder, a commitment to work toward life in the kingdom of God, and a readiness to wait for the richness of the inheritance we've been promised.

Another way to put this is to say that good anticipation often articulates itself as "lower expectations and higher hopes." We need both. "Lower expectations" simply means that we don't expect things to go our way. It doesn't mean "low standards," as if we shouldn't encourage others or ourselves to excel. "Higher hopes" means that even though we don't count on everything falling into line, we still yearn for the best options to prevail. I love to garden. When I plant and water, I know weeds and bugs will come. I have lower expectations. But I hope for tomatoes as sweet as candy and cukes firm and crisp. We live in a "troubled world" in which things can spoil and come to ruin even when we work hard. But we should "take heart," because hope will lead us to our goals—and things will be made right—if not now, eventually, as the kingdom of God rises in its fullness.

A Framework for Hope: From Fear to Courage

Our frames in the "anticipating" essential of the soul are built upon an underlying framework. If the framework has a good store of courage, our virtue of hope is much more likely to be strong and wise. If fear undergirds our frames of the future, we will find it difficult to hope. Fear and hope are often seen as opposites, and cowardice and courage as well—but I'd like to examine fear as a hindrance to courage, as that which moves us to cowardice.

Living in Fear

Most of us have nightmares occasionally. Mine are nothing special. I'm usually running away from something or there's someone who gets closer and closer until they are about to get me. Then, I jump out of a building or I fall off a cliff or a gorilla-alien flies over to me on a motorized chessboard and brushes my teeth. Okay, maybe I exaggerate. The cliff is a bit much.

We all have our daytime nightmares too, some of which we are currently living: our invasive cancer treatment, our child's forty-year drug addiction, a terrorist attack. About baby David still being in treatment, his dad Jason says, "No matter how great my days appear, they are truly never good days. Not with him here in the hospital. Not without my boy at home, with his loving mom, rambunctious sister, sniffing dog, and grateful father. I hate this." Some of our fears seem appropriate to the situation. If there's a fire on the hillside above the house, we shouldn't be casually making a milkshake.

Many fears seem overstated—and we can be paralyzed by our imagination. Some of us are chronically fearful, living in great anxiety no matter how circumstances change. I have a friend who would rarely travel to the snow because she was afraid of avalanches. Another cuts off conversations as quickly as possible to diminish her fear of being a burden. Some have extended their rational fear of being harmed into new situations that don't possess any danger. Fears can oppress and torment.

Perhaps the most insidious fears are those that are manufactured to get us to buy things or to "buy into" various programs. Scott Bader-Saye discusses a fear-for-profit syndrome, how the news and advertising industries overstate danger to the point that our anxiety "leads us to act in ways that override our moral concerns. We spend our money based on fear rather than stewardship. We make political decisions based on fear rather than the common good. We participate in religious life based on fear rather than love." And, I would add, we find it difficult to anticipate the future in hope.

The culture of fear encourages many of us to become even more entrenched in worry, the second of the four problematic self-talk states that Edmund Bourne reviews: "The Worrier creates anxiety by imagining the worst-case scenario. . . . [D]ominant tendencies include 1) anticipating the worst, 2) overestimating the odds of something bad or embarrassing happening, and 3) creating grandiose images of potential failure or catastrophe." Sounds like a lot of us every day.

When our lives are marked by fear, we need hope—but hope can be difficult to summon to our aid. Hope requires a certain amount of risk, even if it is only an intellectual risk, and risk requires courage.

Encouraging Courage

About the only time courage gets discussed in the church is when men's groups get together and celebrate their testosterone. For one of these sessions years ago, I wrote a tongue-in-cheek parody of a Robert Service poem I called "The Manly Ode of Billy McBone." Here's the first stanza:

> I once knew a man named Billy McBone.
> He liked his meat raw and he slept on a stone.
> No napkin for him, and all his wounds gory
> Listen up, lads, and I'll tell you his story.

Since I grew up as the smallest, skinniest kid in every class until I was about a sophomore in high school, I've never appreciated the version of courage that requires you to jump off a cliff into class 5 rapids and then swim until you grab a bar hanging from a biplane that carries you over the desert and drops you onto a camel trotting at full speed.

Not that I don't envy the insanity of the challenge.

Courage is important. After Jesus said we'd have trouble in the world, he said, "Take heart," a phrase that has been translated into variations of "be of good cheer" (be glad, etc.), "take hope" (you need not fear, etc.), and "be courageous" (be brave, etc.). I love how the translations can't quite decide between heart, courage, and hope. Perhaps that indecision says something about the relationship between the ideas. Whatever kind of confidence Jesus refers to here, he doesn't only mean the macho kind. We might not be ready to wrestle a bear, but we can "fight the good fight" of faith because we know the Messiah who has overcome the world.

What is courage? The Cowardly Lion of Oz says it's "what makes the elephant charge his tusk, in the misty mist or the dusky dusk." Other definitions might be more helpful, even if they can't be as easily sung. I think of courage as a kind of high-heartedness, an undaunted movement toward a goal. G. K. Chesterton says courage is a "strong desire to live taking the form of a readiness to die." Less dramatic forms of courage might involve initiating a hard conversation or continuing to comfort a crying baby. In any case, we know that courage suppresses the fear of a bad outcome in order to pursue a good outcome.

Courage is important for the virtue of hope, because hope is risky. It involves setting out in the direction of a vision without the surety that the vision will be fulfilled. Every fall I look out at the latest group of students and think, "I wonder how things will go this year?" Of course, I *hope* things go well, but teaching is uncertain and I have to find the courage to take action in the hope of true learning. If I'm overcome with fear of student rejection or apathy, I will be stymied from the start. Courage helps me to anticipate the future in hope.

———

The soul essential of anticipating the future with hope is highlighted in how we frame the story we are living. Do we speak as if our sorrows will be redeemed? Do we frame the future in the hope of eventual mercy and justice, a peace that we are walking in as we love others as Christ loved us? Are you in a hopeful story? When you frame your future, what's in the picture?

Because she was a mother before she had David, Jill knew that her feelings were not just the result of having a child with an extra chromosome. "The overwhelming love, the complete obsession, the desire to fight anyone who would say anything disparaging about your precious miracle: I feel all of this for Ella (my daughter) and for David," she notes. "I don't ever see Down syndrome when I look at him. I see happy smiles and a pointy little chin and the most sparkly eyes." Jill's family was changing into people who don't see a person's disability first, but instead notice all of their amazing qualities. "And I hope I am becoming the kind of person that I've always envied, a person of grace and warmth who reserves judgment and welcomes all."

Crowning Up on the Cane

I stripped
the roses yesterday.
      Every leaf.

Most gardeners do this
after winter's work is done,
when the plants begin to push out
their buds and blooms. But
I did my deed in June.
      I had to.

Little worms had eaten the Cecile Brunner
down to its skeleton, with leafy carcasses
hanging on in the desert
of the once rich river of green
      and creamy pink.

I blame myself. Just too busy
to look after them. Priorities,
important ones,
      I keep saying.

So, with penance pruners
in hand, I snipped them back
      to stark bare canes.

Boldly, whimsically, I announced,
      "Without their food supply,
      the devil worms will curl and die!"

It was my mantra, my shearing cheer.
Some worms I found
hiding, skulking and nibbling
on the back sides of the veiny leaves
      —I squished these demons

between my fingers,
them and their eggy sacs
        full of future devourers.

Near the end of my sad task,
a neighbor wandered over. He took in
the carnage and said, "These blooms will
        rise again."

I nodded. "Yes. You are right. Maybe we should
        call it the Resurrection Rose."

I heaped the remains into the trash
and put my tools away, thinking about
the comfort this vision brought me,
        this confidence

that roses will come back, that roses—those lush,
delicious flowers, so difficult to keep
without rust or pest or mold—have such
        hardy botanical bones.

They just keep coming back,
crowning up on the cane
like a baby's birthing head.
Rising, rising,
        always rising.

Dwelling

within

Ourselves

in Peace

CHAPTER ELEVEN

Dwelling

*My frame was not hidden from you when I was
made in the secret place, when I was woven
together in the depths of the earth.*

—Psalm 139:15

When I was a boy, I was not only the shortest kid in class, I was also the skinniest. I was called Beanpole, Shadow, Runt, Short-stuff, Pipsqueak, String-bean—and other epithets not suitable for public consumption. During lunch, when all us boys would line up to get picked for teams, I'd fidget, hoping the inevitable would not occur.

But it did.

Time after time, I was picked last. Years later, in high school, I didn't relish co-ed trips to the beach. My ribs showed. I was the "starving child" poster boy.

At the same time, my wife Janet was growing up across town, tall and "large" for her age. A "friend" actually called her "Janet the Planet," and the geeky boy in class, the one she had been kind to (in part because no one else was), signed her annual: "Roses are red, violets are blue. If you were skinnier, I'd like you." One time, her mom took her to Sears for school clothes, and they walked over to the (I'm not making this up) "Chubby Girls" fashion line.

When we found each other, I had filled out my six foot body a bit and she had lost forty-five pounds. We've had good laughs imagining ourselves as elementary school versions of No-fat Jack Sprat and his No-lean wife.

But, sadly, we haven't had to use as much imagination as we'd hoped. Though our weight has changed, the ways we dwell within ourselves have often been stuck in those earlier frames. I still think I need to prove myself, to show I'm masculine enough, worthy of attention, a valiant competitor. And Janet wrestles with the body consciousness of many contemporary women, who judge themselves by the fit of their jeans and think about food more than is healthy. Somehow, we ended up in a beach town, two folks too insecure to feel comfortable sunbathing in the open. I know, I know, you'd gladly switch places.

How we frame ourselves matters. The question "Who am I?" is a conundrum to us—but it is never far from our minds.

In this third section on a soul essential, we are moving from the two related to time (remembering the past and anticipating the future) to the two related to space (dwelling within ourselves and engaging with others). We live in time, in the present with a past and a future. And we also live in space, with an inner life, an indwelling experience of contemplation, imagination, and self-dialogue; and with an outer life, a socially engaged experience of interaction, community, social framing.

It may sound a bit abstract but, very simply, this is where we live—in the intersection of time and space. We are chronological (time-bound) beings and we're geographical (space-bound) beings. Being "in space" has nothing to do with *Star Wars* or *Journey to Mars*. Here's an example: During his senior year in college, Patrick was my TA. He was intellectually and physically active, rapidly growing into a richer sense of himself. Then the accident happened. While rehearsing for a dorm skit, Patrick was flipped as part of the choreography. His partner lost his footing and Patrick landed on his head, breaking his neck. His paralysis was instant and permanent. Though his physical space changed radically, it took him years to name himself accurately in relationship to his new physical situation. He struggled to come to terms with the word quadriplegic. We live in physical space, and we live in the ways we frame that space.

Patrick's story is a reminder that "there is no immaculate perception." We all have different views of the same event, even if only slightly. So, we would do well to examine how we frame our "inner" lives, how we discern the ways we dwell in our identity. Might we reach a physically incorrect conclusion? Sure. I could say I'm well suited for the life of a heavyweight bodybuilder—but I'm not. Though some things are driven more by nature, as in how our brains are predisposed, even our brains are influenced by the ways we frame our natural tendencies. When I frame my inner life, what is in the picture? Am I friendly, depressed, extroverted, introverted, artistically sensitive, quietly strong? Am I repulsive? Beloved?

Voices That Call Us to Reframe the Self

We don't frame ourselves in isolation. We're influenced by our culture, especially through media; our *friends*, how they reflect to us who they think we are; our circumstances, which might call us to reframe in dramatic ways; and our transcendent beliefs, which, for many of us, are drawn from the Scriptures.

Cultural Voices

"Know Thyself" marked the entrance to the ancient Temple at Delphi. Whether we've succeeded in obeying this command or not, recent generations are famous for trying. Some say we've taken this injunction too far, succumbing to compulsive self-centeredness. Though results change constantly, a search for the word "self" on Amazon Books yielded over a million hits, while "God" brought up 484,000. From Christopher Lasch's *Culture of Narcissism* to Nina Brown's *Children of the Self-Absorbed*, critics have increasingly seen our times under the shadow of the selfie stick.

Even if we aren't more selfish than previous generations, we love to label ourselves—and seek clarifying names. The four classic temperaments, the Myers-Briggs test, and the Enneagram help us find categories for explanation. About myself, I might say I'm tightly wound (naturally caffeinated), creative, impatient, passionate about teaching and about communicating well, perfectionistic, funny, an accomplish-aholic. I have a bad back and good stamina. I enjoy family, gardening, tennis, hiking, reading, and good conversation. I'm an apprentice to Jesus. Do I know myself? Have I spent too much time attempting to know myself? Would my description of my strengths and weaknesses be similar to those who know me well?

As contemporary Americans, we're encouraged to believe in ourselves but not necessarily to *know* ourselves, to seek pleasure for ourselves but not necessarily to create loving community for others. In the media and elsewhere, we often hear about the importance of freedom, fun, individuality, appearance, and success. Many of these themes are placed before our eyes and ears through advertising. All day, everywhere. On TV, radio, every website, social media, in the mailbox, on billboards, in public bathrooms, sides of buses, sides of buildings, sides of golf and tennis hats, maybe soon on sides of beef. "Get two ribs for the price of one when you carve up this cow!" As a powerful cultural influence on the self, advertising is worth an additional excursion.

Excursion into Advertising

In 1759, well before mass media as we know it, the great essayist Samuel Johnson said, "Promise, large promise, is the soul of an advertisement." Though the presence and style of advertising have dramatically changed over the centuries, the primary promise has remained the same: our product will solve your problems, even problems you didn't know you had. A woman on the edge of her bed eats a bowl of cereal while her husband sleeps behind her. The ad for Shredded Wheat says, "What satisfies a hungry woman?" No problem is too great for Post, Nabisco, or General Mills.

Advertising is successful because it links products with our identity. It defines the self in the context of a particular car or phone or style of vacation. If we want the suave image of luxurious living, we need a BMW sports car or Dior perfume to get us there. Michelob Light says, "This is your beer." We identify ourselves with certain brands and, overall, as "consumers," a frame that implies "using things up," not "building things up." Nordstrom claims, "In the end, I'll only regret the stuff I didn't buy."

To convince us that we are what we buy, advertising capitalizes on metamessages, indirect assertions that go beyond the main message of an ad. I'm a lonely man walking the streets, but then I chew Extra gum and a beautiful woman appears at my side. The message is "Buy Extra gum," but the metamessage is "Extra gum is the way to romance." In addition to the primary slogans and appeals, we are told two metamessages in almost every ad: "We are happy when we buy" and "We are inadequate." John Kavanaugh notes that many TV shows portray people as "unfulfilled, unfaithful, unhappy, frustrated, foolish. The only times that persons are presented as uniformly happy and ecstatically fulfilled are in commercials: purchasing, collecting or consuming products that resolve problems, deliver self-assurance, win friends." And, of course, we never measure up without *this* deodorant or *that* diamond ring. Besides high-fashion photos, people smile in almost every ad. What else would they do?

Advertising often convinces us that some nonmaterial good thing (love, success, happiness, etc.) can be acquired through material means (cars, beauty products, toilet paper). Coke means happiness. Dentyne gum promotes romance. Lingerie leads to sexual intimacy. Laundry soap leads to sexual intimacy. Computers, coffee, everything leads to sexual intimacy! Values themselves can be purchased: Life cereal. Eternity cologne. Barilla spaghetti gets you perfect harmony. Wisconsin cheese says, "Welcome to the Meaning of Life." Cartier (diamonds): "True love has a color and a name."

In recent years, ads have leaped from making spiritual claims (we can build romance in your life) to religious claims about the nature of faith. Note the religious language in these ads: Belvedere Vodka: Believe. True Religion (a clothing brand). SK-II lotion: Touch the Miracle. Pro-Glow Foundation: Infallible. Levi's: Cut with Grace; Go Forth. Some have said that advertising functions as a consumer religion, providing salvation through purchasing. We are encouraged to find our redemption in things and in our bodies. We must be attractive, thin, beautiful, sexy, and "flawless beyond any stretch of the imagination." And we should never age: "What if you could grow young?" and "Correct every sign of age."

It's so hard for us not to get these perspectives into the ways we frame ourselves, how we frame what is important to us. Sadly, even becoming media savvy won't keep us from believing ads. Our desire to be a certain kind of person, a disciple of Jesus, gets co-opted by all these messages. As we dwell within the self, the words we use need to be clear, developed, true, and ready to compete with the contradictions to them that come to us thousands of times a day.

— End of Excursion —

More than ever, due to cultural frames such as those from advertising, "comparison" rules. Though jealousy is not new, social media has taken jealousy to greener and greener heights. We love to see what's happening with our friends, but the comparison can drive any of us to the despair of not measuring up to others' beauty, vacations, weddings, or picnic lunches in the backyard. We can become addicted to "likes" and followers. Increasingly we feel the need to manage our self-image, to see the main task of our life as self-promotion. Some have taken to abstaining from social media for their mental health.

We also hear a lot about sex. After interviewing 200 adolescent girls in the United States, Nancy Jo Sales concluded, "Much of the culture of social media is, in a way, an ongoing expression of 'hot or not,' liking or rejecting people and things, and the physical appeal of women and girls." Far more than most moms and dads realize, norms of attractiveness are driven by online porn. Sales quotes John Chirban of Harvard Medical School: "With porn, you're not looking at the meaning and value of a whole human being. Girls take away from it the message that their most worthy attribute is their sexual hotness." The sexualizing of almost every sphere of contemporary culture powerfully influences personal framing.

Friendly Voices

Our culture tells us what's important about ourselves. So do our friends and family. We may like to think that we just "are who we are," but we are constantly negotiating who we are—in concert with others. According to Cooley, Mead, and many other theorists, we develop the self, at least a significant part of it, by looking at ourselves through the eyes of others. Someone says, "You are such a creative person," a term we haven't used to describe ourselves—so we entertain the idea, "Maybe I'm more creative than I thought." Many of us are in vocations because of the "blessing" someone gave to our teaching, business instincts, or cheerful service of others.

Friend-framing can be confusing too. One person says I'm humble, another that I'm arrogant. One person says I'm good with people, another tells me I don't read situations well. Years ago, after my mom died, my dad came in his fifth-wheel trailer to stay with my family for several weeks. Though he helped me with some larger house projects, he seemed oblivious to our three daughters—and he never volunteered to help with daily chores. We thought he acted like a king waiting to be served, and I wanted him to engage with the kids. He stayed with us long enough that I felt compelled to talk with him about it. We had one of our best conversations ever. We said important things carefully and honestly. At the end, we hugged. In the morning, we saw that he was gone. A few days later, we received a letter saying that he had never been treated so poorly in his life. Just the night before, I thought I'd made a breakthrough as a son. Now I was a bad one.

The power that friends have to influence our "dwelling within" leads to the question, "Who are our friends?" If I get a large part of my sense of self from my friends, do I surround myself with friends who tell me what I want to hear? On one level, of course I do. No one wants to live with a constant barrage of naysaying and rebuke. How would I ever be funny if none of my friends thought I was funny? But do we also choose friends who are willing to challenge, to confront in love? Do we have friends who draw out of us good qualities that "don't come naturally"? Do we have friends to whom we could go and ask, "Was I out of line?" Good friendships can work this way, as iron sharpens iron, as long as the attempts to sharpen aren't constant, like that squeak in the family-room chair.

We all have our inner demons that tell us we don't measure up in some way, that we aren't any good at X (whatever it is we are trying to do), that we should spare the world our failures and just withdraw. Praise can also disturb our inner life, sometimes in life-changing ways, as in "I will never forget how you took me aside and told me you thought I should be a writer." However, as John Gottman's research substantiates, we tend to pay much more attention to criticism. He discovered that stable married couples maintained a ratio of five positive interactions to one negative during conflicts, whereas those who divorced used nearly an equal number of positive to negative comments. Sometimes we zero in on the critique that wasn't said: "Why didn't Morgan call? She must not like me."

Circumstantial Voices

Home with a five-month-old, Erin waited for her husband Jason to get home from work. At a new job forty minutes away, he often stayed late, but Erin had an app that allowed her to track Jason's drive. It gave her a little extra security. On this night, Erin saw that, ten minutes from home,

Jason was stuck on Highway 31. Was there traffic? An accident? Had he run out of gas?

Strangely, he wasn't responding to texts. Time passed. Too much time.

Eventually, Erin learned that a woman, Angela, had rear-ended a car going seventy miles an hour—and that another woman had stopped to help. For some unknown reason—maybe because of what she'd seen in the accident—this second woman had collapsed on the freeway, probably in shock. It was a chaotic scene, with cars zooming over the hill above the accident.

Jason was in one of those cars.

As he came down the hill, he could see in front of him the two cars that had collided, and this woman in real danger, lying on the busy highway. He pulled over to see what he could do, and so did another man. The two of them dodged the traffic and went out to lift the woman off the road to safety. As they did so, a teenager, driving way over the speed limit, came over the hill and hit Jason and the other man and killed them both.

We have a way of framing the world, our lives, our self—and then events, sometimes enormously tragic events, come to disturb our sense of order, our proprioception. Erin said, "I didn't realize what my beliefs were until they collapsed. I must have assumed that if we followed God and obeyed him, he would not take us in death. But now I was asking, 'How could Jason's death be more beneficial than his life?' It's an important question—but it won't bring him back." Erin's new sense of self was as a widow, a "grieving widow," she said, "like Swiss cheese, with holes blown through me." She had tried so hard to be "together," to be in control, to achieve her way to whatever she wanted—but now, she said, "If Jason could die, anyone could. Nothing felt safe."

Having walked for a few years past this event, she says she is a more discernibly broken person—but that many people relate to her more freely in this brokenness. Appearances don't matter anymore. She says she's learned that "God isn't fair, but he's just. All that matters is eternal relationship. I just don't have time to waste over things that aren't true. I have a certain kind of peace, but also an urgency."

We don't have to have stories this painful to know that our circumstances have changed our sense of self over the years. A marriage, a new job, a disease, or just about anything could lead us to feel the need to reframe.

Kurt Vonnegut's short story "Who Am I This Time?" explains how Harry Nash seems to be a "nobody" until he gets a part in a play. Then he comes alive, embracing the role and staying in that character until the play is over. When challenging circumstances arise, we might ask the same thing, "Who am I now, after these events? What roles am I playing?" At times, we do feel like Swiss cheese, and all we can see are the holes—but other times we feel broken but renewed, full of holes but healing, a person with an identity in God.

Transcendent Voices

We all operate according to certain overarching beliefs, including values that affect how we dwell within. When a Christian friend of ours stayed with locals in Holland, the hosts immediately announced that they were "totally secular," that they raised their son "totally secular," and that the country was "totally secular." My friend assumed that "totally secular" meant that the church was not allowed to run public institutions—but the hosts said "totally secular" meant that "all intelligent, educated people know that there is no God." They seemed proud to not need a God to help them or define them. Then, pointing to the crucifix on the church across the street, one of the hosts, the wife, said, "They just put that gross, hideous thing up where we have to see it every time we leave our house." My friend said, "Yes, it is gross and hideous, but it is also beautiful." She looked dumbfounded. Then my friend told her the story of a schoolteacher in the Midwest who placed her body over the children when a tornado struck the room, sang with them throughout the storm—and then, tragically, lost her life from falling debris. "That's the cross," my friend explained. "Gross and hideous, ugly and full of pain. But beautifully sacrificial, a death for our sake!" The woman seemed taken by the story. "That's such a new way to see it." Later, as they hugged and left for the train, she remarked, "Now you have to leave just when our conversation gets good."

What does it mean to be a person? Are we just atoms set loose in the cosmos? Are we locked in evolutionary destiny? Are we made in the image of God? Some get their sense of self from beliefs in natural forces. Others believe in various versions of divine activity.

Those who follow Christ look to the Bible for its messages about the self. Two of these messages can be seen with the "*this*, not *that*" format

Jesus often used, messages that will help us see how the gospel calls us to reframe.

Not self-centered but other-centered. Many scriptures remind us that we should not be self-seeking but truth-seeking, other-seeking, God-seeking. Here's one passage: Paul says, "Do nothing out of selfish ambition or vain conceit. Rather, in humility value others above yourselves, not looking to your own interests but each of you to the interests of the others" (Phil. 2:3–4). In contrast to most cultural frames about the self, Christians are to move the self from the foreground, the focus of attention, to the background, the part of the frame that might be out of focus. Jesus says, "What good is it for someone to gain the whole world, and yet lose or forfeit their very self?" (Luke 9:25). Understanding the proper place of the self is a consistent biblical theme.

Another part of how we are to regard the self is related to our need for personal discipline. When we think of our actions, Jesus calls us not to indulge ourselves but to deny ourselves (Matt. 16:24). We are to "pick up our cross," sacrificially to do what is the most loving thing in a situation—hold our tongue, suffer persecution, serve those who are ungrateful or unresponsive—acts that require tremendous self-control, a quality so important it is listed among the fruits of the Spirit (Gal. 5:23).

When we can run ourselves into the ground serving others, being other-centered can be complicated. Self-care is important—but my sense is that much of our neglect of ourselves comes from a drive to be perceived as other-centered. When we see ourselves as indispensable, we can't stop to rest or treat ourselves well.

Not the old conception but a new creation. The New Testament is full of reframing messages about a believer's new status and what it means. Jesus and Paul say "not this but that" in a variety of ways. Our new self is:

> not the old sin-bound self but a new creation (2 Cor. 5:17),
> not cursed but blessed (John 20:29),
> not condemned but forgiven (Mark 3:28),
> not an enemy of God but a friend (John 15:15),
> not slaves but children adopted into the family of God (Rom. 8:15),
> not limited by the flesh but liberated by the Spirit (Rom. 8:4).

Each reframing is worth reviewing, but I'll leave most of them on their own, letting the repetition and contrast speak to the power of the change Christ offers. When Paul writes that we should "not conform to the pattern of this world, but be transformed by the renewing of [our] mind" (Rom. 12:2), he recognizes that we who follow Jesus will have different ways of seeing ourselves, that these ways will, at times, conflict with the cultural voices around us, and that our minds are crucial players in these changes. Our transformation depends on our mental activity, much of which needs to focus on the difference between cultural frames and biblical frames. We are not to be reduced to our appearance, to our popularity, to our accomplishments. We are to get our status from being God's children, from being forgiven, from being gradually changed into God's likeness.

When our middle child, Hannah, was three, she announced from her high chair, "Jesus is cold!" "Is that so," I said, "how did he get cold?" "Well," she said, "he's in my heart, and I just drank cold milk that I swallowed right next to my heart!" That's one way to interpret the idea that Christ dwells in us. As we abide in him and he in us, we would be wise to remember the transcendent beliefs that come from the ways Scripture frames who we are to be—not self-centered but other-centered, not the old conception but the new creation.

We dwell within ourselves, and name ourselves. We are being named by others, and we work through how our culture, our friends, our circumstances, and our transcendent beliefs influence our framing. My wife and I keep deciding which voices we will listen to as we think about our bodies. Erin sorts through her need to reframe her place in the world, in God's world, after the death of her husband.

Which names for ourselves will we deny or accept? Which ones will we hold up and hope to live into? Sometimes I think that, like Jacob and Saul, we will all receive new names one day. They might not be written on a white stone, as it says in Revelation (2:17), but when we will hear the name that says all we are and all we hope to be, it will ring true and we will answer it. As for me, I'm Greg Spencer, but you can call me beloved of God.

Sometimes I know why the light is there

When I strike a match, the pungent sparking
punches into my nose like a two-fisted alarm.

Unsettled, I twitch and wince. For the
thrill of the surging flame, I recover

quickly, then I follow the glow moving swiftly
down the stick. I wait till the fire burns right

to my fingers. How long can I hold out?
It's a game, a dare. But I always

blow it down in time and study
the blackened bit that remains.

But the luminous dare Jesus gave
is not this type of gamble. We are not

to watch the radiance till we can't bear it.
We walk under the brightness—and become

children of light.

John 12:35-36

CHAPTER TWELVE

Dwelling Well

*If we were humble, nothing would change us—
neither praise nor discouragement.
If someone were to criticize us, we would not feel discouraged.
If someone were to praise us, we also would not feel proud.*
—Mother Teresa, *In My Own Words*

When Erin heard that Jason had stopped to help the woman on the highway, she thought, "Of course he did. That's just who he is." It made so much sense to her that he followed his principles to the end. But what would she do next? Who was she now? How could she call herself someone who believes in a good God? She said, "People are treating me like I'm 'extremely fragile.' Am I?"

Nearly twenty years after the accident that left him with the punishing combination of paralysis *and* pain, Patrick still had not come to terms with his condition. He said, "I kept trying to force fit what I wanted onto my body. I said, 'I can keep my dreams alive, can't I? I can be the same person I was before.' But I couldn't be that person. I had to admit that I had shut myself off emotionally, that I was angry, that I really did not know how to surrender."

Amy, an extremely bright and capable student, struggled with relationships after graduation. She had always been the kid who did the right thing in a conservative Christian household. Now she was working through the unthinkable, that she was not heterosexual. There was no room in her mind for a reframing. The only space she had was "Gay is bad."

Who am I? On one level or another, all of us wrestle with this question. We grapple with labels that describe us, and may feel pinned down by them. To dwell wisely within ourselves, we must frame ourselves well, even though, as the last chapter reviewed, many forces bear down upon us and within us, doing their best to persuade us toward their ends.

Dwelling Well Is Essential

Not very many parents need to tell their children to think more about themselves: "Oh, sweetie, don't forget. You really are the center of the known universe!" But "thinking about ourselves" is not the same as "dwelling well." Some folks are famously self-centered. Others seem utterly unaware of who they are. Often, these two types are rolled into the same person.

To help us think through the self, three aspects of dwelling wisely will be reviewed. We improve our indwelling if we frame ourselves as minds and bodies, doubters and believers, and resilient.

Remembering We Are Minds and Bodies

Olivia can't figure out what's wrong. She sleeps three hours Tuesday night, eight hours Wednesday night, and two on Thursday night. She eats like a bird for two days, then gorges herself like a bear at a salmon feed. She never exercises unless forced—and drinks away her Friday and Saturday nights, sometimes hooking up with a new guy. On Sunday, she goes to church and prays that the Lord would "take away" her tiredness, stomach issues, and unrelenting psychological stress.

Truth be told, we are astoundingly promiscuous about many things. We often act as if nothing we do to our bodies will have any effect on our spirits, as if the body were only something we carry along as a piece of luggage. As the devil Screwtape tells the junior tempter under his tutelage, "You must always remember that they are animals and that whatever their bodies do affects their souls." But we try to act as if no cause-and-effect relationship exists between our life choices and our bodies. I confess that one of my images of heaven is that we can eat whatever junk food we want—with no physical consequences. (Cheetos all day! Doughnuts till dawn!) But in the meantime, promiscuity usually catches up to us and we suffer the results.

We can't just compartmentalize our spiritual lives to some nonmaterial box of our lives, as if we are all "head" and no body, like aliens from Mars are often portrayed. In my academic community, heads can get really big and bodies can be dismissed. I wonder if this dismissal of the body is related to the number of divorces we've had in recent years. Some faculty seem to ignore the physical reality of too much time spent in their offices, away from spouse and family. Maybe this is one reason James says that faith and deeds are inextricably bound together (James 2:14). We can no more say we have faith without some physical manifestation of it than we can say we are minds with no body attached. Though I say I believe something "in my mind," I can't be sure unless I also believe it "in my feet."

Playing the Doubting and Believing Games
What is your reaction to the following ideas? Marxism is the most biblical economic system. If everyone packed a gun, the world would be safer. My next job will be fulfilling and financially rewarding. Can you believe each or doubt each—for a time?

English professor Peter Elbow suggested that when learning anything new (even learning about the self), we should engage in twin strategies, or "games." We should "play the doubting game" by looking for any problems, issues, or errors in what we hear. We should ask, "What's wrong with it? Why won't it work?" No matter how sympathetic I am to Erin's ordeal, the doubting game might lead me to challenge her conclusions (to myself and maybe to her) about "what God was doing" in the midst of the accident or how she framed her new life without Jason. Some of us are quite skilled at asking these questions of others, exposing flaws in logic and articulating doubts.

Elbow says we should also "play the believing game." We suspend judgment and ask, "In what ways is this true? How is this perspective believable?" The goal in the believing game is to understand, to clarify, to empathize. How might Patrick's fears and reluctance to accept his situation make sense, even if his quadriplegic experience is not remotely like mine? What parts of Amy's story can I accept? The believing game creates a lens for seeing and hearing what we might otherwise shut off.

As you consider these games, you might find yourself suspicious of one of them. "Oh, those cynical doubters, they are so negative," or "Some people are so undiscerning that they accept everything." I'm guessing we all lean toward one game more than the other—and that we will be richer, faster learners if we play both games. If we typically doubt, we will learn a lot by also asking, "What's right about this idea?" and if we typically believe, we will learn a lot by asking, "What's wrong with this idea?" Elbow says that the best approach is to play the believing game first, because we won't be fair with new ideas unless we have attempted to understand them as if they were true.

When it comes to understanding who we are, we would be wise to play both games. Many writers, including Blaise Pascal, have called human beings a paradox: part angel and part beast. If I doubt myself too much, I might struggle to "believe" anything good about myself (I'm rotten, despicable, unworthy, a constant failure). If I tend to trust myself too much, I might not sufficiently doubt my own motives or actions (I'm always good at heart, don't mean any harm, believe the best about humanity).

Playing these games can open us to knowledge about ourselves that we have resisted. Here's a teaser I've turned over and over in my mind: Is it harder to believe what you typically doubt or to doubt what you typically believe? You might find out by doing the exercise I've explained in the discussion questions for chapter twelve at the back of this book.

Being Resilient

In our age of anxiety, we often surprise ourselves by how fast we get back up after we get knocked down. Writing books could send anyone over the edge. Twenty-five years ago, after I received my first manuscript back from the editor, I thought I had received a D. Years later, an editor said about my novel that it "started on page sixty-six." Another book had to be reduced by almost one-third. (Hmm, there's a pattern here.) But, besides the troubles with my drafts, what amazed me every time was—after a short period of self-loathing—how quickly I was back at it. Just a few days into the editing, I'd think, "She's right. This is going to be a much better book." My resilience surprised me.

About nine months after the Santa Barbara Tea Fire, in which thirteen of forty-one homes in our neighborhood burned to the ground, a number of us attended a session on post-traumatic stress disorder. The therapist reviewed PTSD's symptoms, especially the sentiment "I'm not safe." Then she suggested factors that aided resiliency, ranging from our history of coping with stress (children of alcoholics don't typically do well) to our ability to reframe negative situations (children of alcoholics don't have to do poorly). She stayed on this point, that despite our sadness and depression, we tend to bounce back.

Filmmakers get this. From *Star Wars* to *Shawshank Redemption* to *Sully* (and other films not starting with S), human beings find a way to endure, to rise above, to triumph over difficulties. It could be that we just enjoy watching these victories, but I think they appeal to our inner resilience, *an ability to recover* that we need to name about ourselves. Suicide is shocking for many reasons—but one is that we struggle to believe that someone actually, thoroughly, totally gave up. We may feel like giving up, but we usually don't. We seem to have built into us a God-given buoyancy. As Paul says in Romans: "We also glory in our sufferings, because we know that suffering produces perseverance; perseverance, character; and character, hope" (5:3–4). This is part of how we frame ourselves as people of faith.

Dwelling well within ourselves may feel mysterious at times—but it includes straightforward goals: pursuing our embodied, doubting and believing, and resilient selves.

Dwelling Well as an Essential of the Soul

When I frame myself, is it "me" who is in the picture—or someone else? If I'm "out of sorts" with myself, feeling insecure, traumatized, or depressed, everything is affected. Just taking a step out of the house can seem overwhelming. I need more than the suggestions under "dwelling well"; I need to connect to the soul. Maybe this is one reason God seems to care so much about how we frame ourselves. Dwelling within is an essential of the soul that draws from our sense of home, our use of verbs, our inward life with Christ, and the fullness of our discernment. Erin, Patrick, and Amy have taken these qualities to heart.

Being at Home with the Self

With our cultural emphasis on privacy, we don't often get a knock on our door. If we do, our first thought is probably, "Yikes! This house is a mess!"

But being at home with ourselves is a different issue—though we may still throw up our hands and say we're a mess.

When discussing welcoming others (an issue I'll address in the chapters on "Engaging"), Henri Nouwen says that a hospitable host must "be at home in his own house—that is, he has to discover the center of his life in his own heart." We can see what he means when we contrast those whose comfort with themselves helps us to be relaxed around them and those who are so uneasy about themselves that we find ourselves anxious and looking for a way out.

Feeling "at home" does not mean all is well within our soul. But it does mean that we aren't always looking to others to compensate for our insecurities. It means we know who we are. We know our strengths and weaknesses and we understand that spiritual and moral progress takes time. The key is that, even though we aren't perfect, we are liberated enough to be focused on others.

Erin didn't like being exposed as "fragile," Patrick as "paralyzed," Amy as "outsider." To be at home in their own house, they had to have ways to frame these issues, frames that didn't lead others to feel unwelcomed in their presence. Erin learned to say she was strong in the new weaknesses she felt after Jason died. Patrick came to understand that his paralysis gave him a calling to tell his story. Amy claimed new ways to talk about her sexuality.

Replacing Nouns with Verbs

Years ago, when I was in the midst of my back problems, I was asked to speak to a group of soccer players. I wanted to identify with them by talking about my own athletic life, but I realized I could not say "I am a tennis player" because I wasn't playing tennis at the time. This got me thinking that "being" a tennis player was too large a part of my identity—and perhaps I should be saying "I *play* tennis" rather than "I *am* a tennis player."

And that got me thinking that the soul essential of dwelling within carefully chooses its "I am" statements. The framing of "I am" presents the self as static, unchanging, living in labels such as "*I am* an idiot" or "*I am* amazingly successful" rather than "I couldn't solve this problem" or "I helped my business grow." Since everything that exists changes, *nothing* remains exactly the same, not rocks, not nations, not me. Everything is dynamic, in process.

Maybe that's one reason God calls himself "I AM"—because he is the only one who can say it with confidence (Exod. 3:14). The rest of us are in flux. Because it is in our nature to change, we recognize that we are not yet what we are going to become. Perhaps we should reframe from "I am a writer" to "I write," from "I am a student" to "I'm learning."

In a similar way, in *Your Body Believes Every Word You Say* (great title!), Barbara Levine says that when it comes to physical ailments, we would be better off using verb frames rather than noun frames. Rather than "I have cancer," we should say, "I am cancering." She says that "I have cancer" seems too definitive; it sets up cancer as a condition over which we have no control. This noun-to-verb advice seems helpful when it comes to most aspects of the self. I tell my students that I don't grade them, I grade their *exams*. So students should say (if they failed an exam), "I failed the exam," not "I am a failure."

Maybe this frame-shift is too clumsy—but the idea is fascinating. Patrick resisted saying "I am quadriplegic" because that would mean his state would be unchanging—but he needed to find a way to come to terms with his condition. Maybe we can say "I am" if by it we mean "I am in process." And there are biblical exceptions to this rule, including how we refer to ourselves as part of the family of God. I take this up next.

Living in Christ

Unlike my daughter Hannah when she was three, I don't think Jesus gets cold when I drink milk. Even so, the nutrition of my soul depends on living in Christ and Christ living in me. This self-defining frame, "in Christ," is mentioned over 150 times in the New Testament. James Bryan Smith says that this status liberates us to say, "I am free to make choices about what I do and do not do. But pay attention to this: *Those choices should be made in light of who I am, not to determine who I am.* I am one in whom Christ dwells, and that should guide my decisions." Would a child of God, secure in a Father's love, bicker incessantly or cheat others in business? As we are in Christ and Christ is in us, our new identity is a guide.

This is the main point of the gospel: "union with Christ," knowing and loving God, and living out the fruit of that union. Jesus says as much in John 15:1 and 4: "I am the true vine, and my Father is the gardener. . . . Remain in me, as I also remain in you." Staying grafted to Jesus is an "I am" part of my identity. Or, to pick up Paul's metaphor (Rom. 8:15), I am adopted into the family of God. I may not always act like a family member should, but I'm no longer a spiritual orphan. I'm a son of the Son of God, a child of the heavenly Father. This is my new self. I signed the papers when I answered the call to come home to God. Jesus signed the papers when he died on the cross and rose again.

Living IN Christ connects well to what I said about the nature of language in the first chapter. Words are not merely tools we pick up and put down. In fact, we live in them. We live *in* the words we choose, and we live in these words: living in Christ. When we frame our soul as living in Christ, we see Jesus as big enough to live within; he holds the grace that makes our lives possible and we walk in that grace. I can try to pick up the words "in Christ" and just put them down, but unless I am utterly insincere, this frame becomes a way to see the world.

As Erin worked through the months that followed Jason's death, she said, "I've learned that all that matters is our *eternal* relationship. I now know the cost of life, of wasting life." She knew where she wanted to dwell and the difference it made. J. I. Packer put it this way: "What were we made for? To know God. What aim should we set ourselves in life? To know God. What is the 'eternal life' that Jesus gives? Knowledge of God. . . . What is the best thing in life, bringing more joy, delight, and contentment, than anything else? Knowledge of God."

I am learning to be "at home" with being an adopted child of God, living in Christ—and I'm in the process of learning what it means to be a son. The noun of adoption helps me learn to live out the verb.

Discerning the Self Well

The fourth part of dwelling within as a soul essential helps us work through the mass (and mess) of contradictions about the self. Sometimes I'm confident. Other times a quivering nabob of nothingness. All day long, we have to contend with the cultural, friendly, and circumstantial voices I mentioned in the previous chapter. Just when we frame ourselves as stable, our sense of order is disrupted by sickness, an unexpected gift, doubt, or accomplishment—but especially by criticism and praise.

Constructive and destructive praise. Most of us can point to a marker in our lives that helped us to reframe who we say we are and what we would pursue: "You are so in tune with children. You should be a teacher." "I'm so impressed with your mechanical ability. It's like you can solve any problem that involves moving parts." We can name the date and source of these encouragements—and we know we were never the same afterward.

We hear a lot about the importance of praise, but we aren't always sure how this translates into our framing of ourselves. I tell my students "Good job!" and "You are compassionate," but I struggle to tell myself. In the back of my mind are verses such as Proverbs 27:2: "Let someone else praise you, and not your own mouth; an outsider, and not your own lips."

On the one hand, it seems silly to stand in front of the mirror and tell ourselves we have a cute nose or we are good in our hearts. On the other hand, we tend to pay far too much attention to criticism. Those of us who read evaluations on a regular basis often ignore most of the positive comments and brood over the negative ones.

Is this also true for our self-praise and self-criticism? A good rule of thumb may be to praise graciously without dismissing it or having it puff us up. If I tell James, "You are an excellent storyteller," I don't want him to think, "You are such a liar." Nor do I want him to think, "I am so amazing, I should corner everyone and tell them a story." I want James to be encouraged and to use my appreciation as a counterpoint to his own irrational doubts. So it should be when *we* receive praise.

Praise can hurt too. Much has been said about parents who overpraise and children who underachieve, about those who are unprepared for competitive circumstances because they've been "trophy-worthy" all their lives no matter what they did. Advertising can get our self-image off-kilter as well: "Find your greatness. Nike." "So inspired, so desired, so you. Cache." Deep down, we know this inflated malarkey just isn't true. Dwelling within builds our soul when we have an accurate self-image, not a falsely positive one.

An old adage is "Competence builds confidence." In our times, we tend to reverse it, thinking that "believing in ourselves" is more important than what we can actually accomplish. Praise requires discernment so that we encourage others and ourselves to fulfill what we were made to do—but not overpraise so that we become praise-seeking, praise-desperate narcissists.

Constructive and destructive criticism. Though we often see criticism as nagging negativity, it has many benefits. Okay, I'll admit, it wasn't good timing to critique the musical *Wicked* immediately after seeing it, when our daughters were giddily dancing along the sidewalk and singing the songs. But we seem so afraid of giving and receiving criticism that we end up acting as if we approve of everything. Disagreement is such a no-no at my college that some students set up a debate club so there would be a "safe place" for criticism.

At the same time, we know it's difficult to improve at anything without evaluation. Every musician and athlete needs correction and coaching. So do fathers and mothers, husbands and wives and children, supervisors and workers, pastors and churchgoers. A new colleague came into my office during her first year and asked, "Do you have my back?" She said that if I was supportive, she could accept all kinds of important critique from me—but if I let others smear her, she would not be able to listen. I realized I had not been vocal enough that I was on her side.

Sometimes criticism crushes. When I was in a sixth grade "accelerated" summer school, Mrs. Trowbridge took me into the hall to tell me she didn't think I belonged there. For all I know, I had been saying smart-alecky things for weeks, but I took it to mean she did not think I was "gifted" enough for the class. The remark cut me to the core—and sometimes I wonder if this criticism played a subconscious part in my decision to get a PhD. I guess I showed her.

We all have our stories that sting, those sticks and stones that keep breaking our bones. Words have power, power that is difficult to control. Proverbs 18:21 captures this concern: "The tongue has the power of life and death, and those who love it will eat its fruit." May we discern how to use the tongue wisely, including the ways we frame ourselves.

———

Curiously, though we have been "studying" ourselves all our lives, we might not pass a test about ourselves. Thus, the soul essential of dwelling within calls us to learn to be at home with who we are, to frame our identity more with verbs than nouns, to live in Christ, and to discern how to negotiate praise and criticism.

These tasks can seem daunting, like being asked to jump who-knows-where through an open door. But I'm much more likely to open that door when I know that, no matter what, someone is there to catch me. If I know I'm loved, I can confront how I've been living. That's why it's so important that I frame myself in relationship to God, as a child and friend, and to others, as my neighbors.

I want to get to the point where my frames for the self are good and solid and true—but when they are, I won't be studying the frame. I'll be looking out through it. For that, I need some measure of contentment, of peace.

In Search of a Duck's Back

I knew he wouldn't like it,
this poem about his distaste
for all I do; not
all, no that's not fair, but
Much if not Most, at least,
especially the images of water rolling,
flowing, soaking deep, filling the hollows,
drowning me in their rising curse.

CHAPTER THIRTEEN

Dwelling in Peace

Love and faithfulness meet together;
righteousness and peace kiss each other.
—Psalm 85:10

No giant tragedy, no dramatic event: Kelly's life was moving along just fine. Her gifts and passions fit into ministry, so that's what she pursued. She was well liked and effective, but she felt unsettled, as if she was on "cruise control." She thought her job was too tied to her identity. "I always feel like, unless I can accomplish something, I am just a wasted space. Are you, God, asking me to give up my job? If so, you're going to have to make it a lot clearer than this."

Giant tragedy, dramatic event: Tim and Rhonda's relationship began in typical fashion. As undergraduates, they fell in love and married. Not long afterward, when Tim was a grad student, he "cold-called" a woman from a phone book, made an appointment, went to her house and propositioned her. She called the police. He was booked. It was a huge flap because everyone knew. The college said they would "handle it," and they did so by sending him to a counselor. Cleverly, unbelievably, Tim dodged the whole business.

Kelly's story and Rhonda's story show that all sorts of circumstances may lead us to feel uneasy in our spirit. It doesn't take a catastrophe to interfere with the ways we are dwelling within ourselves—but catastrophes happen too. We often lack peace and feel the need to reframe.

What is this peace we desire? Is it unfettered happiness, deep contentment, absence of conflict, harmonious feelings of exuberant joy? These qualities seem remarkably elusive. A contemporary Jeremiah might want to cry out, "Peace, peace, . . . when there is no peace" (6:14). Even so, we want it. Kelly and Rhonda wanted it. We know peace is the virtue that will help us to dwell within ourselves as an essential of the soul.

"Go in Peace," but Where Are We to Go?

At the end of a recent church service, the pastor said, "Go in peace." I thought, "Okay, here I go. I'm walking out in peace." Was I not to fight with anyone? Was I to avoid feeling anxious or guilty or insecure? Is there some way that I could "go with peace" whether I felt it or not?

What is peace? Robert Pirsig says, in effect, that a problem is a lack of peace of mind. Hmm. If I think of what I consider to be a problem (like gophers in the yard), I can see how I am not at peace about the situation (I want to trap the little buggers). But Pirsig implies that to get more peace of mind we just need fewer things we think of as problems. I know I'd be better off if I did not see losing my reading glasses or getting stuck in traffic as "problems"—but some things should be thought of as problems, no? What about unreconciled friends or wandering refugees?

Scripture presents a variety of ways to think about peace. Jesus says, "Do not suppose that I have come to bring peace to the earth. I did not come to bring peace, but a sword" (Matt. 10:34). Following Jesus is not a foolproof path to peace. Though divisiveness can't always be avoided, Scripture also describes peace in positive terms: as an action to be pursued, a consequence of other choices, and a blessing. (The following italics are mine.) Peace as a choice: "Flee the evil desires of youth and *pursue* righteousness, faith, love and peace, along with those who call on the Lord out of a pure heart" (2 Tim. 2:22). Peace as a consequence: "The mind governed by the flesh is death, but *the mind governed by the Spirit is life and peace*" (Rom. 8:6). Peace as a gift: "*Peace* I leave with you; my peace I give you. I do not give to you as the world gives. Do not let your hearts be troubled and do not be afraid" (John 14:27).

We can see these categories in Kelly's and Rhonda's situations. To address her internal uneasiness, Kelly made some tough choices. She quit her wonderful, comfortable job and moved to Oregon. Her husband landed an amazing job and—even though she is still working out who she is in a new place—she wanted to be able to tell her kids that it was okay to take risks. Kelly did not have peace, so she made choices she hoped would lead to peace. Rhonda suppressed her anxiety about Tim's crazy behavior. She knows she should have walked away then, but she had some core beliefs that kept her in the relationship. Her guiding frames were that marriage was for life, that repentance and forgiveness would eventually come—and she had picked up from her family that "if it's negative, you can't act like it exists." In the midst of heartache, she chose peace—but it would not last. More violations would come. Eventually, peace arrived as a gift.

Peace is important in Scripture and in life. It is something we do and something we receive. Just as gratitude and hope are virtues that guide the ways we frame remembering and anticipating, peace is the virtue for dwelling within as an essential of the soul.

Peace as a Virtue

I've come to see peace as a "cluster virtue," as a lake fed from a number of streams. Though we usually think of peace as something we simply have or we don't, we can learn to see it as a practice—and not just the task of keeping conflict from escalating. As part of this "dwelling within" soul essential, *peace is the practice of learning the truth about ourselves, having a charitable view of that truth, and in the context of brokenness, doing our best.* The streams that feed the lake are humility, compassion, and contentment.

Humility

In the last chapter, I discussed the importance of being at home with ourselves. Part of being at home is what Frederick Buechner calls dealing with our "nakedness." We must come to terms with who we are without the clothes of accomplishments, our reputation, and the image we show the public. Buechner says, "If there is ever to be a true healing and helping, a true sheltering and clothing for any of us, it is with our nakedness and helplessness that it has to start." I believe Buechner—but, remember, I'm the guy too skinny to want to take off his shirt.

I'm reminded of this common nightmare: discovering that you are naked while giving a speech or walking along a promenade. Kelly did not want to admit her identity was so tangled up in her success in her job. Rhonda did not want to see her husband as an adulterer or herself as a victim of abuse. But they needed—and we need—to tell the truth. To develop peace, we can't be trying to fool ourselves about ourselves. What vices grip me? Where do I seem to flourish? What secrets keep me from living freely? Humble honesty is a good place to begin.

Not surprisingly (as a college professor), my identity is wrapped up in being "wise" (intelligent and moral). One of the most significant challenges to this framing occurred in 2006, when Janet and I invested in a condo. We did our due diligence before we made the decision. I asked friends in business if the decision would be shrewd and how much we should risk. I was anxious about it, very anxious. But Janet and I bought the condo and became proud owners of an investment that lost money every month. We fixed it up and rented it out. We strongly disliked being landlords—but we told ourselves all would be well in the long run.

It wasn't.

When the financial crisis of 2008 hit, the condo's value plummeted, adding to our mounting losses. I blamed myself. "How could I be so stupid?" (an intelligence frame). "Why were we so greedy?" (a moral frame). But we kept writing checks. Then a financial advisor told us, "Here's your choice. You can cut off your arm or bleed to death." The advisor said we should default on the loan or do a short sale. We would just have to suffer the consequences. I was in agony. "How could I admit this folly? And how could I say I'm a person of integrity?" We talked to lawyers and pastors and businesspeople—and eventually decided to "give the condo back to the bank." When I confessed to our church small group about the moral torment and the feelings of incompetence, helplessness, and shame, they wept with me. I learned what Thomas à Kempis said: "A true understanding and humble estimate of oneself is the highest and most valuable of all lessons. . . . We are all frail; consider none more frail than yourself." The condo ordeal was a hard, hard lesson—and I'm still not certain it was the "right" choice.

For peace to grow, the stream of humility must flow into the lake. Self-deception won't help us dwell well within ourselves, and we will need to confess our struggles if we hope to make our way toward peace. The ride can be rough in these identity waters, but it helps to know that Someone will be there if we overturn.

Compassion

Paul tells us in Ephesians to "speak the truth in love" (4:15). We understand the admonition when we need to say hard things to others, but we sometimes struggle to apply it to ourselves. We can be magnanimous toward messed-up friends, but we are often merciless toward ourselves. Just listen to athletes: "Good shot!" to others and "You idiot!" to themselves. It's hard to practice peace when we are constantly at war within.

When I was in counseling some years ago, the therapist asked me to write a letter to "young Greg," to address "him" directly about "his" experience. When I wrote to "young Greg" about growing up as the shortest, skinniest kid, when I spoke to him about dealing with alcoholic parents, when I addressed his distant relationship with his dad, I grew in compassion. The letter helped me see how irrationally and destructively hard I was on myself. Why did I treat myself worse than I'd ever think of treating another human being?

Once we have the courage to tell the truth about ourselves, forgiveness, charity, and compassion are in order. Sometimes we worry that if we take this stance, we will excuse all our behavior. But that's not usually how it works when we are compassionate toward others. As a parent, I have tried to tell the truth about my kids—not always to them, but to myself. The negative parts of these truths did not make me want to punish them. Most of the time, their poor choices drew out of me deep empathy and love. I'd been a teenager at one time, too. I wanted to help them gain the character and faith to overcome. So it is as we walk with ourselves. We follow humility with compassion.

Contentment

Finally, Rhonda's husband Tim had a major, public affair with a co-worker at the college where he was teaching. Rhonda confronted Tim and told him he needed to repent. Tim was furious. After all, he was tenured and beloved by his students and peers. "Why did I stay with him for so long?" Rhonda wonders. "I suppose because, I thought, that's what you do when you have faith. I kept believing he would change." She hung on to the relational frame that "Everything will be fine if we all just work hard enough." She said, "How could he not see that he was wrong?" But Tim didn't—and finally, they were divorced.

Crises like these—and far less eventful ones—strain our ability to be content, our sense of peace in the moment. I've written about this quality in *Awakening the Quieter Virtues*. There, I define contentment as "the strength hope gives us to pursue the unsatisfied life in satisfying ways." The world (including ourselves) is fallen, wounded, broken. Our lives here will never be fully satisfied. Even so, we keep trying to do our best. We pursue the good and true and beautiful. Contentment is not complacency; we are still ambitious for righteousness. But we can better deal with our worry along the way if we remember we are children of God and that nothing can separate us from his love.

For Rhonda, contentment grew through reframing. She learned that Tim had been abused by an older brother when he was ten—and his mother was pathologically repressive about anything remotely sexual. She reflected on all that she was learning about sexual addiction. What was her role in all of this? What was the church's role? Though Tim did not change, Rhonda grieved for his brokenness, her woundedness, and held out hope.

Peace involves a freedom to accept the truth about ourselves, the wisdom to treat the self with the same spirit with which we treat others, and the drive to pursue the unsatisfied life in a satisfying way. Humility, compassion, contentment. What upholds these frames? What framework makes our house stronger?

A Framework for Peace: From Perfectionism to Grace

I make lists. I get much more accomplished because I do. A friend of mine used to put one task on a small Post-it note and line up each of these on his desk, maybe two rows of four. When he finished one task, he didn't like the fact that one row had four notes and another row had three, so he moved some of them to make one row of seven. I don't do that. But I do mark items on my lists with boxes and stars to denote stages of urgency—and if I accomplish something and it (heaven forbid!) wasn't on my list, I write it on my list and draw a box around it and cross it off, just for the deep and beautiful pleasure of covering that box with ink.

What happens when I finish everything on my list? Do I dance for joy? Do I enter into the leisure of the day with freedom and delight? Not usually. Instead, I conclude that I hadn't put enough on my list—for the law of the perfectionist is that you must accomplish things to become perfect; but you can never become perfect, so you must keep trying to be perfect by accomplishing things. It's such a great system.

For each virtue in each soul essential, I have suggested an undergirding framework. If we lean toward forgiveness instead of bitterness, we'll more likely frame our memories with gratitude. Here, in the dwelling within soul essential, the framework is the continuum from perfectionism to grace. The closer we are to the grace side of the framework, the easier it is to frame ourselves in peace.

Perfectionism

When we hear the word, we have no trouble rejecting it. Who thinks they can be perfect? Well, actually, most of us. Though we deny the theory, we *accept* the practice. And for good reason: we need a strategy for managing our insecurities, incompetencies, and self-criticism. We're supposed to try to get better, right? So, we accept the strategy that all we have to do is measure up.

Messages promoting perfectionism come from everywhere in our culture: The boss says, "I care deeply about your family life, but please get these fifty tasks completed by tomorrow morning." Beauty ads promise we can be "flawless beyond any stretch of the imagination" (Maybelline). We are told hundreds of times a day that we ought to be excellent. At school, work, and on social media, we must deal with performance reviews and constant comparison.

Even in the church, we can't escape. Jesus said to "Be perfect," didn't he? Even if he meant "perfect" as in "mature," not "flawless," we know which believers are admired the most for their wisdom and faith—and we know who the Christmas-and-Easter-only slackers are. Much of this assessment is inevitable, but some of it is destructive.

If we live by the need to achieve, we must always show ourselves worthy. We must find some rule or law against which to measure our accomplishments. It's an ever-present pressure. As Anne Lamott reminds us, "Perfectionism is the voice of the oppressor, . . . [it] means that you try desperately not to leave so much mess to clean up. But clutter and mess show us that life is being lived." We can become paralyzed, unable to complete projects for fear of not measuring up.

Whatever we set up to achieve (beating Devon in ping-pong, making the promotion, getting married), we are not satisfied when we reach the goal. Our innate perfectionism leads us to "up the ante," to make higher goals (beat Chris in ping-pong, win an award at work, have stellar kids). It's our natural bent—and it can make us miserable. Edmund Bourne adds that the Perfectionist is always saying *I should* be better at everything and is focused on external affirmations, leading to chronic stress and burnout.

Far too often, my life mimics these themes. I *must get this stuff done*, but, of course, a perfectionist's work is never done. During my years of significant back pain, I learned I needed to be open to the idea that one possible cause of the pain was emotional, not physical. My chronic pressure on myself was manifesting itself in my body. When I focused on accomplishment, little "good" came from success but plenty of "bad" resulted from failure. When I began to work on some longstanding stress and anger in my life, I made gradual progress. I reframed my problem from something "purely physical" to something "significantly emotional." I worked at reframing "I must measure up" to "I am not my accomplishments."

Scripture calls perfectionism "living under the law." (You can read about this throughout the book of Romans.) It is a system of relentless tyranny. It appeals to our arrogance that we can finally get it right, that we *really can* measure up. We think we're on a good road that just needs occasional repair. But the problem is the whole system: the road, the car, and the driver. Perfectionism might drive us to certain accomplishments, but it is a slave driver that cannot be pleased. We have to find a new road, a road that allows us to enjoy driving in the context of loving support, not gripping the wheel in the context of unrelenting scrutiny—and the road is not found by our excellent map-reading skills or our superior internal GPS. The on-ramp comes as a gift from the Holy Spirit.

During my agony over the loan default, I knew I didn't measure up. I had failed as an investor. I had failed as a promise-keeper—and my system did not allow for failure. I needed a better inner language, the language of grace.

Defining Grace

On the framework supporting the virtue of peace, on the side opposite perfectionism, is grace—an idea that sounds too good to be true. Grace is love that is not dependent on others doing what is right. Grace says, "I'm going to love you, and you can't stop me." It allows us to live gently with what isn't fully right—because it doesn't demand perfection as a condition.

We are often scandalized that God's love is free. We are hard workers, and we'd prefer to earn it. When grace circumvents deservedness, it exposes the tyranny of the perfectionist system—and we resist losing the justification for so many things we do.

Nine years after Tim and Rhonda's divorce, they remarried. I'd like to be able to say that Tim radically repented, that he reframed his past in light of new convictions about sexual choices. But even though their reunion didn't happen that way, reframing was critical in their journey. Rhonda said that Tim had a new humility. He had lost everything—job, marriage, children—and now he had cancer. She said, "I felt God telling me, 'Israel never apologized for all the wrong done to me. I just changed their heart.'" This is scandalous—and maybe unwise—but Rhonda forgave Tim. She said she felt more loved in those last five years than she had in the first thirty, and that remarriage was truly redemptive for their children. When I told a friend about my disappointment that Tim never confessed, never asked for forgiveness—and how irrational it seemed to me that Rhonda took him back—he said, "I've seen it before. It doesn't make sense from the outside, but I chalk it up to the power of love." Rhonda was saying, "I'm going to love you, and you can't stop me."

Grace Assumes Imperfection

In Second Corinthians, Paul said he had a "thorn in the flesh," some disability of body or character that he could not shake and that God would not remove. Maybe he had an itchy rash, or maybe it was the prickly thorn of lust or anger. Whatever it was, the Lord's response was, "My grace is sufficient for you, for my power is made perfect in weakness" (2 Cor. 12:9). Paul learned that the grace he received to endure his "thorn" was a better foundation than his accomplishments or some sort of "perfection." And that's the way our world is: imperfect. One way to think about grace is that it only exists when things aren't quite right and can't be made perfect. Since ours is such a world, we might accept these circumstances by moving to the grace side of the continuum. Paul did.

What Grace Is Not

Sometimes we fear that if we move toward grace, others will take advantage of us or we will lose our motivation to do well. But grace does not cause the relaxing of all boundaries. When late for an essay due date, students sometimes ask, "Will you give me grace on this paper," as if the issue is my willingness to be grace-full, not their discipline to respect the deadline. Grace is about unconditional love, not unconditional boundary-breaking. My sense that "I'm going to love you, and you can't stop me" might be better expressed by holding to the rule, for the sake of the student's learning.

Grace is also not something we *do* so that we can add it to our spiritual résumé. I'm not more acceptable to God because I exercise grace. This would just be more perfectionism. God's system is not like a business based on commission.

And grace doesn't provide an excuse not to work hard or to care about excellence. It changes our attitudes during the work. Grace liberates us toward practicing peace as a virtue. When we know we are loved, we can fail. We have the security to express our humility—and we gain permission to be compassionate and the freedom to be content.

The Difference Grace Makes

A friend once asked me, "Are you okay with not being the smartest person in the room?" I interpreted the question to mean that *he* was not okay with being less than number one. When we live in grace, we can accept imperfections in ourselves. We can admit we have a thorn in our side, that we have many thorns, or that on special days we are a wall of thorns, poking others all the time, even if we don't notice it. We may begin to believe Thomas Merton: "A man who fails well is greater than one who succeeds badly."

I'm not very good at this. One time when I was beating myself up for not having enough faith to endure a trial, my friend Ben reminded me that

God was not disappointed in me. He said, "Grace means you don't work for it. You don't earn grace by how much faith you have." I've realized we can't bring our improvements to the bargaining table with God and use them to ask for his favors. He offers his gifts freely. We don't have to avoid failure at all costs, to live as if there is no margin for error.

Grace also helps us endure the imperfections in others. The peace that grows because of our humility, compassion, and contentment allows us to extend grace to others, to remember our own thorns as we get irritated by the thorns of others. Paul ends all of his letters with some variation of "Grace to you." It is a worthy way to frame our time with others.

To Kelly, Rhonda, and all the others in this chapter, including myself, I say, "Grace to you."

Preemptive Kindness

We received the call
as we loaded the car.

Just minutes earlier we had driven
home in eighty-degree high winds,
in November, to see the hill above us
ablaze in colors we had hoped never to see.

Too bright, too alive, the glowing reds
in the fire raced through crackling coyote bush
and dried-up sage, roaring its way
to our wooden house, its kindling-sides waiting.

We hadn't time to think about where
we would go that night. We would just
get in our cars and drive away—
away, away, that's all that mattered.

The phone rang when our hands were full of things
we thought we wanted to keep wanting,
photos and computers and so much stuff.
That's when we heard it, a bell pealing

for vespers or compline, a call so full
and holy—sacred, yes, though we did
not know this yet. How could we?
Not till we answered and the song

of our friends said, "Come."
I still weep when I think of that mercy-minded
ringing, that leap of preemptive kindness,
the one that anticipates. Not the one that says,

"How can I help?" but the one that says,
"I've made soup and it's for you.
It's already made and you can't
do anything about this gift except receive it.

Come, come, all of you,
for as long as it takes."

Engaging
with Others
in Love

CHAPTER FOURTEEN

Engaging

"How could you love [me,] such an ugly,
ill-tempered, rude, hateful little wretch?"
"I saw, through it all, what you were going to be,"
said the wise woman.

—George MacDonald, *The Wise Woman*

It was a typical lunch with my friend. As he sat down, he set his phone face up on the table. My shoulders slumped a little—and I grimaced inside. I knew what would happen. The phone would ring or buzz. Compulsively, my friend would look at it and decide whether he should respond immediately or not. Usually, he did.

But this time, I did the unthinkable. I asked him if he would put the phone away.

Even though we were close friends, I worried that he would be offended. Would he bristle inside? Would this be our last lunch for a while? Because my friend is the open-minded, nondefensive man I took him for, what followed was a terrific conversation about technology, relationships, and the pressures of time.

As we come to the last of the soul essentials, engaging with others in love, technological changes need our attention. Few contemporary shifts have affected interpersonal life as much as our phones. Among other things, we've increased our framing of things in relationship to time—mainly our need to respond quickly, and we've decreased our framing of things in relationship to space—mainly the ways we interact in one another's presence.

These technological choices matter. As Neil Postman reminds us, "Every culture must negotiate with technology, whether it does so intelligently or not. A bargain is struck in which technology giveth and technology taketh away." When we put our phones in front of us at lunch, we gain access to other people (and others gain access to us), but we lose some things too: uninterrupted conversation and undivided attention with our companion. And we don't have to feel these losses to actually lose. Although some say, "I don't mind that my friends are on their phones when they are with me," that doesn't mean the conversation remains the same as it was before. Community life is different and in some ways diminished.

An extended biblical passage that addresses "engaging with others" is Ephesians 4. Paul reminds his readers of what makes for a strong community. Overall, we are to maintain unity by living peacefully (3) and fulfilling our various roles and callings (4–13). We do this by putting off the old self and putting on the new self (22–24, some obvious reframing here), feeding certain character qualities—humility, gentleness, patience, bearing with one another in love (2), industriousness (28), compassion and forgiveness (32)—and by starving sensual indulgence (17–19), extended anger (26), bitterness, brawling, slander, and malice (31). I'm particularly taken with the admonitions to speak the truth in love (15, 25) and to talk for the sake of building others up (29).

Of course, Paul doesn't apply these standards to cell phones, social media, modern medicine, or space travel. That's up to us. As we negotiate with technology, we can't help but put some ideas and values above others, to hold some frames higher. Given the rewarding possibilities in a conversation (compassion, genuineness, truth-telling, neighborliness) and all the destructive possibilities (slander, rage, bitterness, alienation), when do our current choices most likely lead to beneficial ends? In our times, how can we keep love as our highest goal when we engage with others?

How Our Phones Are Calling Us

When my friend and I were at lunch, we talked about the pressure he feels to look at his phone frequently and to answer messages immediately. He worries that his wife or adult kids might need something "right away." Our culture tends to prize aspects of time—speediness, urgency, and efficiency, over aspects of space—being in lively proximity to one another, sharing our deeper selves, supporting one another with personal presence. Because of our communication technologies, time has risen as a moral commitment. We are more interested in fulfilling the demands of time than respecting the needs of space. As we negotiate with technology, at this point, time frames the debate, not space.

In the not-so-old days, when the phone rang at dinner, any of us might interrupt a meaningful conversation to take the call. "It might be important," we'd announce. But, usually, we'd trot back to the table and mutter sheepishly, "It was only a telemarketer. Now, . . . what was it we were talking about?"

Then we got caller ID, so we no longer had to take those calls. We said, "How wonderful!" We ignored calls for a while, but what happened next? What did we do with this freedom from interruption, this freedom to engage with others around the table? We each got a phone, thanks to the invention of cell phones. Then we all put our phones on the table, screens up, and gave higher priority to the phones (to calls, texts, emails, the Internet, social media) than to the others in our presence. We claimed, "It might be an emergency!" and compulsively checked our messages. There have never been so many would-be emergencies!

Don't get me wrong. I like phones. Talking across a distance is terrific. Texting can be incredibly convenient. Other communication technologies make a positive contribution too. Social media keep us connected. I love those apps that allow me to see friends, relatives, children, and grandchildren. And, of course, because of work, I'm on email all day.

But if we frame every technological innovation as an advance, as Postman reminds us, we may miss the corresponding retreat. How does participation with our technologies play out?

All forms of communication get us leaning in certain ways. Watching a lot of television gets us leaning toward the importance of entertainment, which becomes a lens for evaluating nonentertainment situations such as friendship, church, school, and presidential candidates. Advertising moves us to appreciate pithy slogans (whether they are in ads or not) and to think that buying something, anything, will make us happy.

Though these media sometimes harm us, we can become educated about how each one pushes us, and do our best to push back when necessary. If we don't pay attention to how each technology is acting on us, we will blindly follow in the direction each technology encourages. Framing technology well will aid the way we approach engaging with others.

Time Is "Up"

The more that cell phones and other quick technologies are important to us, the more we expect to be in control of our time, and time itself has a new morality. We can be "chastised" for not responding quickly enough to a text or for staying away from Facebook. Increasingly time seems to be running our lives. That must be why Sophie checks her phone during her own birthday party, while guests are talking to her—and why Dylan constantly sends photos during an outdoor concert, though it clearly irritates his friend sitting next to him.

We prize efficiency (communication is short and to the point). We value speed (of output and response). And we feel a sense of urgency around our devices. When we hear the ding of a text or an email, we feel anxious until we see what it is. We can become compulsive, even physiologically addicted.

Some researchers say that not only is our attention span decreasing, but our brains are actually getting rewired toward flitting and scanning, toward short bursts of attending—and away from thorough thinking, deep reading, and intimate relating. We live a shallower experience, skimming over various surfaces, but not able to sustain a trip to the depths. We struggle to focus on anything complicated (just ask teachers about their students).

Typically, we don't mind because we love the power over time that our devices give us. We want to send and receive messages quickly—in ways we can control. We exercise power by managing our texts, editing photos, and by avoiding circumstances that might decrease our sense of control, such as interpersonal interactions with unpredictable responses. We don't want to deal with uncertain facial reactions to our messages. (That's one reason some of us look down at our phones when approaching people in public. We use our phones to avoid eye contact.) Perhaps it is no accident that Facebook and other applications were created by introverts for introverts. One friend says, "It's great! I never have to actually be in conversation!"

Engaging with others can be a markedly different experience these days. We feel the pressure of higher digital standards and the need to control our own images, pressure that can cause so much anxiety and depression that some users take a sabbatical from social media for their mental health.

And our focus has changed. Sherry Turkle, a sociologist at MIT, has addressed these concerns in her books about screen time and being "alone together" in American culture. In *Reclaiming Conversation*, she says, "Our mobile devices seem to grant three wishes . . . first, that we will always be heard; second, that we can put our attention wherever we want it to be; and third, that we will never have to be alone . . . that we will never have to be bored." Increasingly, as the saying goes, we'd rather text than talk. In part, I think this means that we'd rather do what keeps us in control: send a text, a Snapchat, an Instagram, or Pin it. We shy away from what's open-ended.

Imagine a lunch with three friends. Everyone is on the phone for part of the time. Some for a lot of the time. Friends interrupt conversation to show others their texts or pictures or videos—and never, during the entire lunch, are all of you paying attention to each other. Doesn't take much imagination, does it? These choices change the ways we engage with others and may make fulfilling Paul's Ephesian values more difficult. How can we speak the truth in love when no one is listening?

Space Is "Down"

Our attention to time has come at the expense of personal space, how we act in one another's presence. See if you resonate with the following situations. Would you frame it this way?

In public, there seems to be a conspiracy against conversation and solitude. TVs fill our eyes and ears in restaurants, coffee shops, even gas stations. Music, blaring music, shouts us down in stores and at sporting events. At a recent Rose Bowl, the music was so loud during halftime that I had to shout whatever I wanted to say—to the person right next to me. Eventually, I just gave up. Our environments often say, "Whatever you do, don't talk! Don't be present with one another!" While we wait for a movie to begin, ads and factoids occupy our attention. I'm sure a few teenagers on first dates have thought, "What a relief! No awkward silences!"

Then there are the choices we make that are related to human presence. We are so often focused on our devices, and not on those nearby. We show that "space is down" at lunch with friends, on hikes "in nature," in committee meetings (at which we might complain about the poor attention spans of our employees), and at church services, making sure that worship, too, wasteth not any time. Many of my students wake up each morning to their phone alarm, then spend the first minutes of the day in bed scanning their messages and social media. They set the tone of their day with this information. They begin the day "on" and stay "on," sometimes ignoring their roommates. Parents are often on their phones when they are with their kids. One teacher I know says that parents often do not even acknowledge their children when they pick them up after school—because they are looking at their phones.

Time Is "Up" and Space Is "Down." So What?

As I engage with college students these days, things have changed. When I walk across campus, far fewer students say hello to me or each other. They are looking at their phones. If I'm feeling mischievous, I walk toward them until they notice and dart out of the way. Before class, almost no students talk with their peers. They are—you guessed it—looking at their phones. In one class, I do a little coaching. I interrupt their phone-gazing and suggest a question they could ask their neighbor. Instantly, the class erupts with conversation. After class, it's back to the same. Most students reach for the phone because, probably, some message came in that "just cannot wait." I encourage them to look at it later and talk with the friend in their presence. My reflections have led to five ways of framing significant interpersonal developments due to recent technology.

The Norm of Interruption

Too often, no matter how much effort was made to be in someone's presence, the phone is the highest priority. Urgency undermines the quality of human interaction. Scanning trumps attentiveness. When things are not this way, we might think, "The conversation feels different—rich, but more intrusive. I'm not used to going so deep." Not that long ago, people said, "Would you mind if I took this call?" Now, they just pull away, even in the middle of a meaningful exchange, even in the middle of a walk that has been scheduled for weeks, on Christmas, even if there is absolutely nothing urgent about the text. I keep thinking, the president isn't calling—and Jesus isn't on the line either.

A New Sense of Competition

Don't you sometimes feel a rivalry with the phone on the table? I do. I wonder, will I be able to keep the other person's attention? Will the phone be a preferable, more arresting, more compelling, more entertaining option? How can I "up" my game, make myself more interesting than the other person buzzing in? My presence isn't as sufficient as it used to be. Sometimes, in restaurants, one person scrolls through their phone while the other one looks around awkwardly. Then the other person, after being ignored, sighs with resignation and joins in.

Being Connected but Disconnected

We think we can have it both ways—be fully present and be fully linked-in elsewhere—but we often end up with superficial connections. We wave the banner of "Champion Multitasker," even though researchers have repeatedly shown how poorly we multitask. Sometimes we rationalize our detachment by telling ourselves, "Hey, there are a lot of people here. No one will notice me withdraw." At the college where I work, "whenever two or more students are gathered," someone is on the phone.

We tend to forget about the power of metamessages, that "extra" communication that accompanies the primary message. If I say I'm fully listening but I watch the TV or computer or phone screen, my metamessage conflicts with my more overt message. If I think I'm saying that being in your presence matters, but I keep opting out of your presence, my metamessage is that I have other priorities. The result is that though we might be more regularly connected to some friends and family, we are often detached from those close by.

Accidental Arrogance

In our minds, we say we are only "stepping out" of the conversation for a moment—but this withdrawal makes an unintentional narcissistic statement: "I'm the one who matters here. My tech messages are more important than our interpersonal ones." In addition, the lack of courtesy in many of these choices has a way of asserting that "I will be in charge of our communication."

The fifth consequence of time being up and space being down is a lack of inquiry. This contemporary feature is so significant, so pervasive, so relevant to all four soul essentials, that it requires a final excursion.

— Excursion into Questions —

I've been teaching the following maxim for thirty years: *Nothing will influence your social and intellectual life more than your ability to ask good questions.* The problem with this maxim is that most people think, "No problem. I ask lots of questions." But most people don't. We think we are more inquisitive, curious, and other-centered than we are.

Here's an experiment: In a conversation with a friend, see how long you can go only asking questions. The idea is not that other forms of communication are wrong, but that if we can't fulfill this exercise for over ten minutes, we may need to take a good look at our ability to ask questions—and, I'll say it again, *nothing* will influence our social and intellectual life more than our ability to ask good questions.

The following has happened more times than I'd like to recount. We invite someone to dinner and chat together for three hours—but the guests leave the house without knowing *anything* about us they didn't already know. Why? They asked no questions. None. When my wife and I returned from eight weeks in Europe, my mom and dad took us out to dinner. We were excited. Here is the total number of questions they asked about our trip: zero. Nothing about England or France, nothing about the food, nothing about meeting Janet's relatives in Holland. Or, we meet up with old friends we haven't seen in ten or twenty years. In several hours, they ask us little to nothing. It happened again as I was working on this chapter. We chatted with some folks in an airport when our flight was delayed. They were happy to talk about their three residences (British Columbia, Arizona, and Hawaii!), their interest in Wimbledon, their children. They did not even return the simplest question: And what about you?

Is it us? Are we so uninteresting? Possibly. We have spent ample time in self-doubt. Do we ask too many questions? One very private couple told us so. Are we impatient, like radio hosts filling the dead air with this and that? Perhaps. But we have also waited and waited in awkward silence—and sometimes this *is* a helpful strategy. Are many folks just uninterested in others? Maybe, but I'm more convinced that too many are simply unpracticed and unskilled at asking questions. We can do better. Is it too much to ask that we could improve our level of inquiry?

In the context of a discussion about "fights and quarrels," James 4:2 says, "You do not have [what you desire] because you do not ask God." Though James focuses on petitioning God instead of being envious of others, the principle can be expanded. *We do not have because we do not ask*—because we aren't going to get an answer unless we ask a question. *We do not have because we do not ask*—because the quality of a question directs the quality of the response. If I ask a clichéd question, I will get a clichéd answer. "How was your trip?" (a perfectly acceptable question) usually gets us the answer, "Good." But if we ask, "What was a highlight and a lowlight of your trip?" we often get more interesting details. The question "What are some defining moments in your life?" elicits a very different answer than "Tell me about yourself." The point is not to feel the pressure to ask a perfect question, but to realize that the way we frame a question has everything to do with how the answer is framed.

I'm worried that the tone of this section sounds judgmental. I don't mean it to be—but I *am* concerned about our lack of inquiry, our diminished curiosity about how others live and what they believe. I'm worried that our natural self-orientation is being encouraged by our technologies, our selfies, and postings. It's always been hard to "get out of ourselves" to care and learn about others. With our cell phones and computers, we need to work all the more to love others well by asking about them. The quality of the question speaks to our compassion and frames the way we engage with others. Rudyard Kipling's simple poem is a good reminder:

> I keep six honest serving-men
> (They taught me all I knew);
> Their names are What and Why and When
> And How and Where and Who.

This is a good reminder too: *Nothing will influence your social and intellectual life more than your ability to ask good questions.*

—— End of Excursion ——

———

Time is up and space is down. Practically, this means that key frames about what is important in relationships has changed. We talk about relationships differently and we talk differently. We engage with others in keeping with a norm of interruption, a sense of social competition with technology, an overstated feeling of connection, accidental arrogance, and a lack of inquiry. That's a lot to overcome. Learning to engage with others well is as important as ever.

Coffee Break

I came for peace

to The Daily Grind, for just enough
noise to keep me focused

on quieter things. I thought
if I created my world

out of dark brew and hard chairs,
sweet smells and a buzz,

I'd find the center
of the universe and get all things

needful accomplished. But then
the jackhammer started up, woodpecking

incessantly through the asphalt outside,
cutting a line—though never seeming to find

the bottom of that damn hole. It kept rat-a-tatting,
rat-a-tatting away. It had to stop sometime,

didn't it? Then the espresso machines whirred in,
as did the deaf retirees to my left, the whole roasted

wonderland becoming a Great War, a cacophony
of crushed beans and chatty teens, like a giant box

of Christmas drums delivered to the quintuplet
boys next door, ever marching round my house,

banging, banging, snaring my life
as they searched for the Western Front.

CHAPTER FIFTEEN

Engaging Well

Using words, God reveals himself to us. Using words,
we reveal ourselves to God and to one another.
—Eugene Peterson, *Tell It Slant*

Engaging well. Sounds like my friend who got pulled over when taking his girlfriend to dinner. The cop asked him to get out of the car and told him he matched the description of a jewel thief who had just robbed a store in the area. My friend said, "It's not me. I just drove into town from a half-hour away." The cop patted down my friend and pulled a ring box out of his jacket. "Then how do you account for this?" My friend opened the ring box and showed it to his girlfriend. "But, officer, it's not my fault. She stole my heart." True story. The cop was a friend of the guy. The girlfriend said, "Yes." Cheesier than most proposals—but, still, engaging well.

Being somebody's fiancé is not the point of the chapter. "Engaging well," in the sense of relating, caring, or conversing, is. In fact, engaging well is on our minds much of the day. What can I say to ease the pain of a depressed friend? How can I be witty enough to attract that cute somebody? How do I deal with my bickering children?

We all want to relate well with others. Occasionally, we get in a snit and dream of a malicious, expletive-enhanced, back-stabbing, boatload-dropping shout-fest. But that only lasts a tiny minute . . . right?

Engaging Well Is Essential

Tom and Alicia's marriage was in trouble. From Tom's point of view, Alicia seemed to wake up one day and decide that the relationship was over. She brought up how oblivious of her needs he had been since their first year of marriage. She said he had increasingly treated her as a servant. He said she was stuck in a "follow the rules" mindset and that she dodged meaning-ful conversations. For twenty-five years, their conflict stayed beneath the surface—but when it rose in power and urgency, it erupted volcanically, spewing out all over. Having been good friends with them for many years, I flew up to see if I could help. As much as I wanted to be their Marriage Messiah, I was not. They were divorced in the coming year.

But I did my best. I went for a walk with Tom for an hour or so and listened. His story was perfectly believable. Sound arguments. Good evi-dence. I came back to the house thinking, "That Alicia really needs to work on some things." Then I went walking with Alicia—and was just as impressed with her perspective and examples—a viewpoint *utterly at odds* with Tom's. I realized how complex their situation was and, perhaps, how complex everyone's situation is. Their framings of the same events were so radically different, I couldn't help but conclude that both had significant truth and both of them had significant reframing to do. Sadly, it was just too late. Too many wounds had festered for too long. They were not inter-ested in reframing or reinventing their marriage.

I learned a lot from that visit: that everyone has a story, that it is diffi-cult to say no in a yes culture, and that choosing the more humane option is important.

Listening to the Other's Story

No matter what one person tells you, no matter how airtight their case seems to be, there is always, always, always another way of looking at it, another (not necessarily equal) way of framing. Years ago, we had an eighteen-year-old college student as a renter. It did not go well. We thought she had some serious issues. She thought we had some serious issues. After three months, we came home one day to discover that her mother had swooped in from out of town and moved her out. There was no warning or conversation, no questions or confrontation—but we did receive a scath-ing email from the mother, who had wholeheartedly believed everything her daughter had told her. We sent an email back, accepting responsibility where we could and offering different evidence here and there. Mainly, we pled with her to consider the idea that there might be another story, a story from the perspective of adults who had rented successfully for years, that "it's often unfair to listen to just one side." We never heard back from either of them.

Much of the time, we struggle to remember that the stories others tell make sense to *them*. Some stories we hear are so contrary to our ways of framing that we are flabbergasted. But it is immensely helpful for "engaging well" to listen appreciatively to a different version of the story, to listen to others the same way we want to be heard, with respect. Though intentional deception is always possible, more often than not, people have their reasons for framing their story the way they do. We might disagree—even strongly—but unless we hear the story out, we are unlikely to work things through. We thought our renter and her mother betrayed us in a number of ways, but we tried to extend grace by reminding ourselves that our renter was young and immature and the mom was just being a mama bear.

Listening respectfully to another's story is a way of playing the believing game, the idea I introduced in a previous chapter. We need to be open to the idea that our way of framing might not be complete, that we may have misunderstood the story. And even if our view is confirmed, our listening helps the others involved to "be heard." Tom and Alicia did not want to hear the other's story even though they wanted to be heard. A little more self-denial would have helped.

Saying No in a Yes Culture

I've reviewed the cultural trend that "time is up and space is down." Another trend is that "yes is up and no is down." Saying yes is celebrated in our times. Be free, open, tolerant—and embrace all your desires. "Follow your heart" is the YES of our times. It's one of our culture's favorite frames, as evidenced in about every other film to come out of Hollywood. Want to break tradition or fight injustice? Follow your heart. Want to be the rock star or have an affair with the boss? Follow your heart.

And sometimes we *are* too conformist or fearful for our own good. We want to write poetry or work at an orphanage overseas or run for city council, but we are just too worried. The message "Follow your heart" comes along to motivate us. And, of course, if we don't say yes frequently and with joy, we might devolve into curmudgeonly negativity. "Yes" is a wonderful word. Our heart should be followed when what our heart wants is worthy—but that's not always the case. And even when it is, we still need to learn to say no to competing desires.

Popular culture tends to link "no" to being oppressed, closed, subservient, unfulfilled, even though a simple fact of life is that any improvement requires discipline, often through moral struggle. As columnist David Brooks puts it in *The Road to Character*, some vices can only be tamed through "habits of restraint." Sadly, "train your heart" is the NO of our times.

But unless we train the heart (by saying no to some things), we can't even truly follow it when the need arises (by saying yes to other things). We can't get better with our anger problem without working at restraining it. Finishing any project requires denying other projects. Real training matters, not virtual training. We don't get the courage of Martin Luther King Jr. by watching the movie *Selma*. We have to get off the couch, go where we are needed, and perhaps even accept a beating for the sake of justice.

We learn to engage well with others through disciplines of restraint. What makes a community work? In part, we live together in peace by saying no, by denying the impulse that says, "Go ahead, act on everything you feel." We must train our heart to not follow our heart. For example, saying no to lying builds trust, saying no to gossip fosters confidentiality, and saying no to cynicism encourages hope. A large part of "living in community" requires holding the tongue, enduring the irritation, practicing forbearance. Though YES can be wonderful and NO can be terrible, LOVE is what helps us decide between the two, not freedom. We must not merely follow our heart—which could lead us anywhere—but train our hearts according to the demands of love.

In my twenties, I had a deep, nonromantic relationship with a woman. I greatly admired her ability to ask compelling questions and to create welcoming spaces for honest conversation. She was amazing, but she was in a personal crisis that led to a repetitive pattern of her emotional outburst followed by my attempted rescue, which usually involved a long, stressful, weepy conversation that did not end until late into the night. The more I listened and prayed with her, the more frequent and exhausting the conversations became. I felt trapped. I feared seeing her because it meant that the pattern would repeat itself. Finally, a mentor told me, "Greg, you need to tell her no. You need to say that you won't see her under any circumstance for two weeks." I called my friend. She was furious, but I stuck to the plan. When we met two weeks later, she said, "That was the best thing that could have happened to me. The cycle had to be broken." I learned that I shouldn't always say yes, even when I sensed a need. Sometimes the more loving response is to become less entangled, to say no to the impulse to talk everything out. Following my heart was not the wisest direction in this situation.

Choosing for the Fullest Flourishing

I am a sucker for white tablecloths. To me, they say a lot about the difference between eating and dining. Good food helps, but if it comes in a rusty bucket, I'm less than thrilled. When you think about it, much of what makes dining "dining" is not the taste of the food. It's all the other communication choices involved: an inviting setting, cheerful staff, excellent presentation of the meal. In fact, most of what moves us in all areas from the human to the humane, from the "merely existing" to the "wonderfully flourishing," involves communication choices, including our framing.

In addition to listening to the other's story and saying no in a yes culture, engaging with others well means that we seek what is humane, what is the higher fulfillment of our humanity. Some might say that to become a father or a mother is merely human; it just shows that the plumbing works. But to become a parent—to love for the best interests of the child—that requires our whole person. Consider the differences between these ways of framing:

It's human to	It's humane to
talk	commune
hear	listen
memorize	learn
label	name
think	contemplate
father/mother	parent

There's a double layer of framing here. We can reframe particular goals in more humane terms. We can *state* that we'd rather commune than talk.

We'd rather be a musician than just play an instrument. We can also *make the framing choices* necessary to get us from one to the other, from mere hearing to deeper listening, from seeing Jesus as an interesting person to seeing Jesus as the Son of God.

When John was in college, he spent hours and hours on his computer, writing papers, emailing friends—and looking at pornography. It was his way of coping with his anxieties and "spitting in God's eye" for bringing pain into his life. He lived in these sexual fantasies as often as he could, imagining that these women wanted him, that they would gladly give themselves to him. He framed these choices as "entertainment" and as the "fulfillment of his desires." He did not really think of these women as people with their own lives, with ordinary worries and dreams. He did not imagine one as a mother whose child was struggling at school, or another as a niece distraught over her uncle's pancreatic cancer. After much reflection and prayer, John was transformed. He said, "God revealed to me that I was looking for a woman based on the way she made me feel, not based on who she was." John began to see the difference between an object and a person, between "the idol of feeling validated by women" and "the confidence of being loved by God." He began to choose the humane, the "fully flourishing" view of women—and he made word choices that helped him get to that new perspective: He reframed himself as a worshiper who needed to find the right object of worship, and women as fully human persons made in the image of God.

As I learned in my experience with Tom and Alicia, my way of framing the nature of marriage or their relationship could not be forced on them, nor could I insist on change—but I could listen to their story, train my heart to avoid their pitfalls, and choose the more humane aspects of life. Well, I could try. I couldn't transform their vision, but I could transform my own. That's the best we can do when we seek to engage well with others.

Engaging Well as an Essential of the Soul

When Billy Baker wrote an article on loneliness in middle-aged men, he was shocked by the outpouring of resonance. Thousands wrote to agree with him. Typically, women manage to stay connected but men don't. "When [men] become overscheduled," he said, "they don't shortchange their children, they shortchange their friendships." We need to be in community.

Research shows that the elderly live longer if they are in relationship with others. A number of recent books argue that people are happier if public spaces are designed with more conversation-encouraging walking areas. None of this need for connection surprises us. We might even conclude that we were not meant to live alone (Gen. 2:18).

But we are living alone. If we lived in the dorms in college, no matter how life-giving that experience was, we strive most of our lives to avoid repeating that experience. We move into an apartment with a few friends, then into larger and larger living spaces, sometimes isolating ourselves on sizable properties, sticking to ourselves, and rarely having anyone to the house. Privacy becomes the key value.

Though true solitude is indispensable for sanity and spiritual life, being alone is not necessarily the same thing. And no matter how introverted or contemplative we are, we are still called to engage with others, to "carry each other's burdens" (Gal. 6:2). Engaging well is an essential of the soul.

How we frame this engagement matters. Are we aiming for peaceful coexistence? Friendly contact? To live and let live? Given current pressures we face on our time, we need to give more attention to space, on personal presence, on the frame of "hospitality." Why? What's so good about hospitality? What's so good about personal space that we should raise it up?

Framing Hospitable Presence as a Gain

Affirming the company of others offers the potential of a high and holy reward: the gift of *undivided attention*. When I was in graduate school, I frequently went to see my favorite professor in his office. Most of the time, someone got there before I did. So, I would wait. And wait. After what seemed to me to be "long enough," I paced back and forth in front of his door so he'd be sure to see me. I'd think, "Don't you know I'm waiting out here? Can't you wrap up this conversation?" No matter what I did, he never acknowledged me in the hall. He never even made eye contact. The nerve! After many such sessions in the hall, I finally figured it out. When it was my turn, when I sat in the longed-for chair, he gave me the same uninterrupted attention he had given the previous student—that, in fact, he gave to every student. He valued immediacy. Being in another's presence meant something important, something to protect. And I felt valued by him because he gave me this gift of undivided personal interest.

Hospitable presence also involves *a dynamic uncertainty*: open-ended conversations, interesting lines of inquiry, and a lack of predictability. In his book on improvisation in art and life, Stephen Nachmanovitch says that "Every conversation is a form of jazz." I love this metaphor. You lay down a topic, a theme. I take it up and play my variation, then send it back to you. You add your riff on the refrain—and on and on it goes. Our most forgettable conversations are formulaic scripts:

> "Hey, what's up?"
> "Nothing. How are you?"
> "Good. What are you doing over the weekend?"
> "Just hangin' out."
> "Cool."

These scripts aren't evil; they are often just extended ways of saying hello, one part of our daily rituals. And though they aren't immoral or destructive, they also aren't usually meaningful. Occasionally, memorably, we play our vocal instrument in a jazz conversation. The dialogue moves and grows and creates tunes we never dreamed we'd hear. Framing conversation as jazz can be liberating.

When we choose hospitable presence, *the whole person gets involved*: emotions, intellect, values, and the senses: eye contact, sound, smell, touch, even (at a meal) taste. It's the whole enchilada of humanity—well, if that's what you ordered. Emailing and texting are so easy and efficient that we can work for years next door to someone and never cross the threshold of their office door. One rule of thumb is to choose for more, not fewer, senses. Going next door adds sound and possibly touch to the sight of an email. We are not just our words. We are bodies. Remember to smell the roses. Don't just Instagram them.

As attractive as undivided attention, spontaneity, and wholeness sound in theory, they are often framed negatively in practice. To some, hospitality is a threat.

Framing Hospitable Presence as a Loss

For all its benefits, a deeper connection with others can feel like just more intrusion, chaos, and too much risk. In fact, one tragic irony of our times is that the three rewards I've mentioned are *the very reasons* we avoid deeper presence. The costs of hospitable presence can seem overwhelming and frightening.

For Robyn and Byron, these costs dominated the first fifteen years of their marriage. Though wives don't usually think about whether they are being "hospitable" to their husbands, Robyn consistently struggled with the intimacy of Byron's "presence." She dodged his probing questions. She dodged him. By not admitting her feelings or "even having feelings," she kept a "safe" distance. Whenever he asked for her opinion, she said, "I don't care." Over and over again, Byron said, "But I know you have an opinion. Just say it."

But Robyn wouldn't. She hated the whole idea of intimacy. She didn't want to deal with the messiness of her family pain, the raw exposure of her emotions, the risks of being held responsible for a decision. Byron was not welcome here, in these places. So she criticized him regularly and even prayed "that Byron would die in his sleep so our conflicts would just go away." But Byron kept loving her. His natural inclination was to give, so he gave. Robyn's bent was to take, so she kept taking. Gradually, Robyn came to several revelations—that life is going to be difficult, that Byron was not going to stop loving her, and that she had, for years, "been treating Byron like crap." When she faced her weaknesses, she reframed her role in the marriage. She could change from taker to receiver. She could let the barriers down and let Byron in. Together, they sought forgiveness, and Robyn grew into a giver too. Hospitality transformed from a loss to a gain.

Several themes touch on our resistance to hospitable presence. First, until we address our self-centeredness, we will not want to give the gift of undivided attention. Consumed with herself, Robyn had no room for Byron. She had to reframe herself from "taker" to "receiver" and then to "giver." Second, many of us struggle with spontaneity because we want control. We fear unpredictability. Robyn did not want to express her feelings because she feared what would happen if she opened that door. In a technological age, we want others to see the edited version of our experience, the touched-up and happy photos. We like to watch the unstructured, unpredictable, and spontaneous, but we don't want to live it. We are too busy managing our image. And, third, when we lean away from presence, we feel increasingly insecure about and wary of engaging the whole person. Robyn preferred the safety of isolation to the risks of intimacy. It's a vicious cycle. The more we keep others out, the harder it is to let them in. We can see this with our phone behavior. As the use of texting increases, the pressure *not* to call increases. The caller worries that the voice is an intrusion, even when the voice is desired by the other or when a call would be a better resolution than a dozen texts. Strategically, we avoid more intimate contact. Confronting our resistance to presence will help us become more open to hospitality.

Public and Private Hospitality

We need a renewed commitment to hospitable presence, a pledge to cherish it, to truly love our neighbors as ourselves. We understand face time. We need to revive face space. We've drifted so far from this framing of space that the phrase seems curious, even foreign. Public hospitality involves respect for place. Public areas are not the same as private areas—so we should not act as if we are alone at home. A classroom is not a bedroom, a restaurant is not an isolated reception desk, a shared meal is not a solitary meal. When my mother-in-law met a food server or a cashier or a bank teller, she usually asked for his or her name. She treated those in her presence as persons, not as robotic servants. I know what you're thinking. What's a bank teller?

Might we muster the courage to speak to strangers when we are in line? Could we get off our phones long enough to treat a cashier as a valued person? Some might say that this kind of initiation is only for extroverts, but given the losses in public communication, I think that most of us can find ways to be hospitable, even if just to smile.

We could also affirm personal presence by remembering private hospitality. What can we do to invite others in, to help them to flourish? As we reflect on our community experiences, surely we can conclude that meaningful conversation is one of life's greatest goods and highest pleasures. It's not as flashy as Disneyland or a sunset cruise—but most of us would say that some of our best human moments have involved sitting around a table and talking, learning to know others and getting known ourselves. At a recent birthday dinner for a peer, the table was composed of an uncommon intergenerational mix. Though it was my friend's birthday, he wanted to bless his guests with surprising conversations. That's who he is, someone who values hospitality.

Like many good things, conversation asks of us risk and skill, perseverance and creativity. It also requires compassion. How can we invite others
in without dominating and without disappearing? How can we help others
feel strong enough to share their stories? If "every conversation is a form
of jazz," we can lay down a theme and listen to how the others riff on the
theme. We'll hear the joy of improvisation.

———

Since we tend to lean where technology pushes us, we will need help to
resist where it's important to resist. We need countercultural desires, new
frames, and support from our community. Let's lean into "engaging well."
Let's listen to hear deeply, and choose to be fully attentive, with all the risks
and joys therein.

The Rhetoric of Spring

I had another argument
with a mockingbird
this last April. She said
the point was definitely
tweetle-doo, but I retorted
that it was clearly tweetle-dee.
As you know, these debates
cannot be easily resolved

with bookish references
to golden throats or tufted
crests. So we chirped and
squawked and cheeped and
talked—until she settled
the question as she always does.
I stood my ground.
She flew away.

CHAPTER SIXTEEN

Engaging in Love

*It is all a big mess, I think to myself quite often, . . .
But today I suddenly wondered why I used the word
mess in the first place. It is so much hot air and
doesn't make things any better.*

—Etty Hillesum, from a Nazi camp in Holland

Two weeks before she was shipped to Auschwitz in 1943, Etty
Hillesum wrote about the heartless Nazi guards: "I study their faces. I try
to look at them without prejudice. . . . In what punishment camps were
they trained? For after all, this is a punishment, isn't it?" In her diary and
letters excerpted in *An Interrupted Life*, Etty reveals herself to be one of
the most remarkable people I've met in print—so much so that it seems
I should refer to her by her first name. Though she experienced horrors
beyond what most of us can even imagine, she maintained that life was
beautiful and meaningful. She consistently asserted her frame:

> Many feel that their love of mankind languishes at [the holding
> camp] because it receives no nourishment—meaning people
> here don't give you much occasion to love them. "The mass is
> a hideous monster; individuals are pitiful," someone said. But

> I keep discovering that there is no causal connection between people's behavior and the love you feel for them.

Etty suffered and saw great suffering. From Westerbork, the holding camp designed for 1,500 prisoners but occupied by 40,000, a train transported a thousand Dutch and German Jews to Auschwitz every week. One day, after a young boy tried to escape, fellow inmates were forced to round up fifty others to be sent off immediately—or be shipped off themselves. Mind-numbing tragedy was their daily food.

Yet somehow Etty loved those she felt God had put in her path each day. To the very end, she brightened the lives of fellow prisoners. She sent letters home expressing her gratefulness. I'm not sure how she remained so faithful—but I'm inspired by her affirmations to herself and others.

Engaging well as an essential of the soul means that we learn to love well, as fully and richly as we can, as significantly as words permit us. We can't *make* our words have particular effects, but we can consider our listeners as we speak. Etty and many others show us how.

Loving Appropriately through Speech

So much has been said about love. Dare I say more? I'm not sure we need *more*, but we do need to be reminded of extravagant and steadfast love—at least I do. We give credit to St. Francis for saying, "Preach the gospel at all times. When necessary, use words." Even if we accept Francis's perspective (and I would want to qualify it), the subject of love makes words necessary, words about love and words of love. One of the highest motives for speaking is to help others delight in what has delighted us. When Janet and I saw the largest, reddest harvest moon rise in the east, we went door to door to tell our neighbors to come out to see the astronomical wonder. As we learn something inspiring or important or entertaining, we want others to know.

When it comes to engaging with others, a laudable goal is to love appropriately with our speech. In this application of love, the word *appropriately* reminds us that love is situational and personal. When my wife is sad, I put on one of her (many) favorite musicals and give her a kiss. This strategy won't work with me. I need more time to brood, plus (ironically) I need more assistance with my framing. Appropriateness also relates to our moral choices. If I make a power play by publicly shaming my leering uncle for being "a disgusting, oppressive pig," I've probably missed the morally appropriate choice. And though f-bombs may make you feel strong and daring, they often offend and alienate.

Part of loving well is learning the difference between framing relationships as a power struggle we must win, and framing relationships as the fabric of community that all of us weave together. It's the difference between the Critic and the Lover.

The Critic

A wise man told me, "Be careful when you hear someone say, 'I have no regrets.' You are in the presence of a fool." So, at least you will not take me for a fool when I confess a regret, maybe the most significant regret of my marriage. I have been and can still be crushingly critical of my wife, not just of her, to her, sometimes in public. I can ask a demeaning question that implies she is ridiculous for not knowing the answer. I can dismiss her words with arrogance and disrespect. It is the very opposite of loving appropriately through speech—and I am ashamed I have too often treated gold like tin. Thankfully, Janet has had enough strength of character to endure and to push back, but her resistance grew gradually, after suffering plenty of surface-level and deeper wounds. Slowly, my awareness of my critical framing has improved and I have learned to love her better, more appropriately, with my speech. I still have room to grow.

The Critic is the last of Edmund Bourne's negative self-talk styles. Though Bourne focuses on how the Critic speaks about himself or herself, I want to translate these ideas to our speech to others. Bourne says that the Critic points out flaws and limitations wherever possible, jumps on mistakes to remind you that you are a failure, and often implies, "That was stupid!" Sadly, too many of us can identify with these ways of framing, at least if we can stop blaming others long enough to see ourselves.

The book of James admonishes the Critic: "With the tongue we praise our Lord and Father, and with it we curse human beings, who have been made in God's likeness. Out of the same mouth come praise and cursing. My brothers and sisters, this should not be" (3:9–10). When we "curse" others, they often feel the betrayal and hypocrisy implied by James. The verbally abused person might think or say, "I thought you loved me."

Critics do not love appropriately through speech. They are not think-ing of the receiver's response, only of their power. If they saw themselves as the recipients of their criticism, they might recoil in shame and anger. Such an abuse of verbal muscle! Such a revelation of some perverse need to frame oneself as superior, as witty, as armed and ready to dominate. Ultimately, a framing of oneself as the Master.

Part of the problem is that—consciously or subconsciously—many of us consistently frame any sort of interpersonal conflict as war. We take sides, resist an opponent, fortify our defenses, and on and on. Framing disagreement as a battle is so "entrenched" in our thinking that we have to "fight" to imagine any other metaphor. But Etty did. She found it dif-ficult to frame relationships in terms of war—even during war, even in a Nazi camp: "I love people so terribly, because in every human being I love something of You [God]. And I seek You everywhere in them and often do find something of You." Love indeed has a better way.

The Lover

Instead of "arguers as soldiers," Wayne Brockriede suggests we see "argu-ers as lovers." Instead of "How can we triumph over others?" we could ask, "How can we romance others?" Even if we do so, not all love well. Some passive-aggressive lovers think they can seduce their way to romance: they use deception and create an illusion of choice. Some domineering lovers attempt to force themselves on others: they act aggressively and rely on threats. The best lovers, the most sensitive, woo their beloved: they regard the other as an equal and seek to be inviting rather than demanding.

Whereas the Critic blames and shames, the Lover supports and serves. Whereas the Critic delights in the power of the put-down, the Lover rel-ishes the freely chosen answer to an aptly posed question. When I deny the Critic in me and allow the Lover to flourish, I can get off my high horse. I can meet Janet face to face and then we go riding together. Years ago, she showed me how this works—and her story has nothing to do with romance.

"We have a problem," announced the elementary school principal to his staff. "Karen is nine years old and has not been attending school for months. We're supposed to see that she gets an education."

Two days earlier, Karen's father, an unemployed truck driver, forced Karen to come to school. After Karen kicked out the windshield on their way into the parking lot, the father and the principal decided to lock Karen in a waiting room so they could talk more peacefully about the problem. When they returned, they discovered that Karen had ripped the door molding off with her bare hands.

Clearly, Karen wasn't quite ready for a classroom experience.

So, in the staff meeting, the principal swallowed hard and said, "I'd like a volunteer, someone who would be willing to go out to tutor Karen in her home."

My wife, Janet, raised her hand. In so doing, in her small way, she imitated Christ in the Incarnation.

In Philippians 2, Paul writes that Christ "did not consider equality with God something to be used to his own advantage; rather, he made himself nothing by taking the very nature of a servant" (6–7). Although God could have tyrannized his creation, he humbled himself as a poor, rural carpenter. How might we imagine the measure of this sacrifice? What if Rembrandt were to become a shadow in one of his own self-portraits? Or Rosa Parks became a seat cushion in the back of the bus? These examples border on the absurd, but perhaps that's what it takes to begin to frame the distance traveled in the Incarnation.

If we use the Incarnation as a model for communication, Jesus shows us that we should not automatically exercise the power we possess. Often Jesus *stooped* before he *stood*. He lived as a dependent child before he went to the synagogue to talk with the rabbis. He allowed John to baptize him before he, himself, baptized others. He addressed the poor before he confronted local magistrates. Jesus often left his "rightful place" so he could speak on the level of others.

To connect with Karen, Janet acted in a similar way. She thought about how she had to be willing to leave prepared lessons, classroom rules, and the predictability of her school's structure. When she made this leap and entered Karen's house, things weren't easy. "I couldn't believe my first day," she said. "In a dirty kitchen, Karen sat at a table while her mother yelled at her. Karen didn't say one word."

Janet worried about how she, a sheltered, suburban teacher, could hope to reach Karen and her parents. A few routes were clear. She should not condemn them in her heart or pretend to be superior or keep her distance from all their pain. She knew that being there meant taking significant risks.

This is what lovers think and what they do.

A Framework from Defensiveness to Empathy

On her second visit to Karen's house, Janet suggested the tutorial take place away from the mother, away from the house. As the two walked through the yard toward the barn, Karen picked up a stick, poking the ground with it and hitting things. Then she raised it and threatened Janet. Just when Janet thought, "What's going to happen next?" Karen's imposing father appeared. He was angry. Karen ran into the barn, and Janet followed. As Karen sat on an old dirty mattress, Janet gently spoke to her. And just when Karen began to open up about her struggles, her father burst into the barn, his tall frame silhouetted ominously in the morning light. He screamed at Karen for assaulting Janet. Frightened about what he might do, Janet calmly assured the father that things were fine and that she and Karen would probably do better alone. Reluctantly, he left. Her heart racing, Janet turned around to see Karen shaking, curled up in the fetal position on the spider-infested mattress.

We return for the last time to the idea of frameworks, those structures that support the way we frame each essential of the soul. If our framework is grace instead of perfection, we are much more likely to frame ourselves in peaceful terms. To respond with love, Janet drew upon her framework of empathy. If her starting place had been defensiveness, she might have yelled back at the dad or stormed out or simply withdrawn. Our ability to frame our engagement with others in terms of love is dependent on which side of the framework is stronger: defensiveness or empathy.

Defensiveness

We all know this quality when we see it, except maybe in ourselves. When we are threatened, our natural reaction is to protect ourselves. On a San Francisco street years ago, a strung-out man leaped in front of my teenage daughters. In my mind, I grabbed him and threw him into a nearby store doorway. Thankfully, it didn't come to that—but Janet told me later that I had thrust my chest out. This from a guy who has *never* been in an actual fistfight.

But often, we fight as if genuinely threatened when we actually aren't, like when someone says, "Do you want a muffin?" and we growl back, "Don't you know I'm on a diet?!" Defensiveness makes choosing for love more difficult, because insistence on certain frames drives us to see danger where none exists. If I must be seen as competent, I'll challenge whatever seems to me to reinforce my incompetence. If my frame is perfection, I'll be defensive about any criticism. "How dare you imply I'm prideful! You are an arrogant pig!" It's back to life as war. If I perceive a battle, I'll fight to win it. But if I realize life is a woven tapestry, I won't have to be a warrior. I'll be looking to weave my thread with the threads of others.

Defensiveness applies to virtuous frames too. In *Undefended Love*, Jett Psaris and Marlena Lyons say that even if we frame ourselves as generous, sensitive, and helpful, we might have too much invested in others seeing us in these ways—and we'll feel the need to defend ourselves whenever someone frames us in some other way. They use the acronym REACT to show how we try to get others to reinforce our self-asserted personal characteristics. The letters stand for Reciprocity (expectations of equal give-and-take), Entitlement (demands about our deservedness), Approval (the need for external validation), Consensus (expectations of agreement), and Trustworthiness (how others must be dependable). We all REACT at times, but if reaction is our primary style, love will be inhibited.

When one of our daughters was in high school, she returned to her car parked on the street and found herself boxed in. As she tried to get out in the stick-shift car, she "tapped" the bumper of the car in front of her. Not long after she drove back to the house, a police officer pulled in and asked to see the driver of the red Nissan. The officer explained that someone watched her hit the other car, reported her license plates, and that he had been tasked with coming over to tell her she had just executed a "hit-and-run." Our daughter was furious. Raising her voice, she said sternly, "What do you mean? I did nothing! That car jammed me and all I did was bump it to get out." Appalled, Janet and I looked at each other in disbelief as the officer's anger clearly climbed from his neck to his face. "Young lady, this is serious. You have disobeyed a law by not leaving a note on the other car. I could have you arrested!" As our daughter burst out to protest once again, we ushered her into the house and told her to keep her mouth shut. We apologized to the officer and did what we could to get him to leave without issuing a citation. He did.

When I went inside, I said, "What were you thinking? You were egging on a POLICE OFFICER! He could have nailed you. The only appropriate response was to admit what you did. You are lucky we saved your skin!" She yelled back at me and stormed upstairs. I stood confounded by the whole thing. She was so defensive when she was so obviously in the wrong. Thankfully, she grew out of this irrational stage and into a very thoughtful woman and loving mother.

But I was defensive too. And come to think of it, the officer was as well. Our daughter felt the need to defend her Entitled self. I reacted because I wasn't getting Consensus or Trustworthiness from her—and the officer was steamed because our daughter didn't provide the Reciprocity and Approval he expected.

And this is what defensiveness often does. It enlarges a small rock in our path until it becomes the largest thing in our universe in that moment. How might we reframe to get out of our defensiveness? We might see that our best self doesn't need to be defended.

Empathy

On the other side of the framework scale is empathy, our capacity to identify with one another, to "rejoice with those who rejoice and mourn with those who mourn" (Rom. 12:15). Instead of reacting, we reach out. We reach in. Empathy is not just about finding ourselves in others, but finding others in ourselves. When I am defensive, I frame others as threats to my identity. When I am empathetic, I frame myself as a resource for the encouragement and healing of others. We empathize as we identify.

When the Messiah came, he did not come as a lizard. Although God could have taken the shape of a reptile or a rock, Jesus was "made in human likeness" (Phil. 2:7). We have heard this scripture so often we might miss its dramatic implications for empathy. We think, "Well, of course the Son of God became a person to reach persons." It seems so obvious. But wouldn't it have been easier to call out commands from heaven? Wouldn't it have required less suffering?

In the nineteenth century, Hudson Taylor left England to start missions work in China. When he returned, he sported a braided ponytail and long, curling fingernails, signs of a spiritual Chinese person. To his critics, he said that Paul commanded we should become all things to all people. Was Taylor overdoing identification? Did he overstate the importance of appearance or was he bravely empathetic?

Although we can't *look like* every person we encounter, we can look for them. Where? Inside ourselves. As we better learn how to love God, and our neighbors as ourselves, we can put off our "right" to see the world only through our own lens. We can use our imagination for one of its intended purposes, to become like others so we can better understand them. Isn't this what divided husbands and wives often long for—a sincere effort on the part of one to find ways to appreciate the other?

Sometimes I worry that our culture knows how to create distance but not how to reduce it—or we reduce distance superficially with happy faces and false praise. We isolate ourselves behind our phones and computers, within temperature-controlled walls, and search for websites that reinforce to us how terrible our "foes" are. We tell ourselves it's a dog-eat-dog rat race out there, and we shouldn't monkey around by sticking our necks out. But these animal frames might keep us in separate cages. With more face-to-face eye contact and some good coaching, we could increase our empathy. We have more in common with "those people" than we realize.

Henri Nouwen wrote, "The man who has spent many hours trying to understand, feel, and clarify the alienation and confusion of one of his fellow men might well be the best equipped to speak to the needs of the many, because all men are one at the wellspring of pain and joy." Can a beautiful mother of toddlers empathize with a young male's doubts that he will ever find a mate? Can a healthy Latino man identify with the fears of an elderly Japanese woman dying of cancer? Can a middle class, sheltered, suburban teacher "find in herself" a poor, abused, rural young girl? Yes, by God's incarnational grace.

On the third home visit, Janet discovered Karen in her room, lying silently on her bed. Karen would not speak to Janet, but she allowed Janet to speak to her. This felt like good progress. For the entire hour, Janet tried to imagine what it would be like to grow up with an unpredictable, violent father and an incessantly critical mother. What might Karen need to hear?

She spoke softly to Karen, affirmed her, talked about school, and stroked her hair. Nothing else occurred. Janet did not insist that Karen do her homework. The real lesson was the work of tender empathy.

The Incarnation moves us to see our deeper bonds with others, to frame ourselves and others as *all* made in the image of God, *all* longing for meaning, in need of grace and forgiveness, living in a moral universe, and under the supervision of a loving God. To know the human soul is to recognize that temptations and virtues reach rich and poor alike, the talented and the incompetent, both the faithful and the untrusting. Recognizing our own pride and jealousy can help us understand the motives of those who take those sins to more extreme ends. When we frame ourselves in this way, it is harder to be defensive about what others say. We connect to the pain, not a perceived attack. "I'm so irritated by those idiots who have affairs," Alex said. He affirmed the virtue of fidelity, but he could have had more compassion. We can do both.

In the early years of my friendship with Jose, I heard a lot about what he didn't like. Extroverts, theatrical people, fast-paced people, popular and insecure people or, really, anyone who wasn't like him: a quiet introvert, a nuanced thinker, an institutional rebel. As a people-pleaser, I tried to change my ideas and tone to conform to his. But at some point, I saw his egotism, his defensiveness, his need to be seen in a certain way. And I realized that his constant criticism of others was a slightly veiled way of criticizing me. His first genuine compliment felt like a miracle. But over the years, Jose gradually grew softer. He stopped demanding that everyone be like him—and he increasingly appreciated gifts he did not find in himself. He became more and more empathetic, and his love has followed stride for stride.

Unless we find a way to move our framework from defensiveness to empathy, our engagement with others will suffer from pride, jealousy, and bitterness. Empathy encourages "the believing game"; it gets us inside ourselves, looking for what might motivate others, how they might be feeling and thinking. Empathy is good for love.

Janet showed this quality day after day with Karen—and Karen began to be responsive. As Janet reframed her role from "the teacher up front" to "the teacher who gets inside," Karen flourished. Soon regular lessons began. After a few months, to the amazement of staff and faculty, she returned to school. Though Karen's life continued to be marked by struggle, she was indeed influenced by the love of her teacher.

———

We might read these stories—of Etty and the Nazis, of Janet and her student—and feel how far we have to go to truly engage with others in love. And we may in fact be entrenched in patterns of defensiveness. But we can at least attempt to frame our goals well: articulating that we want to respect others and not shame them, that we want to be willing to see in ourselves the weaknesses we gossip about with others. As we reframe in love, we can step into that frame and live in it. It's what my daughter did when she gave me permission to tell the story about her hit-and-run. She laughed at her teenage self. It's a good place to begin.

Griefing

I know we have a perfectly good word
for naming sorrow's soul
but some days it doesn't push in deep enough
to get at what must be found.
I need my own word
for my own wounds, something
I can take to memory's gravestone and grasp hard
till it grows into something I can grip,
a rope for the vertigo I feel on the mountain pass
of my mourning.

Little Jacob fell into a pool. He was two—
while his brothers played in the water
and his mother ran to check the laundry.
No doubt she said, "Watch him, boys," as she tried
to get one more thing clean and dry.

As has happened before,
I got stuck on this trail. Too steep, too much
slipping down. So, just before the summit,
as others go up, I trundle off
to an untainted alpine lake. It seems cold and stark
enough to meet my griefing. I cup my hands
and bring water to my lips
but mostly it seeps out. I'm shaking.

Jacob died, and all my strength
can't make the hollow hold. Then,
just when the pressure overwhelms,
your fingers fold over mine. You stop the leak
in my cup and I lean into the sweet, dark
drink and we walk down together.

The Practice
of Reframing

CHAPTER SEVENTEEN

Finished and Unfinished Frames

Good stories often introduce the marvelous or
supernatural, and nothing about Story has been
so often misunderstood as this.
—C. S. Lewis, "On Stories"

I have one more story to tell—and I hope by now the idea of telling a "good story" does not seem at odds with a high view of the truth. In fact, how we frame our inner stories reveals our commitment to telling the truth. My story is about a family rescue involving guns, beer, and a golf club. It's not a tidy little tale. It's as messy as all of us. As the chapter title says, some of our frames are unfinished; they still need work. I tell my unfinished story because it is a full-bodied example of reframing principles and, I believe, touches on basic human experiences, and on all four soul essentials. Perhaps along the way, you can look for issues of remembering, anticipating, dwelling within, and engaging with others.

When my dad moved into a rehabilitation facility for the elderly, my brother and I were told that Medicare would cover his expenses indefinitely, at the very least for six months, until June. We knew Dad's independence would end at some point, so we were relieved we had some time to figure out what would happen next. We anticipated a future of transition. Imagine our surprise when we received a call in February that Dad's aid would be ending. "When exactly will he be cut off?" I asked. The answer came, "Tomorrow." "Really? You mean tomorrow as in Saturday." "Yes. It will be $240 every day after that." Wow. What to do? My brother negotiated a few days' extension on the aid, I booked a flight—and by Monday I was on my way to the Northwest to "rescue" my dad and bring him to California.

It had all started with a trailer the previous December. Dad, 94, his wife (my stepmother) Helen, 92, and her short-fused son, Steve, 65, had driven into a restaurant parking lot. Dad and Helen had been at odds for years, and Steve was solidly in his mother's camp. When Dad was not interested in Steve's advice about how to back up the trailer, Steve felt seriously slighted. He rushed over to Dad, grabbed him, lifted him up and shook him so hard, he knocked off his hat. Then Steve stormed away, excreting expletives, and walked six miles back home.

The next day Dad had severe chest pain and was taken to the hospital by an ambulance. After examining him, the physician said, "Your heart is fine. All your vitals are strong. Sir, you had a panic attack, and I'd like to know why." Dad resisted and resisted but finally came out with the story. The physician said, "That qualifies as abuse, and I'm required by law to call in a social worker." Dad was not allowed to go home—to a dangerous situation—so he was sent to the rehab center, for which his money had now run out.

In conversations before I left, Helen had been agreeable. We didn't debate which version of the trailer story was correct, and she seemed fine with us taking Dad away. She may even have been thrilled. Dad was self-consumed and a compulsive spender. That was her frame. To Dad, Helen was ungrateful, unloving, and whiny. Those were his frames. To complicate things, just before I left for the airport, I learned that Steve had been indicted for elder abuse. When I arrived, I wouldn't only have to deal with Steve's ever-bubbling rage—but Helen too would be hopping mad.

I arrived at night at a neighbor's house where I would stay. Ted and Debbie greeted me warmly, with something like, "How the #%^&! was your flight?" I really do mean warmly. They were great hosts: friendly, helpful, gregarious. But I'd never heard so much profanity in my not-that-sheltered life. I wanted to count the words so I could get the profane/non-profane word ratio. "That #%^&! Helen wants to know why you aren't staying in a #%^&! hotel. Well, #%^&!, I don't want you staying at some #%^&! hotel!" And on it went, with fouler things said by the minute, all with obvious love for Dad and an endearing acceptance of me. At dinner, Ted said grace with a fervor I'd not heard around many tables. How could I reconcile these things? With his stories about Vietnam and his six beers a night, I was getting more of a cultural education than I had anticipated.

I called Helen about when I could go over to get Dad's stuff. "Your father started the whole thing, and my Steve didn't do anything. It's all made up. Your father lies all the time." Ignoring the bait, I asked when I could come and if she would arrange for Steve not to be there. After another rant about what that would cost, we set a time for the next day.

In the morning, I called Dad that I was coming to pick him up. By the time I arrived, he had lost a hearing aid, so I sorted through the garbage that went out with the morning breakfast trash. No hearing aid. Just like Dad, I thought, unconcerned if someone else was paying the bill or doing the work, like the way he orders the most expensive thing on the menu if he knows you are paying for it. Finally, bags in hand, we headed to the bank so he could withdraw half their savings before Helen took it all and froze the account. I kept looking around for some undercover police agent who would arrest me before we got out the door. We made it.

Back at Ted and Debbie's, I prepared for the trip to Helen's. Would Steve really be gone or would he be hiding behind a door and fly at me with a hatchet? I wondered, how did I find myself in this spot? I'm not a martial arts master—or even a good wrestler. I play tennis. Ted had told me the day before that if Steve set one foot on his property, he would "send Steve to God"—then Ted asked me if I'd like for him to come along to Helen's. I said, "I guess so." "Well," he said, "do you know how to grab someone by the Adam's apple and 'put them down'?" "Actually, no, I don't." "Okay," he said, "then I'm coming." On the way over, Ted lifted one pant leg to reveal a pistol in his boot. He said, "I mean this: If anything happens, just get out of the way." I thought, *don't worry*.

Walking up to the door, I wasn't sure who I was more afraid of, Steve or Ted. Then I knocked. With the iciest stare you could imagine, Helen let us in. "I don't know why you are here. And why are you mooching off Ted? We pay our way!" Ted said that he wanted me there. "I should never have married that man," Helen continued. "The things I could tell you. He's hit me with things. He spent all my money. What do you need these papers for?" As Ted threw Dad's clothes in boxes, I explained as calmly as I could that Dad should have a copy of every document that both she and he had signed. Reluctantly, she let me go through things. My heart pounded hard. Ted was edgy. "Let's get this over quickly," he said. In a few more minutes, we were out.

That night, at dinner, Ted talked about a meeting he'd had with the social worker and the physician. He said he told them, "#%^&!, Helen! Get all the evidence you can to crush her." I'm just not around very many people who frame things this way, who admit these kinds of desires. Make that no one.

As I talked about the papers with my brother over the phone, we realized I had to go back—and my heart sank. Again, into the rage and open wounds! He said, "While you are at it, if it's not too much trouble, could you get Dad's Big Bertha?" (a golf club). I said I'd try. So I went back with Ted. Helen showed me a scar she said Dad had caused in a fight—and reiterated that Steve had done nothing wrong with the trailer business. I ignored her and got the golf club from Dad's bag in the closet. When Ted went to get something from Dad's shop, Helen and I stood awkwardly. She softened her scowl and said, "Give my love to Janet." Amazed by this sudden warmth, I said, "I'm so sorry things are ending this way. It's not what we wanted. We love you." Then, more amazingly, we hugged. Her shoulders drooped and she sobbed and sobbed in my arms. I held her and savored the miracle of this moment.

In the airport the next morning, as I wheeled Dad through security, golf club in hand, I handed my boarding pass to the TSA guy. He said, "You can't bring that on the plane." I said, "I was hoping I could put it the overhead bin. It didn't fit in my suitcase." He looked at me with befuddled disdain. "It's a *club*." Oh, yeah, that's right.

We had a few minutes, so I went looking for a way to send it home. That was not going to happen, so I thought, what am I going to do? I got this idea and wheeled Dad to the bottom of the escalator, where arriving passengers were coming down. I yelled, "Hey! Anyone play golf? Anyone want a free club?" After many odd looks, I finally got a taker. A young guy, maybe 17, said, "Yeah, I'll take it. This is fantastic!" Then his father came up, asked why I was giving it away, and said he would be happy to mail it to me. I gave him my last $20 in cash and we boarded the plane.

The club arrived at my house the next week. It turned out I had grabbed the wrong one.

As I lived this experience, one of the most astounding and troubling weekends of my life, I brought with me my frames—and I was challenged to reframe hour by hour. How did I proceed? How should I proceed? My weekend intersected with all four soul essentials, as indeed most things do most of the time. Although I've treated the essentials separately, we live them out all at once. In light of our labels for ourselves, we bring our frames of the past to how we anticipate the future, which affects how we engage with one another. And even this description is too linear, because everything impacts everything else in ways too complicated to plot out clearly. Framing is more like a web than it is a line.

Though my situation was complicated, I wanted to frame well. Truth-telling and attitude-making matter. When I boarded the plane, my mind was swimming in the past and diving into the future. Long-term memories with my dad included his era of heavy drinking (slurred speech, absentee parenting)—but I framed more recent memories as "open sharing about marriage" and "important confrontation in love." Metaphors about family life relate here. Is the family a garden where we learn to grow and flourish? Or is it more like a hospital? The residents have various diseases, but some gradually find better health. All of us are patients in search of a good doctor and an encouraging diagnosis. My wounded-but-healing frames from the past helped my attitude about the future, giving me the courage to ward off paralyzing worry, and to approach the weekend's encounters with hope.

I knew that my arrival at my dad's place had the potential to reduce relational conflict, but I was nervous about the interaction and afraid of Helen and Steve's volatility. I needed to be truthful when I thought about my own ability to "make things right," and when I described Helen and Steve. It would have been easy to frame them as opponents to defeat or as heartless ogres. And I could be influenced by images and lines from commercials, ads that mock authentic love by telling us to "just do" whatever feels good or even to pursue "the right amount of wrong." In past visits, Janet teamed with me to strive toward greater love in my dad's household. I was less confident going solo. I brought frames of a dutiful son learning to be a friend, a child who was becoming the parent, as often happens when parents age. I wanted to be a helpful mediator.

My faith informed all four essentials, at least in theory. I came to this situation and these relationships "in Christ," which meant that because of my allegiance to Jesus, I accepted the importance of forgiveness, empathy, courage, and grace. I did not want my difficult past with my father to dominate my actions. Though shocking, Ted and Debbie's outlandishness was not beyond my empathy. God's promises could give me courage to navigate the chaos of my dad's world. And perfect decision-making was not required of me; I could give myself grace. Of course, I did not fulfill each of these leanings. I judged my dad for his self-centered life. I stumbled through difficult conversations with Helen. My courage wavered with each new threat, and I blamed myself for stupid things I said or loving things I left unsaid. And into my busy brain swarmed a dozen clichés, from "when God closes a door, he opens a window" to the idea that we should "hate the sin but love the sinner." To frame well, I needed to listen well—to God and to the Scriptures, not to overused and often trite phrases.

Even with these many challenges, God led me to frame the experience with gratitude, hope, peace, and love. I was grateful I didn't get shot by Ted (!), and thankful for the tender moment with Helen. My tone of voice probably softened some hard edges in a number of conversations. As my brother and I worked through the details, we certainly hoped that the decision we made for my father was a good one—and that he would end his days with less stress. Though I did not feel much peace during that weekend, I settled into a "satisfied acceptance" after reflecting on all that occurred.

We all have our reframing stories, though most are not as dramatic as this one. Yet my uncommon story taps into common experiences of interpersonal conflict, relationships with parents, cultural differences, faith-informed decisions, and blatant vulgarity. Since questions drive the kinds of answers we receive, good inquiry can take us deep into our reframing—and into all four soul essentials.

Remembering the past: How do you discuss family and friendship memories, your work and faith history? How would you *like* to frame your past? Would a change from bitterness to forgiveness lead to more gratefulness?

Anticipating the future: How do you imagine your work and creative life in five or ten years? What fears frame the way you anticipate? Can you articulate the courage available to you because Jesus has "overcome the world"?

Dwelling within the self: What do friends and family say about you? How does your life with God influence your personal sense of order? Do you see yourself as a warrior, a manager, or a lover? Do you lean more toward perfectionism or grace?

Engaging with others: What roles do you play with others: a negotiator, an agitator, a nonparticipant? Which scriptures call you to reframe your interactions? Who upsets your sense of order? Who brings you stability?

Though I have reviewed this story extensively, my reframing isn't that important for you as you finish this book. Your reframing is. I don't know what your questions are, or which of your broken frames need mending. But I do know that we are called by God to reframe. Jesus gives us gospel words: redemption, inheritance, adoption, unconditional love. Will we choose God's THIS to replace our THAT? Forgiveness, not bitterness—so we can remember with gratitude? Courage, not fear—so we can discover hope? Grace, not perfectionism—so we can dwell within ourselves in peace? Empathy, not defensiveness—so we can engage with others in love?

To his disciples, Jesus asked, "Who do you say that I am?" (Mark 8:29). How would we answer? Is Jesus a failed revolutionary? A kind advisor? An irrelevant historical figure? A resurrected Messiah? Our answer to this question determines many of our other frames and directs the path of our soul. When you frame God, who's in the picture?

We choose our frames, and then we live in them. They form the structure of our lives, the "home" we carry around, which includes the "windows" through which we see the world. Though words are not everything, the words we choose matter. We can be transformed by them. They affect our work and play, our faithful and unbelieving choices, our virtues and our vices.

I've asked repeatedly, "When you frame your life, what's in the picture?" But perhaps, as you've reflected and revised your words, the question should be, "When you reframe your life, what's in the picture *now*?"

A Yellow Advent

The finches are here.
We see them come just once

a year—to eat the rosemary berries,
flashing their butter-bright coats

as they flit and flirt from bush to bush.
We don't know why they don't

visit more often. Are we not
sending the right birdly signals?

We've tried thistles and other things
these finches, we are told, enjoy.

But then, I guess, once a year is still
something. The finches come,

open their wings,
inviting us to the feast.

Such lordly hospitality.

Reframing with
the Saints

This exercise is designed to aid your reframing by giving you various models for telling your story. Each writer is a master reframer. The exercise is threefold. First, list a new or ongoing event that has disturbed your sense of order, something that has made your current frames feel wobbly or unhelpful. A new diagnosis, an accident, or a family revelation might have led you to wonder about God's goodness or your own stability, for example. Second, read the paragraph supplied in whichever soul essential is most pertinent. What do you admire about it? How is the author's approach different from your own framing? Third, write out a reframing of your typical description of your situation. The key here is that you attempt to write your new content in the same style as the writer. If you choose Augustine, address God as "You," etc. If you choose the psalm, have your reframing sound like a psalm. You might find that the style of the model reframer helps transport you to new ways of saying things. If you are able, do this exercise in a small group and read your reframed paragraphs to each other.

Remembering the Past with Gratitude

What has challenged your sense of order in the past?

A Model of Reframing: Augustine, *Confessions*, V:8: "It was to save my soul that you obliged me to go and live elsewhere. . . . You applied the spur that would drive me away from Carthage and offered me enticements that would draw me to Rome, and for your purpose you made use of men whose hearts were set upon this life of death, some acting like madmen, others promising me vain rewards. In secret you were using my own perversity and theirs to set my feet upon the right course. . . . You knew, O God, why it was that I left one city and went to the other."

Write out your reframing in the spirit of Augustine (emphasis on God's purposes):

Anticipating the Future with Hope

What has challenged your sense of order of the future?

A Model of Reframing: Annie Dillard in *Pilgrim at Tinker Creek*: "The world is fairly studded and strewn with pennies cast broadside from a generous hand. But—and this is the point—who gets excited by a mere penny? . . . But if you cultivate a healthy poverty and simplicity, so that finding a penny will literally make your day, then, since the world is in fact planted in pennies, you have with your poverty bought a lifetime of days. It is that simple. What you see is what you get."

Write out your reframing in the spirit of Dillard (emphasis on perspectives that influence hope):

Dwelling within Ourselves in Peace

What has challenged your sense of order about yourself?

A Model of Reframing: Psalm 139:7–14: "Where can I go from your Spirit? Where can I flee from your presence? If I go up to the heavens, you are there; if I make my bed in the depths, you are there. If I rise on the wings of the dawn, if I settle on the far side of the sea, even there your hand will guide me, your right hand will hold me fast. If I say, "Surely the darkness will hide me and the light become night around me," even the darkness will not be dark to you; the night will shine like the day, for darkness is as light to you. For you created my inmost being; you knit me together in my mother's womb. I praise you because I am fearfully and wonderfully made; your works are wonderful, I know that full well."

Write out your reframing in the spirit of the psalm (emphasis on God's acceptance and pursuit of you):

Engaging with Others in Love

What has challenged your sense of order with others?

A Model of Reframing: Marilynne Robinson in *Gilead*: "When you encounter another person, when you have dealings with anyone at all, it is as if a question is being put to you. So you must think, What is the Lord asking of me in this moment, in this situation? If you confront insult or antagonism, your first impulse will be to respond in kind. But if you think, as it were, This is an emissary sent from the Lord, and some benefit is intended for me, . . . you are free to act otherwise than as circumstances would seem to dictate."

Write out your reframing in the spirit of Robinson (emphasis on unconditional love):

Discussion Questions

Introduction: Fifteen Years Down the Hatch

1. As you consider the themes of this chapter, do you have a reframing story of your own? When did you:
   a) have a way of framing a situation ("my parents abandoned me"), then:
   b) experience a challenge to this frame (the gospel of forgiveness), which moved you to:
   c) a reframing ("my parents are wounded people who need healing—like me"). How did you work your way through it?

2. Explore what it means that "we frame our story . . . and then our story frames us."

3. What are examples of words you use that help "construct" your "home" and the "windows" for seeing the world?

4. *Faith*-work is often *frame*-work. What does this mean? How has this been true in your spiritual journey?

5. How does the poem "The Beginning of the Road of Ice" tell a reframing story? Discuss the word "home" in relation to the chapter.

Chapter One: Every Word Is a Window

1. Has anyone ever "named" you in a way that changed how you see yourself? Reflect on the power of that word choice.
2. In what ways have you "been framed"? Can you identify frames you did and did not choose? What effects do you see from these descriptive terms?
3. "We live inside the frame." Can you think of an example of how you don't merely pick up a word but how you live (on a daily basis) in your history with that word? What about the terms you use to describe your life with God?
4. What sorts of situations are you being "called to reframe"? How have biblical phrases replaced popular cultural phrases in your everyday speech? Do you see any particular effects from "speaking God's words after him"?
5. How does the poem "Morning Tapestries" speak to the idea of words as windows? Which words in the poem are windows for you?

Chapter Two: There Is No Immaculate Perception

1. What's a recent experience in which you were reminded that "there is no immaculate perception"?
2. When have you wrestled with reconciling perception and truth?
3. Take a major event from your past and discuss the frames you chose in relationship to it.
   a. Did the frames enhance the image or disguise it?
   b. How did the frame create boundaries?
   c. What did it reveal *and* conceal?
   d. How did the size and shape of the frames make a difference?
   e. Would you like to switch out any of these frames for different ones?
4. Think of a situation you framed quite differently from a spouse, friend, or colleague. Given various possible perceptions of the event, how did your choice of words contribute to truth-telling and attitude-making? How did others' words add to or subtract from your description?

5. How does the poem about the lake use different frames to direct the reader? How does it connect with the idea that "there is no immaculate perception?"

Chapter Three: Order, Order, Everywhere

1. Oliver Sacks calls proprioception the "mooring of our identity." How is this true for the body and also true for words and the mind?
2. Words secure us in a narrative. When have you encountered an event that upset your place in your story? How was reframing related to finding new order in your story?
3. Some people have more of a sense of randomness than a sense of order. How do you sort this out?
4. How has your natural "patternicity" (Shermer's phrase) served you well, and how has it led you astray?
5. How has your faith influenced the ways you frame the order you see "out there" (in the world) and "in here" (inside yourself)?
6. "At every turn, Jesus upsets the proprioception of those around him." Has this been your experience? If so, what have you done about it?
7. For Janet and me, the poem "Dementia Road" reviews a disturbance to our proprioception. What are our reframing challenges?

Chapter Four: When You Frame Your Life, What's in the Picture?

1. The title of the chapter is "When you frame your life, what is in the picture?" What strikes you about the ways you frame your life? What is in the picture?
2. Is there a story for you like my story about back pain? What story (in which *something happened*) do you consistently frame a certain way—but now that you think about it, you could certainly frame the story differently? What are the limitations of the words you've used to describe your events?
3. Though many more pages will be focused on the four essentials of the soul, what is your initial response to them? Which one, for you, is most obviously connected to the ways you frame things?
4. Our frames are based on our frameworks—which are more about our fundamental desires than they are our fundamental beliefs. Do you

agree with this distinction? How do your own choices confirm or dis-confirm this idea?

5. Dominic LaRusso said, "You say what you say because you are who you are." When you consider your speech habits, what would others conclude about "who you are" from "what you say"?

6. Explain the title, "Bracing Back." How is the narrator working at framing throughout the poem?

Chapter Five: Remembering

1. What's a sad or embarrassing memory that's become "a classic story" for you? Why did you reframe it?

2. Many scriptures touch on memory. What do the following verses (and others) tell you about life in the kingdom? Psalm 45:17, Luke 12:6,7.

3. Discuss whatever aspects of memory resonated with you: that it's not a container but a stomach, etc. When have you experienced your memory's "superiority complex"? How might this tendency affect a family memory you don't like to revisit?

4. Some say we operate according to our "life" metaphors, that life is a journey, a game, or a dark plot. Which metaphors do you use often? How might they influence your framing of memories?

5. Like my story of my time in the Young Life camp, do you have a story of a redeemed, reframed memory?

6. The poem "Diamond Mercies" recounts a memory. How does the narrator frame that memory—and then reframe it?

Chapter Six: Remembering Well

1. What stories from your past "root you" in the present?

2. In what ways does your *framing* of the past show how your past influences your present and your present influences your past?

3. The Scriptures call us to use our memory in many ways in our relationship with God. Review Psalm 42 for the various references to remembering. How has memory been a part of your spiritual journey?

4. Henri Nouwen calls us "a living reminder of Christ." Of what do you remind others? If in a group setting, members could share what each person "reminds them of."
5. Discernment is a significant part of remembering well. Walk through a "large memory" (a conflict on the job, a friend's sickness, a family's secret), commenting on beneficial and destructive remembering, and beneficial and destructive forgetting.
6. Read the passage the poem is based upon: Isaiah 43:16–21. How does this passage and the poem sort out what it means to remember well?

Chapter Seven: Remembering with Gratitude

1. "Gratefulness is the appreciation for whatever can be appreciated." Explore.
2. When we are plagued by our memories, we see ourselves as the victim. In a difficult story that you tell, what can be appreciated? How do you typically frame yourself?
3. Robert Emmons says that gratitude often depends on a "redemptive twist." When have you reframed an experience in these terms?
4. "Bitterness has its benefits." What are these, and when have you been "held" by them?
5. What do you think about the two explanations of how we would know we had forgiven someone ("wishing them well" and "not thinking they owe you something")? How might these definitions lead you to reframe a memory?
6. What experiences does the poem "I'm grateful for days" remind you of?

Chapter Eight: Anticipating

1. One scripture about the future is Philippians 3:13b–14: "Forgetting what is behind and straining toward what is ahead, I press on toward the goal to win the prize for which God has called me heavenward in Christ Jesus." With all the emphasis on memory in Scripture, why does Paul say we are to forget? What is the prize he mentions?
2. Which version of the Good Life do you gravitate toward? Or some other version?
   a. The everlasting party

    b. What I deserve

    c. Technological control

    d. Peace on earth

3. How does your version of the Good Life connect to its respective "concern": death, anxiety, randomness, or injustice?

4. Jill's story about David speaks to her need to adjust her framing about the future. Do you have an experience that led you to reframe how you anticipate?

5. How does the poem "Terra Squeaka" point to issues of the future—as it speaks about the dawn and routine maintenance?

Chapter Nine: Anticipating Well

1. As you talk about the future, where do you see yourself headed? Does your framing create the path you are on?

2. Take a situation in which you find it relatively easy to "practice paradise," and one in which you find it difficult. How do you account for the difference? How might your framing of heaven influence your reframing of the difficult situation?

3. How does "having the proper time frame" relate to anticipating well? According to the way you talk about the present and the future, what time frame are you in? Would you like to reframe that conclusion?

4. As you think about beneficial and destructive anticipation, and beneficial and destructive "being in the present," which of the four practices is your strongest and weakest?

5. Can you identify with "The Summer of My Gathering Mortality"? Has the resurrection helped you to reframe?

Chapter Ten: Anticipating with Hope

1. What is the relationship between hope and unpredictability? How does Jesus demonstrate this knowledge? Sometimes we treat those in our family worse than those on the outside. How might lack of hope and predictability connect here? Do you see a place where you might reframe?

2. "Hope is the confidence that God has done something that empowers us to wonder, to work, and to wait." Which of these three parts comes

most naturally to you? Which one is the biggest struggle? How would you most like to reframe the way you talk in relationship to hope?

3. What clichés most bother you? What do you wish we said instead?
4. We live in a "manufactured" culture of fear. Respond.
5. How does courage encourage hope? What is an example of courage in your life?
6. Two poems in a row that mention a Cecile Brunner rose! I guess I like them a little too much. How does the idea of "rising" differ from the reference to the resurrection in the "Gathering Mortality" poem of the last chapter? What does "Crowning Up on the Cane" add to the discussion of anticipation and hope?

Chapter Eleven: Dwelling

1. What are a few of your "identity stories," experiences that led to a framing of who you are? Have you done some significant reframing here?
2. Cultural voices, especially advertising, can strongly influence us. What does it mean to think of yourself as a consumer? How have the sexual messages in culture contributed to the ways you think and act (porn and "hot or not," etc.)?
3. What would someone say about you by examining your friends? How do your friends reinforce or challenge your self-image?
4. Circumstances can become voices that disturb our sense of order regarding the self. Have you experienced a dramatic event that has led you to reframe who you are? Or have you been in long-term circumstances (a difficult marriage, difficult singleness, etc.) that have done the same?
5. How have the Scriptures called you to reframe? In what ways do you see yourself as more other-centered or more of a new creation?
6. The poem leads readers to the idea of becoming "children of light." Explore what this says about identity.

Chapter Twelve: Dwelling Well

1. Explore the relationship between the body and the spirit by praying the Lord's Prayer in different bodily positions and different places (sitting, kneeling, standing, in a forest, in a church, etc.).

2. Here's a "doubting and believing game" exercise for two people. You'll have four short conversations (maybe two minutes each). Each person should create two lists of three or four things: one list of things you usually doubt (alien invaders, a perfect government system, etc.) and one list of things you usually believe (Abraham Lincoln was a good president, God exists, etc.). In the first conversation, Person One takes an item off Person Two's list of typical doubts. As Person One doubts this item, Person Two attempts to believe this same item—what he or she typically doubts. In the second conversation, Person One takes an item off Person Two's believe list—and believes this while Person Two doubts what he or she typically believes. For conversations three and four, reverse roles. What does the exercise teach you about your commitments to doubting and believing?

3. What would it mean to feel "at home in your own house"?

4. Which nouns do you use that might be better framed as verbs?

5. The phrase "in Christ" is used over 150 times in the New Testament. How does this phrase frame the spiritual life?

6. The poem "In Search of a Duck's Back" raises issues of praise and criticism. What is your experience with harsh criticism?

Chapter Thirteen: Dwelling in Peace

1. The Scriptures present peace as divisive, a choice, a consequence, and a gift. Does each one make sense to you? Which one is most evident in your life?

2. What's a situation that has taught you humility?

3. If you wrote a letter to a younger version of yourself, what compassionate thing might you say? Where is Jesus in this letter?

4. What circumstances stretch your ability to be content? How is your response related to your ability to act "in peace"?

5. Where would you put yourself on the framework scale from perfectionism to grace? How has your faith affected your placement on the scale?

6. The poem "Preemptive Kindness" tells the story of a phone call we received during the Santa Barbara Tea Fire. Have you experienced a sacred moment such as this?

Chapter Fourteen: Engaging

1. If, as Neil Postman says, every technological gain also represents some kind of loss, what do you think have been the effects of the Internet and social media on interpersonal communication?
2. How is your "engaging with others" influenced by the phone?
3. Would you agree that "time is up"—that there is a moral emphasis on urgency, speediness, and efficiency? Has this affected your faith?
4. Reflect on the idea that "space is down." When have you experienced a conspiracy against conversation?
5. Four of the five technologically encouraged changes in our engagement with others are the norm of interruption, a new sense of competition, a paradox of connection and disconnection, and an accidental arrogance. Do these resonate with your conversational life?
6. Take the challenge introduced in the section on questions: see if you can go ten minutes in a conversation only asking questions. What does that feel like for you and the other person?
7. The poem "Coffee Break" gets at the noises we can't escape. When does the pressure of our culture make its presence known to you?

Chapter Fifteen: Engaging Well

1. An experiment: Share a meaningful story from your past with a friend, then ask him or her to retell it to you with the same degree of feeling and thought. Ask them to keep working on their version until it feels closer to your story. Reverse roles.
2. To what do we say yes in our culture that deserves a no? Also, consider the theme of "follow your heart" in recent films.
3. Jesus says he came that we "might have life to the full" (John 10:10). How does this verse connect to the idea of "choosing for the humane"?
4. We are attracted to hospitality in theory and often struggle with it in practice. Who are some models to you of hospitable presence? When do you resist hospitality?
5. Public hospitality seems like a lost art. What is your experience? How might reframing it lead to a better "engagement with others"?

6. The poem "The Rhetoric of Spring" is a whimsical look at patterns in communication. As you think about "engaging well," which of your patterns are most and least helpful?

Chapter Sixteen: Engaging in Love

1. When, like Etty, have you been in circumstances that challenged your ability to frame others in loving terms?
2. "Loving appropriately through speech." How might this phrase change public discourse?
3. As you compare the Critic with the Lover, how do you identify with each? What are some frames you use that might need to be reframed?
4. Janet loved Karen incarnationally. What does this mean? What are some specific choices Jesus made that we can imitate, so that we might "have the same mindset as Christ Jesus" (Phil. 2:5)?
5. We can be defensive about both petty and virtuous commitments. Explore a situation in which your framing led to a REACTion instead of empathy.
6. The poem "Griefing" attempts to get inside a mourner's feelings. How might the end of the poem also relate to empathy?

Chapter Seventeen: Finished and Unfinished Frames

1. With what parts of my story do you identify? Have you had a major crisis with a parent or a sibling?
2. Walk through your story with the four soul essentials. What frames did you bring to the situation? How did you reframe—or wish you'd reframed?
3. How might God be calling you to reframe your soul? Which gospel values seem most and least alive to you? Retell part of your story using the gospel frames you'd most like to apply more fully.
4. The poem "A Yellow Advent" hints at all four of the soul essentials. How so? How might the poem serve as a metaphor for reframing your soul?

Endnotes

Introduction

page 13 "I am saddened": St. Augustine, quoted in Peter Brown, *Augustine of Hippo: A Biography* (Los Angeles, CA: University of California Press, 1969), 256.

page 18 "make the embarrassing occurrence": George Lakoff, *Don't Think of an Elephant: Know Your Values and Frame the Debate* (White River Junction, VT: Chelsea Green, 2004), 100.

Chapter One

page 21 "What you call 'worry'": Richard Bandler and John Grinder, *Reframing: Neuro-Linguistic Programming and the Transformation of Meaning,* ed. Steve Andreas and Connierae Andreas (Moab, UT: Real People Press, 1982), 49.

page 21 "interpreting people's maladies": Jhumpa Lahiri, *Interpreter of Maladies* (Boston, MA: Houghton Mifflin, 1999), 51.

page 21 "to render the unspeakable speakable": Walker Percy, "The Diagnostic Novel," *Harper's,* June 1986, 40.

page 22 "until we say it out loud": Amanda Hontz Drury, *Saying Is Believing: The Necessity of Testimony in Adolescent Spiritual Development* (Downers Grove, IL: InterVarsity Press, 2015), 31.

page 28 "If you ruminate on imaginary fears": Andrew Newberg and Mark Robert Waldman, *Words Can Change Your Brain* (New York: Plume, 2013), 57.

page 29 "For those . . . who decide": Eugene Peterson, *Tell It Slant: A Conversation on the Language of Jesus in His Stories and Prayers* (Grand Rapids, MI: Eerdmans, 2008), 159.

page 30 "thinking God's thoughts after him": Johannes Kepler, quoted in D. James Kennedy and Jerry Newcombe, *What If Jesus Had Never Been Born?* (Nashville, TN: Thomas Nelson, 2001), 99.

Chapter Two

page 34   "I have a point of view": Madeleine L'Engle, *Walking on Water: Reflections on Faith and Art* (Wheaton, IL: Harold Shaw, 1980), 151.

page 34   "eyewitnesses": See innocenceproject.org and the references listed there; also Elizabeth F. Loftus, James M. Doyle, and Jennifer E. Dysart, *Eyewitness Testimony: Civil and Criminal*, 4th ed. (Charlottesville, VA: Lexis Law Publishing, 2008).

page 41   "If you called a woman": George J. Marlin, Richard P. Rabatin, and John L. Swan, eds., *The Quotable Chesterton: A Topical Compilation of the Wit, Wisdom, and Satire of G. K. Chesterton* (San Francisco, CA: Ignatius Press, 1986), 368.

page 41   "Nearly every student": Chap Clark, *Hurt 2.0: Inside the World of Today's Teenagers* (Grand Rapids, MI: Baker Academic, 2001), 147.

page 42   "This is not my house": Victor Hugo, *Les Misérables*, trans. Charles E. Wilbour (New York: Blue Ribbon Books, 1943), 26. First published 1862.

page 43   "positive thinking": Citing dozens of studies in *The Art of Positive Communication* (New York: Peter Lang, 2014), Julien C. Mirivel says that "Communicating positively can foster your happiness and help you cope with stress and adversity" (6). In *The Luck Factor* (New York: Hyperion Books, 2001), Richard Wiseman wanted to know why some people seemed luckier than others. After interviewing hundreds of "lucky" and "unlucky" people, he learned that the main difference was that "lucky people's expectations of winning were more than twice that of unlucky people" (26). Expectations are, of course, all about how we talk about our circumstances. In the provocatively titled *Your Body Believes Every Word You Say*, Barbara Levine says that "Dis-ease [her use of hyphen] is a process over which you can have more control by carefully choosing your thoughts, your words, your attitude, and your actions" (Fairfield, CT: WordsWork Press, 2000), 53.

Chapter Three

page 45   "The answer, Mr. Perkowitz": John M. Broder, "Seeking to Save the Planet, with a Thesaurus," *New York Times*, May 1, 2009.

page 46   "the fundamental, organic mooring": Oliver Sacks, *The Man Who Mistook His Wife for a Hat* (New York: Summit Books, 1985), 50.

page 47   "appreciative and comprehending critics": Robert Coles, *The Call of Stories* (Boston, MA: Houghton Mifflin, 1989), 11.

page 49   "patternicity": Michael Shermer, *The Believing Brain* (New York: St. Martin's Griffin, 2011), 5.

page 50   "Although true pattern recognition": Michael Shermer, *The Believing Brain* (New York: St. Martin's Griffin, 2011), 62.

page 51   "searching for the perfect word": Kenneth Burke, *Language as Symbolic Action* (Berkeley, CA: University of California Press, 1966), 16.

Chapter Four

page 55 "To change your language": Derek Walcott, "Codicil," in *Collected Poems 1948–1984* (New York: Farrar, Straus and Giroux, 1986), 97.

page 59 "forward to a place": Christian Wiman, *My Bright Abyss: Meditation of a Modern Believer* (New York: Farrar, Straus and Giroux, 2013), 28.

page 60 "Our words must strike a balance": Eugen Rosenstock-Huessy, *Speech and Reality* (Norwich, VT: Argo Books, 1970), 19.

page 63 "You are what you want": James K. A. Smith, *You Are What You Love: The Spiritual Power of Habit* (Grand Rapids, MI: Brazos Press, 2016), 13.

page 63 "Have fun!": Laura Parker, "Why 'Did You Have Fun?' is the Wrong Question," August 19, 2012, http://www.lauraleighparker.com/2012/08/why-did-you-have-fun-is-the-wrong-question/.

Chapter Five

page 71 "To live in the present": G. K. Chesterton, quoted in Robert T. Latham, *A Tale of Boxes: The Role of Myth in Creating and Changing Our Stories* (Tucson, AZ: Wheatmark, 2009), 87.

page 72 "superiority complex": Elizabeth Loftus, *Memory: Surprising New Insights into How We Remember and Why We Forget* (New York: Ardsley House, 1988), 137.

page 72 "memory sins": Daniel L. Schacter, *The Seven Sins of Memory: How the Mind Forgets and Remembers* (New York: Mariner Books, 2002), 4–11.

page 73 "the room where with patience": Frederick Buechner, *A Room Called Remember* (San Francisco, CA: Harper & Row, 1984), 6.

page 74 "all metaphors matter": George Lakoff and Mark Johnson, *Metaphors We Live By* (Chicago, IL: University of Chicago Press, 1980), 6.

page 75 "scaffolding": Andy Clark, *Being There: Putting Brain, Body, and World Together Again* (Cambridge, MA: MIT Press, 1997), 32–33.

Chapter Six

page 83 "means not forgetting him": Nicholas Wolterstorff, *Lament for a Son* (Grand Rapids, MI: Eerdmans, 1987), 28.

page 85 "physical pain in our past": Daniel Schacter, *The Seven Sins of Memory: How the Mind Forgets and Remembers* (New York: Mariner Books, 2002), 139.

page 86 "It is how wisdom comes": Lois Lowry, *The Giver* (New York: Bantam, 1993), 78.

page 87 "To remember a wrongdoing": Miroslav Volf, *The End of Memory: Remembering Rightly in a Violent World* (Grand Rapids, MI: Eerdmans, 2006), 11.

page 88 "To be a living memory": Henri Nouwen, *The Living Reminder* (New York: HarperOne, 1977), 25.

page 88   "Who am I": Henri Nouwen, *The Living Reminder* (New York: HarperOne, 1977), 27.

page 89   "Recalling Bitterness": Frank Dikötter, *The Cultural Revolution: A People's History, 1962–1976* (New York: Bloomsbury Press, 2016), 35.

Chapter Seven

page 93   "When someone remarked": Marilynne Robinson, *Gilead* (New York: Picador, 2004), 31.

page 95   "the Victim": Edmund Bourne, *The Anxiety & Phobia Workbook*, 3rd ed. (Oakland, CA: New Harbinger Publications, 2000), 184.

page 95   "Gratitude maximizes happiness": Robert Emmons, *Gratitude Works! A 21-Day Program for Creating Emotional Prosperity* (San Francisco, CA: Jossey-Bass, 2013), 140.

page 100   "You only have to forgive once": M. L. Stedman, *The Light Between Oceans* (New York: Scribner, 2012), 323.

page 100   "Forgiving is love's revolution": Lewis Smedes, *Forgive & Forget: Healing the Hurts We Don't Deserve* (New York: HarperOne, 2007), 94. First published 1984.

page 101   "Forgiveness has begun": Lewis Smedes, *Forgive & Forget: Healing the Hurts We Don't Deserve* (New York: HarperOne, 1996), 29. First published 1984.

page 102   "Everything belongs": Richard Rohr, *Everything Belongs: The Gift of Contemplative Prayer* (New York: Crossroad, 2003), 130.

Chapter Eight

page 107   "If you come at four": Antoine de Saint-Exupéry, *The Little Prince*, trans. Richard Howard (New York: Houghton Mifflin, 2000), 42. First published 1943.

page 108   "Always the seer": Ralph Waldo Emerson, quoted in Paul Kalanithi, *When Breath Becomes Air* (New York: Random House, 2016), 215.

page 110   "We regard living in the downhill": Atul Gawande, *Being Mortal: Medicine and What Matters in the End* (New York: Metropolitan, 2014), 28.

page 111   "Anxiety is . . . about the self": Joseph LeDoux, *Anxious: Using the Brain to Understand and Treat Fear and Anxiety* (New York: Viking, 2015), 257.

Chapter Nine

page 117   "In order to make sense of": Peter Mendelsund, *What We See When We Read: A Phenomenology with Illustrations* (New York: Vintage Books, 2014), 94.

page 118   "Massive copying": Kevin Kelly, *The Inevitable: Understanding the 12 Technological Forces That Will Shape Our Future* (New York: Viking, 2016), 5.

page 118   "future-blind": Kevin Kelly, *The Inevitable: Understanding the 12 Technological Forces That Will Shape Our Future* (New York: Viking, 2016), 14.

page 120 "the complex interplay between what we assume will be and what is": Chris Berdik, *Mind over Mind: The Surprising Power of Expectations* (New York: Current, 2013), 9, 43, 48.

page 121 "key to thriving is learning to harness": Jennice Vilhauer, *Think Forward to Thrive: How to Use the Mind's Power of Anticipation to Transcend Your Past and Transform Your Life* (Novato, CA: New World Library, 2014), 2.

page 122 "a sudden and miraculous grace": J. R. R. Tolkien, *The Tolkien Reader* (New York: Ballantine, 1966), 86.

page 122 "Earth's crammed with heaven, and every common bush afire with God": Elizabeth Barrett Browning, "Aurora Leigh," in D. H. S. Nicholson and A. H. E. Lee, *The Oxford Book of English Mystical Verse* (Oxford: Clarendon Press, 1917).

page 124 "how we seek to spend our time": Atul Gawande, *Being Mortal: Medicine and What Matters in the End* (New York: Metropolitan, 2014), 97.

Chapter Ten

page 133 "Over the last few days": Oliver Sacks, "My Own Life," *New York Times*, February 19, 2015.

page 136 "grease the hinges": Randall VanderMey, *Godtalk: The Triteness & Truth in Christian Clichés* (Downers Grove, IL: InterVarsity Press, 1993), 14.

page 136 "a dulling of vision": Randall VanderMey, *Godtalk: The Triteness & Truth in Christian Clichés* (Downers Grove, IL: InterVarsity Press, 1993), 13.

page 138 "leads us to act in ways": Scott Bader-Saye, *Following Jesus in a Culture of Fear* (Grand Rapids, MI: Brazos Press, 2007), 21.

page 138 "The Worrier creates anxiety": Edmund Bourne, *The Anxiety & Phobia Workbook*, 3rd ed. (Oakland, CA: New Harbinger Publications, 2000), 183–84.

page 140 "strong desire to live taking the form of a readiness to die": G. K. Chesterton, *Orthodoxy* (New York: Image, 1959), 93. First published 1908.

Chapter Eleven

page 148 "Promise, large promise": Samuel Johnson, "Advertising," *The Idler*, January 20, 1759, https://constantresearcher.wordpress.com/2009/08/02/advertising-1759-by-samuel-johnson/.

page 149 "unfulfilled, unfaithful, unhappy": John Kavanaugh, "Idols of the Marketplace," in Arthur Berger, *Media USA: Process and Effect* (New York: Longman, 1990), 432.

page 149 "even becoming media savvy won't keep us from believing ads": There is considerable research that suggests we tend to overstate media effects on others and understate media effects on ourselves. See Julie L. Andsager and H. Allen White, *Self versus Others: Media, Messages, and the Third-Person Effect* (Mahwah, NJ: Lawrence Erlbaum Associates, 2007).

page 150   "Much of the culture": Nancy Jo Sales, *American Girls: Social Media and the Secret Lives of Teenagers* (New York: Vintage Books, 2016), 17.

page 150   "According to Cooley, Mead, and many other theorists, we develop the self": An introductory summary can be found in Em Griffin, Andrew Ledbetter, and Glenn Sparks, *A First Look at Communication Theory* (New York: McGraw-Hill, 2015), 54–65.

page 151   "a ratio of five positive interactions to one negative": John Gottman. *Why Marriages Succeed or Fail: And How to Make Your Marriage Last* (New York: Simon & Schuster, 1994), 56–62.

page 153   "Harry Nash seems to be a 'nobody'": Kurt Vonnegut, "Who Am I This Time?" in *Welcome to the Monkey House* (New York: Delta, 1998). Story first published as "My Name Is Everyone" in the *Saturday Evening Post* in 1961.

Chapter Twelve

page 157   "If we were humble": Mother Teresa, *In My Own Words*, ed. Jose Luis Gonzales-Balado (Liguori, MO: Liguori Publications, 1996), 53.

page 158   "You must always remember": C. S. Lewis, *The Screwtape Letters* (New York: Macmillan, 1973), 20. First published 1942.

page 159   "play the doubting game": Peter Elbow, "The Doubting Game and the Believing Game—An Analysis of the Intellectual Enterprise," in *Writing without Teachers* (New York: Oxford University Press, 1973), 147–91.

page 160   "part angel and part beast": Blaise Pascal, trans. A. J. Krailsheimer, *Pensées* (New York: Penguin, 1966), 60–66. First published 1670.

page 162   "be at home in his own house": Henri Nouwen, *The Wounded Healer* (New York: Image, 1979), 90.

page 163   "cancering": Barbara Levine, *Your Body Believes Every Word You Say* (Fairfield, CT: WordsWork Press, 2000), 44.

page 163   "I am free to make choices": James Bryan Smith, *The Good and Beautiful God* (Downers Grove, IL: IVP Books, 2009), 161.

page 164   "What were we made for": J. I. Packer, *Knowing God* (Downers Grove, IL: InterVarsity Press, 1973), 29.

Chapter Thirteen

page 170   "a problem is": Robert Pirsig, *Zen and the Art of Motorcycle Maintenance* (New York: William Morrow & Co., 1984), 165.

page 171   "nakedness": Frederick Buechner, *Telling the Truth* (New York: Harper & Row, 1977), 33.

page 172   "A true understanding and humble estimate": Thomas à Kempis, *The Imitation of Christ* (New York: Penguin, 1952), 29. First published 1418–27.

page 174   "the strength hope gives us": Gregory Spencer, *Awakening the Quieter Virtues* (Downers Grove, IL: IVP Books, 2010), 144.

page 176 "Perfectionism is the voice of the oppressor": Anne Lamott, *Bird by Bird* (New York: Random House, 1995), 28.

page 176 "the Perfectionist": Edmund Bourne, *The Anxiety & Phobia Workbook*, 3rd ed. (Oakland, CA: New Harbinger Publications, 2000), 184–85.

page 178 "A man who fails well": Thomas Merton, *No Man Is an Island* (New York: Harcourt, Brace & Co., 1983), 127. First published 1955.

Chapter Fourteen

page 183 "How could you love me": George MacDonald, "The Wise Woman," in *The Gifts of the Child Christ: Fairy Tales and Stories for the Childlike*, Vol. 1 (Grand Rapids, MI: Eerdmans, 1973), 270–71. Story first published 1875.

page 184 "Every culture must negotiate with technology": Neil Postman, *Technopoly: The Surrender of Culture to Technology* (New York: Knopf, 1992), 5.

page 186 "compulsive, even physiologically addicted": See James Roberts, *Too Much of a Good Thing: Are You Addicted to Your Smartphone?* (Austin, TX: Sentia Publishing, 2015), and Susan Weinschenk, "Why We're All Addicted to Texts, Twitter and Google," *Psychology Today*, September 11, 2012, https://www.psychologytoday.com/blog/brain-wise/201209/why-were-all-addicted-texts-twitter-and-google.

page 186 "Some researchers": Nicholas Carr, *The Shallows: What the Internet Is Doing to Our Brains* (New York: Norton, 2010), 122–29 and throughout.

page 187 "Our mobile devices": Sherry Turkle, *Reclaiming Conversation: The Power of Talk in a Digital Age* (New York: Penguin, 2015), 26.

page 189 "how poorly we multitask": Eyal Ophir, Clifford Nass, and Anthony Wagner, "Cognitive control in media multitaskers," *Proceedings of the National Academy of Sciences* 106, no. 37: 15583–87, doi: 10.1073/pnas.0903620106.

page 191 "I keep six honest": Rudyard Kipling, *Animal Stories* (Cornwall, UK: House of Stratus, 2001), 134. First published 1922.

Chapter Fifteen

page 195 "Using words, God reveals himself": Eugene Peterson, *Tell It Slant* (Grand Rapids, MI: Eerdmans, 2008), 10.

page 198 "habits of restraint": David Brooks, *The Road to Character* (New York: Random House, 2015), 56.

page 200 "When [men] become overscheduled": Billy Baker, "The biggest threat to middle-aged men isn't smoking or obesity. It's loneliness," *Boston Globe*, March 9, 2017.

page 201 "elderly live longer": Elizabeth H. Pope, "A Longer Life Is Lived with Company," *New York Times*, September 11, 2012.

page 202 "Every conversation is a form of jazz": Stephen Nachmanovitch, *Free Play: Improvisation in Life and Art* (New York: Tarcher/Putnam, 1990), 17.

Chapter Sixteen

page 207 "It is all a big mess": Etty Hillesum, *An Interrupted Life and Letters from Westerbork* (New York: Henry Holt, 1996), 188.

page 207 "I study their faces": Etty Hillesum, *An Interrupted Life and Letters from Westerbork* (New York: Henry Holt, 1996), 349.

page 207 "Many feel that their love of mankind": Etty Hillesum, *An Interrupted Life and Letters from Westerbork* (New York: Henry Holt, 1996), 323.

page 209 "The Critic": Edmund J. Bourne, *The Anxiety & Phobia Workbook*, 3rd ed. (Oakland, CA: New Harbinger Publications, 2000), 184.

page 210 "How can we romance others": Wayne Brockriede, "Arguers as Lovers," *Philosophy and Rhetoric,* Vol. 5, No. 1 (Winter, 1972): 1–11.

page 213 "REACT": Jett Psaris and Marlena S. Lyons, *Undefended Love* (Oakland, CA: New Harbinger, 2000), 43.

page 215 "The man who has spent many hours": Henri Nouwen, *The Wounded Healer* (New York: Image, 1979), 73.

Chapter Seventeen

page 221 "Good stories often introduce the marvelous": C. S. Lewis, "On Stories," in *Of Other Worlds: Essays and Stories* (New York: Harcourt Brace Jovanovich, 1966), 13.

Reframing with the Saints

page 231 "The world is fairly studded": Annie Dillard, *Pilgrim at Tinker Creek* (New York: Harper & Row, 1974), 15.

page 233 "When you encounter another person": Marilynne Robinson, *Gilead* (New York: Picador, 2004), 124.

Permissions

Ballard Street cartoon panel dated April 4, 2012. Copyright © 2012 by Jerry Van Amerongen. Reprinted by permission of Jerry Van Amerongen and Creators Syndicate, Inc.

"Dementia Road" from *Boundless.com*. Copyright © 2005 by Greg Spencer. Reprinted by permission of the author.

"In Search of a Duck's Back" from *The Cresset*. Copyright © 2002 by Greg Spencer. Reprinted by permission of the author.

"Preemptive Kindness" from *The Penwood Review*. Copyright © 2014 by Greg Spencer. Reprinted by permission of the author.

"The Summer of My Gathering Mortality" from *Windhover: A Journal of Christian Literature*. Copyright © 2013 by Greg Spencer. Reprinted by permission of the author.

Parts of Chapter Fourteen are drawn from "Time Is Up and Space Is Down" from the *Journal of Spiritual Formation and Soul Care*. Copyright © 2017 by Greg Spencer. Reprinted by permission of the author.

Parts of Chapter Sixteen are drawn from "An Incarnational Guide to Communication: S.I.T. Before You Stand" from *Radix*. Copyright © 2002 by Greg Spencer. Reprinted by permission of the author.

About the Author

Gregory Spencer is a professor of communication studies at Westmont College, where he has been teaching and writing for over thirty years. His previous books are *A Heart for Truth*, *Awakening the Quieter Virtues*, and two novels—*The Welkening* and *Guardian of the Veil*. He enjoys tennis, gardening, hiking, writing poetry, and asking ponderous dinner questions at family gatherings.

He can be reached at spencer@westmont.edu. Please visit his website: www.gregspencerbooks.com